BETWEEN DEMOCRACY AND TERROR

THE SIERRA LEONE CIVIL WAR

Edited by

Ibrahim Abdullah

D1620539

CODESRIA COUNCIL FOR THE DEVELOPMENT OF SOCIAL SCIENCE RESEARCH IN AFRICA

ISBN 2-86978-123-7

Cover photography, Revolutionary United Front (RUF) soldiers in Koidu, by Guy Tillim

Typesetting by Djibril Fall

Printed by Lightning Source

Distributed in Africa by CODESRIA

Distributed elsewhere by
African Books Collective Ltd., Unit 13, Kings Meadow, Oxford OX2 0DP, UK
website: www.africanbookscollective.com

CODESRIA would like to express its gratitude to the Swedish International Development Cooperation Agency (SIDA/SAREC), the International Development Research Centre (IDRC), the Ford Foundation, the MacArthur Foundation, Carnegie Corporation, the Norwegian Ministry of Foreign Affairs, the Danish Agency for International Development (DANIDA), the French Ministry of Cooperation, the United Nations Development Programme, the Netherlands Ministry of Foreign Affairs, the Rockefeller Foundation, the Prince Claus Fund, and the Government of Senegal for their support of its research, training and publications programmes.

To All those Who Paid the Ultimate Price

'Yours were the Sacrifices made so that some people will have power while others stay in power'.

(*New Tablet*, Freetown, July 1999)

Contents

Acknowledgements vii

Abbreviations viii

Notes on Contributors ix

Introduction: Between Democracy and Terror

Ibrahim Abdullah.. 1

Part I: Context and actors

Chapter 1

The Political and Cultural Dynamics of the Sierra Leone War

Yusuf Bangura..13

Chapter 2

Bush Path To Destruction: The Origin and Character of the
 Revolutionary United Front (RUF/SL)

Ibrahim Abdullah..41

Chapter 3

Student Radicals, Lumpen Youth, and the Origins of Revolutionary
 Groups in Sierra Leone, 1977–1996

Ismail Rashid..66

Chapter 4

Corruption and Political Insurgency in Sierra Leone

Sahr Kpundeh..90

Chapter 5

State Complicity as a Factor in Perpetuating the Sierra Leone Civil War

Arthur Abraham..104

Part II: One step forward, two steps backward

Chapter 6
In Search of Legitimacy: The 1996 Elections
Jimmy D. Kandeh...123

Chapter 7
The 25 May Coup d'état in Sierra Leone: A Lumpen Revolt?
Lansana Gberie..144

Chapter 8
Unmaking the Second Republic: Democracy On Trial
Jimmy D. Kandeh...164

Chapter 9
Civil Society Against the State: The Independent Press and the
   AFRC-RUF Junta
Olu Gordon...180

Part III: Other players in the drama

Chapter 10
The Elusive Quest For Peace: From Abidjan to Lome
Arthur Abraham..199

Chapter 11
Nigeria, ECOMOG, and the Sierra Leone Crisis
Funmi Olonisakin...220

Chapter 12
'Smallest Victims; Youngest Killers': Juvenile Combatants in
Sierra Leone's Civil War
Ibrahim Abdullah and Ismail Rashid..238

Bibliography 254

Acknowledgements

This project has been long in the making. It originally started as an electronic conversation – Leonenet – on the Sierra Leone conflict in May 1996 following my review of Paul Richards' chapter in Oliver Furley (ed.) *Conflict in Africa*. The Leonenet conversations on the Sierra Leone conflict took a qualitative leap in October/November of that same year after my 'Bush Path to Destruction' was published on the Leonenet discussion forum. An article by Patrick Muana on the *Kamajor* militia also appeared together with Yusuf Bangura's review essay on Paul Richards' *Fighting for the Rain Forest*. These articles together with the contributions from Lansana Gberie on the 1997 coup d'etat, the piece by Ismail Rashid on subaltern reactions, and the article by Arthur Abraham on state conspiracy subsequently appeared in the special issue of *Africa Development* – on youth culture and political violence: the Sierra Leone civil war – at the end of 1997. A CODESRIA-sponsored National Working Group (NWG) constituted the following year made it possible to revise and update the previous articles in the special issue, and to commission seven new chapters to cover areas that were left out in the special issue. The present anthology is a product of that labour. We would like to extend our gratitude to the following for their interest and support throughout the duration of this project: Mamadou Diouf, and Tade Akin Aina for facilitating the publication of the special issue, Achille Mbembe and Ebrima Sall for their speedy response in disbursing the funds after the grant was approved, and Mahmood Mamdani and Adebayo Olukoshi for constantly reminding us of our obligation as scholars. Our thanks also go to the two anonymous referees for their comments and suggestions.

Abbreviations

AFRC	Armed Forces Revolutionary Council
APC	All Peoples Congress
CDF	Civil Defence Force
ECOMOG	Economic Community of West African States Ceasefire Monitoring Group
ECOWAS	Economic Community of West African States
EO	Executive Outcome
IMF	International Monetary Fund
INEC	Interim National Electoral Commission
NIFAG	Nigerian Forces Assistant Group
NPFL	National Patriotic Front of Liberia
NPRC	National Provisional Ruling Council
PDP	Peoples Democratic Party
RSLMF	Republic of Sierra Leone Military Forces
RUF	Revolutionary United Front
SLA	Sierra Leone Army
SLPP	Sierra Leone Peoples Party
SOFA	Status of Armed Forces Agreement Group
UNAMSIL	United Nations Mission in Sierra Leone
UNOMSIL	United Nations Observer Mission in Sierra Leone
UNPP	United National Peoples Party

Notes on Contributors

Ibrahim Abdullah is a historian who specializes in colonial and post-colonial history. He has published in the area of African social/labour history and has taught in universities in America, Canada, Nigeria, South Africa and Sierra Leone. He is currently working on a book length project titled *Youth Culture and Counter-Hegemony in Sierra Leone*.

Arthur Abraham is Professor of History and Eminent Scholar at Virginia State University, USA. He was formerly Professor of African Studies and Dean of the Faculty of Social Sciences at Fourah Bay College, University of Sierra Leone. He is a prolific writer and the acknowledged authority on Mende. His latest book, *An Introduction to Pre-Colonial Mende History* was published this year.

Yusuf Bangura is Research Co-ordinator at the United Nations Research in Social Development (UNRISD), Geneva.

Lansana Gberie is a doctoral candidate in the department of history, University of Toronto. A journalist during the war years, he is co-author of *Heart of the Matter*.

Olu Gordon is a historian by training and a journalist by profession. He is currently the Managing Editor of *Peep Magazine*, Freetown.

Jimmy Kandeh is an Associate Professor of Political Science, University of Richmond, Virginia, USA.

Sahr Kpundeh is a Senior Public Sector Specialist in the World Bank working on Governance and Public Sector Reforms. He is the author of *Politics and Corruption in Africa: A Case Study of Sierra Leone;* co-author of USAID *Handbook for Fighting Corruption;* co-editor of *Corruption and integrity Improvement Initiatives in Developing Countries* and several articles/chapters on issues of governance and corruption. A Sierra Leonean national, Mr. Kpundeh received his Ph.D. and Masters degrees from Howard University, Washington, D.C.

'Funmi Olonisakin holds a Ph.D in War Studies from King's College, University of London. She did pioneering research on ECOMOG operations in Liberia and has published several articles/chapters on gender, peacekeeping and sub-regional security issues.

Ismail Rashid is currently an Assistant Professor of History and Africana Studies at Vassar College, USA. He was born in Freetown, Sierra Leone. He received his B.A. from University of Ghana and doctorate from McGill University, Canada. He has published several articles and book chapters on popular resistance against colonialism and on contemporary social conflicts in West Africa. His latest project is a co-edited (with Adekeye Adebajo) volume entitles, *West African Security Challenges* (Boulder, Co: Lynne Reinner, Forthcoming, 2004)

Introduction

Between Democracy and Terror

Ibrahim Abdullah

After more than a decade of civil war in which 50,000 lives were lost, the people of Sierra Leone, a tiny country in the West African seaboard, went to the polls in May 2002 to elect a new government amidst wild prediction about violence and chaos. It was the second democratic elections in six years; the second since the civil war erupted in 1991. The predictions about violence and chaos not only turned out to be unfounded but the elections were adjudged by most observers to be free and fair – the most peaceful since independence in 1961. The incumbent government swept the polls with a clear and comfortable majority; while the Revolutionary United Front (RUF), the rag-tag guerilla movement that had terrorised the populace for more than a decade failed to win even a seat in parliament (Kandeh, 2002). This is the first example in the history of post-conflict elections in Africa in which a rebel movement, denied outright military victory in war, failed to gain entry into parliamentary politics.

How do we begin to explain the defeat of the RUF and the victory of Sierra Leone Peoples Party (SLPP)? Why were UNITA and RENAMO in Angola and Mozambique respectively able to gain entry into parliamentary politics while the NPFL in Liberia succeeded in coming to power through the ballot box? Does electoral victory or defeat tell us any thing about the nature and conduct of rebel movements in Africa? This volume, the first serious anthology to engage the Sierra Leone civil war, explores the genesis of the crisis; the contradictory roles of different internal and external actors; civil society and the fourth estate; the regional intervention force; the demise of the second republic; and the numerous peace initiatives to end the war.

The chain of events in the Sierra Leone civil war unfolded along a well beaten path: a rebel movement with support from a neighbouring country, the involvement of regional powers, attempt at resolving the crisis by bringing in the OAU/ UN, and the continuation of war despite these efforts. This scenario has been played out again and again in the continent: in Chad, 1977–1983; Uganda, 1979–1986; Sudan, 1973 to date; Angola, 1977–2001; the Democratic Republic of Congo, 1999 to date, and South Africa under apartheid. The above similarity between the crisis in Sierra Leone and elsewhere in the continent has prompted many observers to put forward outlandish explanations derived from these other experiences in understanding the Sierra Leone situation (Richards, 1996; Kaplan, 1994; Reno, 1998). The rule: one size fits all applies with impunity in explaining Africa particularly by Africanists scholars who have made it their business to interpret Africa to the world (Chabal and Deloz, 2000).

Thus we see 'warlords' all over the continent, and in Sierra Leone, battling 'strong men' and 'political entrepreneur' to control 'market and access to resources' in the wake of the collapse of the notorious 'neo-patrimonial state' (Reno, 1998; 2000; Richards, 1996). When youth are suddenly discovered as the central agent in explaining the war and its continuation, they are either boxed in to fit an a priori assembled theoretical formulation, as in the new 'state-within-state' construct, or smuggled in as add-on to recycled notions about 'civil society,' 'neo-patrimonialism', 'excluded intellectuals' or 'anomic slave rebellions' (Reno, 2002; Boas, 2000; Richards, 1996; 2003).[1] To privilege an abstract market centred analysis, or to use the now popular binary – greed against grievance – in explaining the Sierra Leone crisis is to neglect the historical process and the multiple actors in the drama of war and its continuation. The first section in this collection wrestles with the historical and sociological contexts within which the insurgency discourse evolved. The primary analytical focus is on developments internal to Sierra Leone: how lumpen or underclass youth culture and the emergence of a radical student movement coalesced to produce a counter-insurgency movement. For it was these developments, the contributors argue, which laid the groundwork for the emergence of the RUF.

Context and actors

Yusuf Bangura's review essay contextualises a range of issues relevant to our understanding the Sierra Leone civil war. He argues, rather forcefully, against the 'excluded intellectual' thesis put forward by Paul Richards by examining the history and specificities of the Sierra Leone political economy.[2] Bangura not only fails to find any evidence of excluded intellectuals, that is, a group 'with abstract ideas and theories of social change sometimes caught between two opposing realities' but notes the glaring absence of any 'highly educated' individual, another of Richards's construct, in the RUF. It was not the crisis of neo-patrimonialism, per se that was responsible for the collapse of state structures in the late 1970s and 1980s. Neo-patrimonialism, Bangura contends, had generated a relatively high and stable growth rate in Africa during the 1960s and 1970s.

The unanswered question for those who choose to understand the genesis of the war from the point of view of neo-patrimonialism is the specific form of that accumulation and why and how certain forms of political development – such as the centralization of power under the APC, the destruction of civic forms of opposition, the active under- development and destabilization of the countryside, and the deliberate use of state sponsored violence by the ruling APC in settling disputes – provoked a crisis that led to war. Bangura's conclusion brings us back to the larger question: the breakdown of state structures as a result of a particular kind of accumulation in economies that are very rich in natural resources and yet heavily dependent upon foreign aid for public investment programmes. These socioeconomic and political developments and the consequent alienation of the youth, not 'excluded intellectuals', are central to any broader explanation of the context of war.

The chapter by Ibrahim Abdullah explores the social and intellectual linkages between the RUF-to-be, the student movement and lumpen youth by tracing the genealogy of rebellious culture in the city of Freetown. Anchoring his analysis on Sierra Leone's post-independence political culture, Abdullah demonstrates how youth alienation and the absence of a radical political culture was a factor in explaining why rebellious youths generally turned to bland pan-Africanism, and other seemingly radical ideas, such as Gaddafi's Green Book and Kim II Sung's *Juche* idea, in pursuing an ideational alternative to guide their political practice. The absence of a clear ideological direction and the uncritical acceptance of vague populism explain why the burgeoning group of 'revolutionaries' in Freetown and elsewhere had no emancipatory programme. This partly explains why those who were responsible for recruitment turned their attention to any individual, but mostly lumpen youth, willing to undertake military training.

Thus from July 1987, when the first group of would-be cadres left Freetown for Tripoli via Accra, to April 1991, when the RUF attacked Bomaru in Kailahun District, no concrete programme of action was formulated. The *Basic Document*, which came to represent the RUF's message, was drafted in Ghana before the trip to Libya. It was essentially a critique of the neo-colonial regime. Lacking a concrete platform and a broad social base on which to anchor its ideas about society, and what it hopes to achieve by taking up arms, the RUF was left with no alternative but to resort to vague populist formulations about injustice and exploitation. When this message failed to attract any meaningful support from the people, the organization replied with indiscriminate violence against women, children, and at times, whole communities. The wanton violence and the mayhem against the very people it claimed to be liberating, alienated the RUF from the people and provided the objective conditions for a peoples militia to emerge.

Ismail Rashid examines the cultural and social connections between students and lumpen youths and the origins of revolutionary groups. By tracing the cultural connections between students and lumpen youths in the *odelay* (masquerade) societies and the *potes* (a popular rendez vous for rebellious youth), Rashid argues that the culture of resistance that characterised youth in Freetown emerged in the context of non-conformism, student radicalism, reggae music, and drugs. The context within which this vibrant youth culture flourished was also marked by a progressive deterioration of the economy, which meant constricting opportunities for youth, the collapse of public institutions, dwindling revenues from mining – the principal source of state revenue – and an intolerant political culture that drove subalterns into a decidedly confrontational stance. As Rashid demonstrates, students confronted the state on a national scale in 1977 and then again in 1985. The linkages between rebellious youth culture and social change were not only marked by the incorporation of student radicals in the National Provisional Ruling Council (NPRC) military government that came to power after the 1992 coup. In Rashid's analysis we begin to see the social and cultural linkages- shared cultural repertoire – between the RUF and the NPRC. Both used the same 'revolutionary' scripts; both turned to the same constituency to mobilize support. And both would eventually loose whatever support they had after their rhetoric about popular power and political corruption turned out to be anything but that.

The issue of corruption – within the NPRC, the RUF, and the Sierra Leone Peoples Party (SLPP) – is discussed in the chapters by Sahr Kpundeh and Arthur Abraham. Whereas Kpundeh examines the issue within the context of insurgency, Abraham looks at state complicity in perpetuating the war. Kpundeh discusses the war rhetoric of the RUF and argues that greed, not grievance, was the major factor in the genesis of the war and its continuation. This was however not peculiar to the RUF; both the APC and SLPP regimes are implicated in the practice of corruption. Kpundeh's chapter explores the role of civil society in curbing corruption by suggesting alternative approaches to tackling the problem.

The allegation of collaboration between the Republic of Sierra Leone Military Forces (RSLMF) and the RUF is the thesis of Arthur Abraham's provocative chapter on state complicity. Abraham argues that the war was deliberately prolonged because of the congruence of interests between the NPRC and the RUF. This informal understanding was a product of the identical economic interests of the young military officers and the RUF: both were deeply involved in mining diamonds. The involvement of senior officers in diamond mining meant that the rank and file – lumpens recruited into the army by the NPRC – who were not so privileged, were allowed to engage in illegal activities to supplement their meager incomes. In this free for all atmosphere the officers lost control over their men, widespread looting and killing of civilians became the norm, so that in the end the nation was compelled to listen to the voice of the anguished population: the soldiers and the rebels are one and the same. This popular perception from below was strengthened by the NPRC's unilateral declaration of a cease-fire, at a time when the RUF was allegedly on the run, and subsequently, by the opposition of both the NPRC and the RUF to a return to civilian rule. This congruence of interest, dubbed collaboration in local political parlance, was confirmed by the RUF's involvement in the bloody take over in May 1997.

One step forward, two steps backward

The chapters by Jimmy Kandeh discuss the return to parliamentary multi-party politics in 1996 and the unmaking of the second republic. Both chapters reveal the rather weak democratic culture in Sierra Leone and the failure of the political class to learn any meaningful lessons from the war. The ethnoregional alliances that had characterised Sierra Leone politics since independence resurfaced in the 1996 multiparty elections. Ethnoregionalism was compounded by political opportunism and the 'spoils calculations' of party machines built around individual personalities. There were no fundamental differences between the contending parties in the 1996 elections: the party programmes were similar and all pledged to bring a speedy conclusion to the war. The major difference between the parties was the ethnic support of the respective parties and their leaders. As Kandeh convincingly argues, the political landscape remained unchanged in spite of the civil war. President Kabbah's first cabinet turned out to be a 'yawning disappointment'. Before long there were rumours of coups and attempted coups, and in May 1997 the army eventually seized power.

The second chapter by Jimmy Kandeh reviews the activities of the Kabbah administration from the pre-coup period, 1996–1997 to the post-invasion era, 1999–2000. The government's premature withdrawal of Executive Outcomes (EO) under pressure from the IMF, the failure to put together a strategic plan to defend the nation after February 1998, and the excessive reliance on ECOMOG were in part responsible for the January invasion of Freetown in 1999. According to Kandeh, 'Both the May 1997 coup and the January 1999 invasion could have been averted and thousands of lives saved had the president been up to his job as commander-in-chief'. Indeed, some of the shortcomings of the government were used to justify the bloody takeover of May 1997.

The Chapter by Lansana Gberie examines the composition of the coup leaders and their actions in the city and elsewhere, and argues that it was not the militariat – junior officers who lack the clientilist ties of the more senior officers-who were behind the bloody take-over. Rather, it was the lumpen elements, those 'criminally disposed and undisciplined', whom Marxist literature had incorrectly assumed were incapable of doing battle on their own behalf. By privileging lumpen culture in his explanation of the bloody takeover of May 1997, Gberie underlines the salience of this important but neglected category in understanding the crisis in Sierra Leone. His reference to Kabbah's policy of downsizing the military might provide the key to explaining why 95 percent of the army joined the rebellion. This has never happened anywhere in the world. It is indeed tempting to suggest that the bloody takeover was the dictatorship of the lumpenproletariat/riff raffs! The alliance between the RUF and the national army is central to understanding the dynamics of the war and why outright military victory eluded both sides. As the chapter on state complicity reminds us, this collaboration existed long before 1997. If the resistance against *sobels* in the hinterland led to the emergence of ethnic militias, the resistance against *sobels* in Freetown was mounted by the independent press.

Long berated by commentators, both internal and external, for its lack of professionalism and sensational reporting, the independent press, based in Freetown, rose up to defend its much cherished freedom of expression and the right to responsible dissent under military rule. As thousands of Sierra Leoneans, mostly middle class professionals and others who could afford it made their way to neighbouring countries, journalists and reporters devised ingenious ways of bypassing the draconian measures put in place by the Armed Forces Revolutionary Council (AFRC) regime of terror. This 'guerilla journalism,' according to Olu Gordon, enabled members of the beleaguered fourth estate to voice their collective opposition to military dictatorship and to defend democracy. The independent press was stoutly opposed to the AFRC regime, and was arguably, the principal architect in its eventual collapse. And the junta never forgot the heroic role of the press in their demise. There is a double irony here: the independent press that the Kabbah administration wanted to gag unflinchingly defended democracy on pain of death. It is no wonder that when the RSLMF in collaboration with the RUF invaded Freetown in January 1999, they systematically targeted journalists who were opposed to the AFRC junta.

Other players in the drama

The last three chapters deal with the tortous road to peace, the regional intervention force, ECOMOG, and the involvement of juvenile combatants. Not too many people are aware that the initial move to end the Sierra Leone war came from within. Arthur Abraham chronicles this development and argues that the APC regime was reluctant to do anything because it interpreted the rebellion as the work of the SLPP opposition. Instead of mounting a robust counter-attack, President Momoh advised the delegation to use whatever weapons they had, sticks, stones, to resist the invaders. Throughout the tortous road to peace, first to Abidjan, then later, to Lome, successive governments consistently ignored the popular will. The people were neither consulted in the negotiations before or after Abidjan nor were their wishes considered or even tabled in Lome. The NPRC regime was not interested in peace because that would have meant an end to military rule; the Kabbah administration was interested in peace at all cost. Both regimes underestimated the 'wily' Sankoh who knew what he wanted and was using negotiations to buy time to rearm/recoup his losses. This 'yo-yo game' went on and off until the international community, spearheaded by the United States, forced the Kabbah regime, a democratically elected government, to sign a peace agreement with a terrorist organization. If the RUF got some of what it wanted in Abidjan, it got even more in Lome: sharing power with the democratically elected government gave Sankoh and his terrorist rag-tag army the cover they needed to realize the RUF's historic objective of capturing power through violence. Incapable of stopping the RUF's forward march to power through violence, the Sierra Leone government turned to the regional organization – ECOWAS – for an intervention force that would at least keep the RUF at bay.

The initial Nigerian involvement in Sierra Leone occured within the framework of the ECOWAS monitoring group (ECOMOG), and a bilateral agreement, Status of the Armed Forces Agreement (SOFA), between the Sierra Leone and Nigeria governments. The turning point in Nigeria's involvement took place in 1997 when Nigerian troops stationed in Freetown attempted to overturn the bloody takeover by the RUF and the National Army. Those who were opposed to Nigerian presence in Sierra Leone argued that Nigeria was using the regional organization, ECOWAS, to launder the image of General Abacha, while those in favour countered by pointing to the 'illegality' of the AFRC regime. The irony of a military regime intervening to restore a democratically elected government was widely condemned as the personal project of the Nigerian head of state. From the point of view of the people of Sierra Leone, it was a welcomed development particularly at a time when the international community were more concerned with developments in the Balkans.

The Abacha regime was not only instrumental in flushing out the AFRC regime in power in February 1998, but the Nigerian troops under ECOMOG stayed on to provide security after the national army had forced the renegade soldiers to retreat to the hinterland. Stretched to its limit by incompetent political-cum-military officers, the Nigerian state and army could not provide adequate logistic support for its troops in Sierra Leone nor ensure regular rotation for service members. The decline in professionalism and the rampant corruption among some senior officers and rank and file, made it impossible for the Nigerian troops in ECOMOG to perform qua peace-keepers. As Funmi Olonisakin correctly argued, the shortcomings of the Nigerian contingent were a reflection of the internal situation in Nigeria. Even so, their presence in Sierra Leone made a huge difference: they came at a time when the international community had turned their back on Sierra Leone. Indeed when Sierra Leone had no army!

The last chapter discusses the phenomenon of child soldiers. By interrogating the dominant explanation on the subject – the villain versus victim thesis – the chapter argues for an historically informed analysis that situates juvenile combatants within the context of labor appropriation and recruitment in a situation where adults are either unavailable or are reluctant to enlist as combatants. The element of choice, however limited, is also crucial in understanding the whole process of juvenile combatants enlistment in war effort. For, whereas the RUF press-ganged and abducted its under-aged combatant, the national army was swamped by under-age volunteers, who were originally organized as vigilantes to serve as spies and to undertake reconnaissance missions. Yet the differences in the two modes of recruitment have less to do with any fundamental difference between the two military machines. Rather, the differences were a reflection of the dynamics of war: some under-aged combatants flocked to the RSLMF after their communities were devastated and their parents killed, while others were unable/reluctant to do so. Both the RSLMF and the RUF treated juvenile combatants as children not soldiers, though the testimonies of those who fought with the RSLMF and the RUF suggest that the rebels were more brutal. Only a fraction of the children in Sierra Leone took part in the war as combatants, spies, sex slaves and porters. And the majority of them were from the rural areas, not the cities; from peasant families, not the middle class. This finding is true of all armed conflicts in Africa in which juvenile combatants have featured prominently.

It is what propelled internal actors to tread the multiple but conflicting pathways to state power, why the war lasted for as long as it did, and how non-conventional actors were able to inaugurate and sustain an insurgency that called forth the largest concentration of UN peace keepers the world has ever seen that should interest the student of post-colonial Sierra Leone/Africa. To reduce all these happenings, these 'thick descriptions'/histories, to a footnote in a narrative that privileges the economic factor is to devalorise research and scholarship in understanding and changing our reality!

Notes

1   Morten Boas, 'Civil Society in Sierra Leone: Corruption, Destruction (And Reinvention)' *Democracy and Development* 3, 1, 2002, reproduces/copies verbatim Paul Richards application of the neo-partrimonial model in his, *Fighting for the Rain Forest*, London: James Currey, 1996. Paraphrasing Richards, Boas wrote: 'Under the Cold War, the neo-patrimonial logic of rule grew because leaders such as Siaka Stevens used their country's geopolitical position and/or threatened to switch allegiance from capitalism to communism, to extract increased amounts of external aid' p.55. There is no evidence to support this claim about Stevens' ' switch'! See Bangura this volume.

2   Paul Richards has recently abandoned his discredited notion of 'excluded intellectuals' in favour of what he calls 'an anomic slave revolt' to explain the RUF. See Paul Richards, 'Beyond Violence: The Anthropology of New Wars in Africa' 2003.

Part I

Context and actors

Geography of War

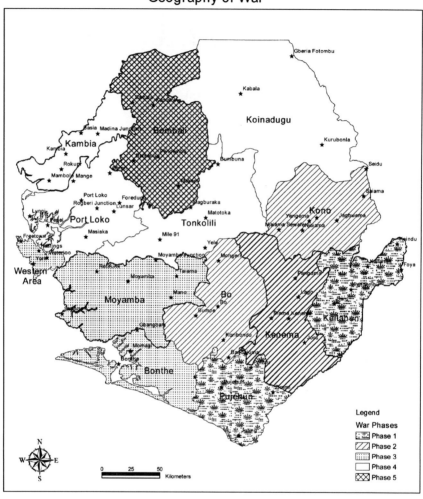

Legend

War Phases
- Phase 1
- Phase 2
- Phase 3
- Phase 4
- Phase 5

1

The Political and Cultural Dynamics of the Sierra Leone War: A Critique of Paul Richards

Yusuf Bangura

Overview

The closing years of the twentieth century witnessed a spectacular rise in new modes of armed conflict, which challenged conventional conceptions of modern warfare. Most wars in the 1990s were fought within countries rather than, as was hitherto the case, between states; the narratives or doctrines of the major world powers no longer define the ideologies and objectives of warring groups; small, highly mobile weapons, often supplied by illicit private dealers, seem to play a much bigger role than heavy conventional weapons in fuelling wars; combatants deliberately target civilians rather than armed opponents in prosecuting goals; and atrocities are freely committed as part of strategies aimed at publicising political statements. In countries that are rich in natural resources, such as diamonds, gold, timber, agricultural produce, drug-generating plants and oil, the political goals of wars often interact with the multiple logics of resource appropriation, the drugs trade, the looting of private property, and vandalism. Such complicated outcomes have led many commentators to portray contemporary wars as being basically anarchical.

Paul Richards's book, *Fighting for the Rain Forest*, seeks to challenge these conceptions of war as they apply to Sierra Leone – a country located in the rain forest region of West Africa, and which boasts of rich mineral resources, forest products, export agricultural commodities and marine resources. Even though Sierra Leone's war has been very viciously fought, with extremely destructive effects, Richards argues that it has nonetheless been highly rational, rather than random and anarchic. He believes that the military methods of the armed groups have been very effective in achieving their objectives; and that the war should be understood as a 'performance' or political drama or discourse, 'in which techniques of terror compensate for lack of equipment'. He analyses Sierra Leone's war as a crisis of modernity, which has been caused by the failed patrimonial system of the All People's Congress (APC) that ruled the country for 24 years.

Richards states that Sierra Leone's youth are part of a modern, Trans-Atlantic creolised culture, with a sophisticated understanding of world events and global cultural trends that are shaped by video, film, radio and the print media. He insists that the war is partly fought by the creative use of these media resources. He argues that the crisis of patrimonialism has had a devastating effect on schooling, social services, jobs, and national communications infrastructure, which has blighted the hopes of most young people for meaningful life in the cities. Young people have been condemned, instead, to a miserable and insecure life in agriculture or as labourers in diamond digging camps. Richards maintains that the fact that the war is fought in the rain forest means that it can only be understood by examining traditional conceptions and practices of forest resource management. He believes that the rebel movement, the Revolutionary United Front (RUF), has a firm grasp of these traditions, and has effectively deployed its knowledge of them in prosecuting the war. This movement is said to be led by a group of "highly educated" excluded intellectuals, many of whom have been living in Liberia as political exiles and economic refugees. They espouse Colonel Qaddafi's Green Book ideology, which is critical of the profit motive, and hold out prospects for a new egalitarian society.

The book is divided into eight substantive chapters, an introduction, and a concluding chapter on war-peace transitions, which examines the prospects for peace and reconstruction. Reconstruction efforts, Richards states, should focus on local 'citizen action', on 'smart relief' rather than high profile assistance, and on the use of traditional cultural institutions and values – such as the accommodationist values of creolisation, initiation into secret societies, and the moral critique in the discourse on 'cannibalism' – which he believes have helped to stabilise these communities in the past.

Richards's book has many positive things to say about Sierra Leone, and challenges widespread misconceptions of the country's war. His discussion of the dilemmas of youth, especially those located in the distressed regions of the forest, and who operate in an environment of a shrinking state, opens up opportunities for further useful enquiry. His insights on the historical dynamics that linked the country's forest region to the world market, including the violent and exploitative exchanges that supported such linkages, are useful reminders about the problems, which external influences have always posed to the livelihoods and physical security of rain forest communities. The brief sections on Pandebu (the last border village in Eastern Sierra Leone) and 'loose molecules', which deal with the formation of mixed diamond-mining communities in the border region, provide very insightful data and perspectives on the problems of social integration in that region. The information in these sections is based on fieldwork material from a previous study on resources and subsistence strategies in the Gola forest reserve (Paul Richards, 1996).

However, Richards's book is seriously flawed in several important ways. As this is the first book-length study of Sierra Leone's war, it is likely to be widely read by Sierra Leoneans and the public at large. It is important, therefore, to discuss these flaws, if only to ensure that future works on the subject do not repeat them. Firstly, driven by a need to prove that the Sierra Leone war is highly rational, Richards adopts only one logic – the RUF's logic of revolutionary change – to explain the dynamics of the war. The logics of resource exploitation, vandalism and random or barbaric violence are completely ignored. Instead, the RUF is portrayed as a highly disciplined organisation, which seeks to transform society on the basis of what it says it will do in its published document, *Footpaths to Democracy.*[1] Without any data to back up his claims, Richards concludes that the RUF was formed by a group of 'highly educated', excluded intellectuals who are capable of making rational decisions about their war goals and regulating the behaviour of their battle field commanders. He does not investigate the social origins of the RUF cadre, which might have opened up other interpretations to the movement's chronic tendency to inflict blind terror on communities in the countryside. I discuss these issues under the first three sections of this chapter. The first section subjects Richards's rationalist framework to critical scrutiny; the second challenges his characterisation of the RUF as excluded intellectuals; and the third highlights the theoretical shortcomings and dangers of his analysis and conclusions about the RUF.

Second, Richards's book is flawed in his uncritical use of the concept of 'the crisis of patrimonialism' to explain the social realities that shaped the conditions for the war. He makes no effort to check whether the general argument about an African patrimonial crisis, put forward by many Africanist scholars, fits the Sierra Leone data and reality. His failure to properly analyse the character of the Sierra Leone state means that he is unable to concretely trace the political processes that made armed conflict and war an option in popular resistance to the authoritarian rule of the APC. Sections four and five of this chapter discuss these issues and suggest alternative ways of looking at the crisis and the political dynamics of the war.

Third, although Richards puts a lot of emphasis on the problems of youth, his analysis of youth culture is rather weak, and his conclusions about youth participation in the war are not always reliable: he is prone to hasty conclusions about, or far-fetched connections between, processes and events that have not been properly investigated. He also does not have a differentiated understanding of Sierra Leone's youths: he is unable to distinguish between the stratum of youth that is often called 'lumpens', or 'rarray boy' in popular discourse, who are believed to be the driving force of the RUF's fighting machine, and other types of youth who, although disadvantaged, remain socially integrated into community and family institutions that guarantee social accountability. Richards uses survey data on the attitudes of non-war youth to make general conclusions about the effects of violent films and drugs on the youth in the RUF whom he has not interviewed. Section six provides a critique of this methodology for analysing youth culture and the conclusions about youth, the RUF, drugs and violence that he draws from his data.

Fourth, although Richards raises interesting issues for debate about war-peace transitions, his recommendations suffer from several basic problems. In his efforts to demonstrate the need to come to terms with local level initiatives, he ignores the point that some local activities, such as the 'attack trade' that he thinks should be privileged over 'high profile relief', have a potential to turn war into a way of life. Richards also demonstrates a poor grasp of the social integration process that he refers to as 'creolisation' of the Upper Guinea Forest region and its role as a cultural resource for peace. Although he states the need to use traditional secret societies as a peace-building resource, he does not explain how this can be done in ways that will involve the participation of youth he has characterised as 'modernist' in behaviour and aspirations. And his recommendation to use the traditional moral critique of 'cannibalism' as an instrument to check patrimonialism is utterly laughable. Since Richards flags the issue of patrimonialism throughout the text as a critical factor that triggered the war, one would have expected a more serious treatment of this problem than what he has offered his readers. These issues of war-peace transitions are discussed in section seven. I conclude the chapter with suggestions about ways of reforming the institutions of state and society that may help the country to break out of the culture and logic of war.

Kaplan versus Richards: A case of double misconception?

Fighting for the Rain Forest is an elaborate critique of Robert Kaplan's influential article, 'The Coming Anarchy', which was published in the February 1994 edition of the popular American magazine, *The Atlantic Monthly*. Motivated by his previous journalistic reporting of the Balkan crisis, Kaplan sought to interpret the emerging post-Cold War order and warn of its consequences for world civilisation if nothing was done to protect areas that were still relatively free of some of its problems. He tapped into a wider current of Western fears about the dangers posed to social integration and global security by uncontrollable population pressures, environmental degradation, drug abuse, disease, crime and ethnic violence. He used Sierra Leone as an archetypal case to highlight the extent to which the forces for anarchy were already far advanced in some societies, which he thought might even be irreversible. In Sierra Leone, he believed, his key variables of disease, population explosion, environmental pollution, drugs, ethnic rivalry, and age-old African 'superstitious' beliefs have combined to produce several unsavory outcomes: a bandit-driven war, youthful military rulers who display a shanty-town style of civic behaviour, and an increasingly strong articulation of an embedded African barbarity. In short, in the eyes of Kaplan, anarchy was already a fact of life in Sierra Leone.

Richards correctly questions this superficial reading of Sierra Leone's war and society. He devotes almost half of the book – four chapters – to disprove Kaplan's argument as it relates to population growth, environmental pressures, and media influences. He also highlights the fact, which most analysts of current African wars tend to miss, that the Sierra Leone war is not caused or driven by ethnic rivalry. Richards convincingly shows that Sierra Leone does not suffer from population pressure or an environmental crisis; and that its urban youth hold very modernist views about society and the world, using video, films and other types of media for self improvement and not, as Kaplan and others believe, passively or as simple-minded copy cats. Indeed, Kaplan would have been surprised to learn that in the space of two years after the publication of his article, his archetypal anarchic society was successfully able to resist army rule, organise two consecutive national elections under unstable war conditions that ushered in a multi-party system of government.

However, despite his forceful and useful critique of the prophecy of the impending anarchy, Richards runs into trouble because of his fixation with Kaplan and his Western audience. In his effort to disprove Kaplan, he introduces a lot more confusion in the 'debate' on barbarism: i.e. by his superficial treatment of traditional values and institutions, his posing of questions that do not allow him to recognise aspects of barbarism that the rebel war has demonstrated, and his 'glorification' or misunderstanding of the violence or atrocities of the RUF. Given the fact that Kaplan did not do any serious research and never lived in the country to understand its history and dynamics, much of what he said about Sierra Leone could have been dismissed by Richards in one or two pages. Like most other serious commentators, Kaplan may have come to the right conclusion about the dangers of anarchy, but his explanations were way off target. Sierra Leoneans who have read Kaplan are hardly concerned about Richards's patronising call 'not to be worried about (the) expatriate intellectual misappropriation' of so-called African ideas from their African social contexts, or New Barbarism (Richards, 1995:163). Instead, Richards's fixation with Kaplan prevents him from probing deeply into the real dynamics of the war as they relate to society, politics and the economy. If one eliminates the issues that do not speak directly to the war, the book could actually have been reduced from its current length of about 200 pages to a journal article!

Richards uses the concept of 'New Barbarism' to construct an alternative reading of the Sierra Leone situation. Where New Barbarism talks of mindless, random, anarchic or irrational violence, Richards posits rationality, organisation, discipline, and calculated visions of social change by a movement that is led by excluded, 'quite highly educated dissident' intellectuals (Richards, 1996:1). In other words, in the rationalist framework of Richards, the RUF is not a bandit group, but an organised movement with a clear political programme for radical social change. Richards's rationalist perspective suffers from three basic errors. First, he does not explain the nature of the old barbarism, which would have helped his readers to assess the validity of the new type. In several locations in the text, Richards gives the impression that there is an authentic old barbarism, but he does not tell us what it is. The New Barbarism thesis becomes a convenient straw on which to weave his very limited material on the war and his more interesting work on the environment to produce a full-length book on the conflict.

Second, by treating all behaviour as rational, even in the most chaotic of conditions, the concept of rationality loses its heuristic value: it becomes difficult to say when a seemingly rational action is in fact irrational, when judged from the stand-point of competing alternatives and the information and resources that may be required to pursue other or more 'rational' outcomes. Every action, it seems, can be explained or justified as rational when seen from the limited standpoint of an actor, even if it can be shown that there are better alternatives to achieving the actors' preferred goal or objective. The cutting off of hands to prevent adult villagers from voting may be a rational RUF strategy, as Richards insists, but one would have to stretch rationality to its limits to explain the logic behind the decision to subject to the same treatment nine- and ten-year-olds who do not vote.

The third problem relates to the deeply flawed view or assumption that rational actions cannot be barbaric! Simply because one can make rational connections between the RUF's strategy of cutting off hands and the goal of preventing people from voting does not mean that the method used to achieve the goal of 'no-vote' is not barbaric. Yet, Richards's rationalist method prevents him from properly scrutinising the rational behaviour of the RUF. Haunted by Kaplan, his main preoccupation gets reduced to one goal: to show that RUF atrocities are rational and, therefore, not barbaric. Apartheid, Atlantic slavery, the Interahamwe call that led to the massacre of Tutsis, the Holocaust, Pol Pot's rule in Cambodia, and the cutting off of Congolese people's hands by Belgian colonial officers, were all very rational responses to problems as perceived by the perpetrators, but they were also barbaric acts of violence against the victims and humanity. The failure to problematise the rationality of the RUF led to a rather poor grasp of the character of the RUF and the nature of its violence.

Mary Douglas's excluded intellectuals and the RUF's violence

Richards's intellectual patron for understanding the RUF and the nature of its violence is Mary Douglas, a social anthropologist who has done general work on institutions, knowledge creation and the behaviour of socially excluded intellectuals. He quotes Douglas liberally in several locations of the book without questioning the relevance of what she has to say for the Sierra Leone situation. Douglas's work forms part of a growing literature on the social determinants of ideas and beliefs as they are articulated in different institutional settings. Excluded intellectuals often hold very abstract ideas and theories of social change, and are sometimes caught between two opposing realities: the pressures of mass equality, which capture the world of the underprivileged; and the social and political hierarchies that serve the rich and powerful, and blight the hopes of radical intellectuals for purposeful egalitarian change.

Excluded intellectuals develop a discourse that rejects prevailing development orthodoxy, calling instead for radical transformations of society. Faced with arbitrary state power and repression, such intellectuals may become small sectarian groups, consumed by their own visions, texts, discourses and constant re-reading or 'deconstruction' of their societies. Exclusion and abstract intellectualism in the face of powerlessness may expose such groups to destructive violence, which itself may become a text to reinforce social bonds among group members as well as to discredit the legitimacy of the existing order. This reading of radical intellectuals and violence has been well analysed in several academic texts under the rubric of discourse theory.

It is significant to note that these types of studies have focused on movements that are led by intellectuals – David Apter calls them 'cosmocrats' – who use violence strategically, and as organised discourse, to open up opportunities for revolutionary social transformations (Apter, 1996). One important logic of such violence is to delegitimise the state, by forcing it to reveal its inherently violent character to the public when it hits back violently at insurrectionary group members. Although not always successful, such movements often try not to provoke violence to the point where their message gets consumed by the violence, and the movements themselves become alienated from the wider public they seek to liberate. The radical revolutionary skeptics who Douglas and similar authors have in mind are 'educated and privileged'

(Richards quoting Douglas, p.xxv), not semi-educated, partially tutored radicals, or individuals straddling the margins of society, who may be prone to random violence or weakly structured responses. Examples of the former are Lenin and the Bolshevik movement in Russia; Mao and the Chinese Communist Party; Che and his Latin American guerrillas; Ayatollah Khomenie and the Iranian mullahs; Cabral and the PAIGC in Guinea Bissau; Machel and FRELIMO in Mozambique; and Guzman and the early Sendero Luminoso, or Shining Path movement, in Peru. One could also mention campus-based radical intellectuals who may be cut off from mainstream national politics. The question is whether the social origins and intellectual content and quality of the RUF fit the Douglas-type model. In other words, how accurate is it to treat Foday Sankoh and his RUF comrades as 'excluded intellectuals'?

Ibrahim Abdullah's chapter (this volume) is the first major attempt to understand the origins and social basis of the rebel movement. Abdullah interviewed a large number of the key individuals who played active roles in the early formation of the movement. He combined this information with his long-standing work on the social history and culture of the marginal youths of Sierra Leone to offer very compelling insights into the character of the RUF. From Abdullah's account, we learn that the RUF does indeed have some intellectual origins: it emerged from the popular struggles of radical students, a large number of whom were expelled in 1985, following violent student demonstrations; three faculty members who were noted for their radical visions of social change also had their services terminated. A section of these students and one of the expelled lecturers ended up at the University of Legon, Ghana and undertook ideological and military training in Libya with a view to carrying out a social revolution in Sierra Leone.

Abdullah's informants state that leading members of the Libya group theorised socially marginal, 'lumpen' individuals as essential elements or 'vanguards' in the strategies for the realisation of the Sierra Leone revolution; and that when PANAFU rejected the armed struggle road, recruitment for the Libya military project became a random exercise – i.e. anybody who expressed interest to go to Libya could do so irrespective of the ideological status or competence of the individual. Not surprisingly, Abdullah finds that the majority of those who trained in Libya were either from the loosely structured 'lumpen' classes, or those with a troubled educational history. They were certainly not the Mary Douglas types of radical intellectuals who remained on the fringes of the political mainstream, but who could buy their way into the power structure if they so wished. Instead, the hard-core RUF 'intellectuals' is drawn from a stratum of Sierra Leonean society that is hooked on drugs, alcohol and street gambling. They have very limited education and are prone to gangster types of activities – sometimes acting as clients of strong 'men' in society or leading political figures and government officials.

Another Sierra Leonean, Patrick Muana, who has done pioneering work on a leading people's militia, the *kamajoisia*, which has played a major role in checking the military advances of the RUF, confirms the point that most of the field commanders of the RUF are drawn from a stratum of society that the Mendes refer to as *njiahungbia ngorngeisia* – unruly youth, or social misfits (Muana, 1997). Muana reports that these were 'semi-literate village school drop-outs', who despise traditional values and authority, and welcomed the violence of the RUF as an opportunity to settle local scores and reverse the alienating rural social order in their favour. Even Richards's discussion of the social dynamics and background of youth in the diamond digging camps of the border region – many of whose youths joined the RUF – suggests that he is dealing with a similar phenomenon of 'lumpen culture' that Abdullah and Muana have described, even though he is unable to make the connection. It is important to note, as we assess the significance of these findings, that lumpens or marginals have been well theorised in Marxist literature as constituting poor material for progressive social change. Indeed, Amilcar Cabral, one of Africa's foremost revolutionary theorists, had warned in his writings on the social conditions of Guinea Bissau that liberation movements should not recruit lumpens for armed activities as they were likely to ignore commands and pursue agendas of vandalism.

It is now widely known that the very few educated individuals, Philip Palmer, Ibrahim Deen-Jalloh, Agnes Deen-Jalloh, Faiya Musa, and Mohammed Barrie were abductees who joined or were coerced into the RUF when the war got underway: they played no role in shaping the ideology of the movement. They were captured in battle or abducted in raids, and subsequently converted into RUF fighters, spokespersons or administrators. Given the fact that Richards attaches great significance to the concept of 'excluded intellectuals' in explaining the RUF's violence, efforts should have been made to spell out who the RUF leaders were, what their history or level of engagement with the movement was, and what kinds of revolutionary discourses informed actual RUF behaviour in the bush.

What we get instead are unverified assertions about the high level of education of the top leadership of the RUF, who are said to number about twenty or more members, and a few quotations from RUF documents, which, surely, were not written by the leading members themselves. Richards provides no evidence to support his claims about the presence of Sierra Leonean radical intellectual exiles in Liberia. There were Sierra Leoneans living on the Liberian side of the border that joined Sankoh to fight alongside Charles Taylor's National Patriotic Front of Liberia (NPFL), and to form the RUF, but these were not intellectuals. The one individual whom Richards cites, Philip Palmer to support his argument, was said to have been gainfully employed in Liberia before he was overwhelmed by the Liberian war and recruited into the RUF (Richards, 1996: 26). Those who knew him in his university days at Fourah Bay College (FBC) say that he was never a member of any radical student movement. And Sankoh, the leader, can hardly pass as a highly educated, excluded intellectual. In short, his movement is not 'incorrigibly didactic', and he does not lead a 'group of embittered pedagogues' (Richards, 1996: 28).

Richards's RUF: The Big Lie?

The failure to problematise the RUF's rationality and use of specific types of violence leads to very serious errors in explaining what the RUF actually does in battle. One is left with the impression that Richards already had formed views about what the RUF ought to be, based on his uncritical appropriation of Douglas's concept of 'excluded intellectuals', and that what he then pro-ceeded to do was to look for evidence that would support his characterisation of the RUF as an organised, disciplined, rational and goal-getting intellectu-ally-driven movement. In chapters one and two, we are told that the RUF destroyed Njala University College as part of a rational plan to 'liberate' other internal 'exiles' or excluded intellectuals. One incident of record burning is enough to demonstrate the rationality of the action since those who did it may have wanted to disguise the fact that they never graduated. The wider issue of why the entire university was vandalised, literally destroyed, and emp-tied of its property was not a subject for serious analysis.

The attack on the rutile and bauxite mines in which buildings were burned and lots of property looted was rationalised by Richards as an anti-APC move, since the mines provided revenue for that party's patrimonial leaders. The fact that the APC was no longer in office when the attack took place, and that the mines' buildings were not only burned but that large amounts of property was stolen by the RUF and some soldiers escapes attention in Richards's rationalist analysis. Richards later bemoans the failure of the RUF to convert the mines into 'insurgent' industries as other guerrilla movements have done elsewhere in the world, and questions the destruction of Njala in a context where educa-tional standards are very low. But in the end, he concludes that the RUF's pre-ferred choice of destructive acts should be seen as 'typical academic responses' (Ibid: 27).

Richards also states that the RUF provided alternative bush camp educa-tion to the rotten or non-existent formal education in rural areas. Tattered revolutionary texts found in RUF camps are held up as proof of the alterna-tive schooling that the RUF offered to youths whose educational aspirations had been aborted by the APC's failed patrimonial system. However, no effort is made to probe how this type of bush education compared with what many students who were captured in battle could have obtained in the schools, which the RUF destroyed. Richards also reports 'neatly planned lines of huts in RUF camps' and interprets this to mean that the RUF seeks to provide 'model housing for all', citing the RUF document, *Footpaths to Democracy*, as proof. (Ibid: 54). The question of why the RUF always sets out to destroy or burn down village houses during its operations is never probed. Richards even claims that the RUF only destroys villages that are not defended (Ibid: 55). But the issue of why any people's-oriented revolutionary movement should seek to destroy only 'undefended' villages is left unanswered. Furthermore, Richards tells us that Sankoh himself lacks presidential ambition (Ibid: 55), is above politics, and that he runs the RUF through a collective leadership. This is rationalised as Green Book ideology, which preaches the importance of people's assemblies in decision-making. It is indeed, very strange that no effort is made to examine alternative explanations to such claims – such as, for instance, the view that these claims could all be a smokescreen, which conceals a naked ambition for power, money and resources.

The RUF's ultimate aim, Richards asserts, is 'to replace Sierra Leone's patrimonial system with a revolutionary egalitarian system' (Ibid: 59). The redistribution of stolen goods to young recruits of the movement is seen as one indication of the movement's egalitarian beliefs. It does not occur to Richards that thieves can also redistribute goods to members and loyal friends and supporters in society; nor does he ponder the kind of rationality that lies behind the decision to forcibly and randomly loot the wealth of poor ordinary villagers in order to create an egalitarian society; or the RUF rationality which says that young villagers should be seized and transformed into modern slaves, subjected to forced labour on stolen RUF farms, and bullied to provide the material and social needs of RUF combatants.

Indeed, because of the simple-minded fixation with rationality, Richards evades or glosses over crucial forms of RUF behaviour that would have helped to shed much light on the character of the organisation: the systematic rape of women, which most people know about, is not addressed; the central issue of drug abuse is treated in just one paragraph; the beheading and systematic maiming of victims is hardly discussed; and the problem of random looting of property escapes serious scrutiny. Richards's last line of defence in sticking to his rationalist explanation is to say that the RUF's acts of violence 'may signal desperation, not terror' (Ibid: 25), and that the mass destruction of the countryside seeks to drive home the point that the wider society 'is dangerous and corrupt', and that victims of RUF violence may then realise that there is no home to return to until the final victory of the RUF and the reconstruction of society along the RUF's vision of egalitarian development (Ibid: 30).

Throughout this strange 'post-modernist' reading of the RUF's violence, Richards pays little heed to the voices of ordinary participants and victims of such violence, who keep reminding him that the rebels are 'evil people' (Ibid: 147, 92), and 'evil thugs' (Ibid: 149) who 'threatened the people to make them give (up) their property' (Ibid: 91). Such voices are not allowed full rein in Richards's analysis even though they are in line with what most Sierra Leoneans think about the RUF. When a wide, indeed, impenetrable gulf exists between the rhetoric of a movement and the reality of its behaviour, it becomes mandatory for scholars to revise their analytical frameworks and confront the reality itself. Failure to take into account the stark social reality, or at least what the majority of victims think it is, risks turning the works of such scholars into simple propaganda texts.

The one significant message of the war is the overwhelming, nation-wide rejection of the RUF's practice, including in areas that it claims to enjoy some support. The displacement of about one and half million villagers from their homes and the failure of the RUF to consistently administer any territory of consequence in the first six years of war should serve as sufficient testimony to its unqualified unpopularity and failure to advance its 'revolutionary' project. The vast majority of rural and urban Sierra Leoneans detest the RUF. Indeed, how rational is a movement whose methods of revolutionary struggle have simply served to alienate the bulk of society from its so-called revolutionary agenda? This is a question that Richards does not confront. The more the RUF uses barbarism to spread its message, the more it drives the people it wants to liberate to the very arms of the state that the movement claims it despises!

What Richards fails to do is to situate the political programme of the RUF in its proper socio-economic context, which should have revealed that the combatants themselves are pulled by a complex of contradictory forces: the pursuit of the long-standing goals of political liberation; the opportunities which war provided to loot the resources of the forest and the property of villagers for personal and collective gain; a 'lumpen' type of unaccountable, free-wheeling behaviour, which drugs and other anti-social behaviour-inducing mechanisms have generated or sustained among RUF fighters; and a tit-for-tat exchange in atrocities between the RUF combatants and government soldiers. In other words, RUF violence does not have only one logic, but several: there is obviously the logic of political violence, aspects of which are covered in Richards's analysis; but this competes, coexists and interacts with the logics of banditry, hedonism and brutality.

Understanding patrimonial rule and state contraction

Richards uses a multiple lense to explain the origins and dynamics of the Sierra Leone war. Unfortunately, several of the explanations – such as those relating to the quest for Greater Liberia, regional competition, and student revolutionary populism – are not pursued in the empirical areas of the text, and appear instead as add-ons intended to enrich the book's sophistication. Throughout the text, however, Richards tried to use the theory and practice of patrimonialism consistently enough as a key explanatory variable for the war. What he calls 'the crisis of patrimonialism' stands out as his most important framework for understanding the factors that led to the war. This, therefore, merits comments as part of the book's problem relates to Richards's inability to ground his analysis in concrete historical and political processes and explore the complex factors that made armed struggle and war an option of political resistance.

Briefly defined, patrimonialism is a system of resource distribution that ties recipients or clients to the strategic goals of benefactors or patrons. In the distribution of 'patrimony', or public resources, both patrons and clients attach more importance to personal loyalties than to the bureaucratic rules that should otherwise govern the allocation of such resources. According to Richards, patrimonialism in Sierra Leone owes its origins to the patron-client linkages that were developed during 'the days of direct extraction of forest resources', which spawned a culture in which the rich and successful protected and promoted their followers and friends (Ibid: 35; this is, of course, highly questionable). In the modern context, 'big persons' at the apex of power compete for the country's resources and distribute them to their followers. Richards singles out one aspect of patrimonial rule, such as the use of resources to resolve conflicts and outbid opponents, as indicative of the nature of patrimonial politics in Sierra Leone. This is illustrated by an anecdote about former president Siaka Stevens, who was said to have been comfortably installed at State House with 'a number of mobile generators', but who always reprimanded riotous students for not having told him about the erratic power supply on campuses, since he could have personally fixed the problem for them and prevented the riots.

Richards believes that patrimonialism thrives in natural resource-rich countries, since the formal mining companies would be responsible for the difficult tasks of state provisioning (such as communication, schooling and health services) in the 'enclave areas', leaving the politicians or rulers to collect rents for their personal use (he forgets that pre-crisis Nigeria and other oil-producing countries with fairly large social provisioning and development programmes exist). Such patron-client arrangements, he insists, can easily lead to a depletion of state revenues, which can only be sustained by foreign aid. Richards states that 'African patrimonial systems of rule grew vigorously under Cold War conditions' as African client leaders played off one Cold War leader against another. But patrimonialism, he asserts, faced a double crisis in the 1990s: a crisis of raw material prices and sharp reductions in foreign aid.

This double crisis created a crisis of legitimacy: the state shrank, both physically ('in terms of communications facilities') and sociologically ('in terms of the groups it can afford to patronise'). Education and social services collapsed, and salaries were unpaid or insufficient to cover living costs, giving the president and a few senior figures in government considerable powers to determine who got access to the limited resources that remained. The crisis affected the 'next generation' located at one end point of the patrimonial chain, which could not afford to pay school fees. Unable to generate resources to help clients to pay such fees, the leader or chief patron, ex-president Joseph Momoh, declared education to be a privilege and not a right. 'A dangerous vacuum' was created, which the RUF then sought to fill by providing alternatives to patrimonialism.

Richards's analysis, which taps into common sense explanations and current discourses of the African crisis, captures some features of the Sierra Leone state and political economy, and is correct in concluding that state contraction or collapse creates possibilities for social unrest or war. However, there are several problems with his analysis of patrimonialism, which fails to explain the kinds of state practices that forced some categories of Sierra Leone's youth to consider war or armed struggle a distinct option of political resistance. Richards is a bit slack in his efforts to transpose broadly held views about the African crisis to the Sierra Leone situation without ensuring that the socio-economic data of Sierra Leone fit the wider argument. Sierra Leone does, indeed, suffer from a fiscal crisis, and the crisis in raw material prices and output (even closure or exhaustion of some minerals), including a heavy debt burden, is an important contributory factor to this crisis. Nationally-generated government revenue did take a dive in the 1980s. However, the same cannot be said for foreign aid flows. Even though global official development assistance (ODA) has suffered a contraction of about 6 percent in the period of the 1990s (ActionAid, 1995), this decline has not negatively affected Sierra Leone's receipt of aid flows. Aid receipts have gone up consistently every year since 1987, except for 1990, which saw a sharp drop. In other words, official development assistance to Sierra Leone went up from US$68 million or 7.3 percent of GNP in 1987 to US$99 million or 10.6 percent of GNP in 1989; it dropped to US$66 million or 8.1 percent of GNP in 1990; but shot up to US$108 million or 10.8 percent of GNP in 1991; US$134 million or 14.5 percent of GNP in 1992; US$192 million or 29.7 percent of GNP in 1993; and US$276 million or 42.7 percent of GNP in 1994 (UNDP).[2]

Contrary to Richards's assertion that Sierra Leone is a victim of the ending of the Cold War in Africa (Ibid: 36) and the drop in global ODA flows to developing countries, the picture we get instead is that of a country that has become astonishingly aid-dependent in the 1990s when the cold war is supposed to have ended. It is important to note also that Sierra Leone never 'threatened to switch allegiance between communism and capitalism' in order to maximise aid from the 'Western and Soviet systems' (Ibid: 36). The APC was not a 'Soviet-style one party' regime, and did not have 'workerist associations' (Ibid: 40). In other words, the APC was never a revolutionary vanguard party, and lacked the kinds of organisational structures that tied the Communist Party in the USSR to associations in civil society. Labour, army, and police leaders were made members of parliament under the APC's one party regime, but this was part of a strategy to prevent unions, army officers and the police from disturbing the APC order. The party's organisational strength was only felt during periods of electoral competition or civil protests. Soviet aid to Sierra Leone came mainly in the form of scholarships, a large number of which went to members and friends of the APC Youth League. Instead, in addition to its links with Western countries, Sierra Leone cultivated closer ties with China, and used the latter's vigorous efforts to break its isolation from the rest of the world, to access financial and technical resources, and to develop trade links between the two countries. Indeed, by the early 1980s, China had become the third most important trading partner of Sierra Leone. The failure to properly contextualise Sierra Leone's crisis throws into considerable doubt the veracity of what Richards believes to be a patrimonial crisis.

It is important to note that the revenue crisis of the 1980s was partly linked to the informalisation of key industries like diamonds, and the collapse of the iron-ore mines, both of which had previously provided much of the state's official revenue. This informalisation of public resources was later extended to other sectors like fisheries and gold, and weakened government's capacity to collect revenue from state enterprises. For sectors, which required heavy capital investment, such as rutile and bauxite extraction, formal large-scale production was allowed, but as Richards correctly notes, state functionaries and company officials set official rents at well below market values with 'unaccountable sums disappearing into patrimonial pockets'. The key point is that leading politicians became dominant figures in the process of destroying the formal institutions for resource extraction, the management of public sector enterprises, and the regulatory mechanism that had ensured the transfer of revenues from such ventures to the state. The value of diamonds alone that were traded unofficially in international markets has been estimated to run into hundreds of millions of dollars a year.

If Richards's argument is that government officials were chief patrons in this thriving informalised market for Sierra Leone's resources, it becomes hard to accept his view that there was a 'patrimonial crisis' in Sierra Leone. The picture that emerges instead is that of a fiscal crisis, which affects general state administration and provisioning, and the fortunes of those who depend upon the state for their livelihood. In other words, the poverty of the state is positively correlated with the affluence of the 'patrimonial' groups. These groups, as most Sierra Leoneans know, were insensitive to the plight of those who operated outside of the 'patrimonial networks', and who, therefore, had been badly affected or humiliated by the informalisation of the country's resources and the astonishing contraction of the state. Rising foreign-aid receipts in the 1990s attempted to make up for the lost mining and parastatal revenues, which now went into so-called 'patrimonial' pockets. Indeed, Momoh's government waged a successful campaign in the UN system to redefine the status of the country – from that of a low income country to an LLDC (least of the less developed countries) in order to qualify for more loans and grants.

These efforts were pursued at a time when the APC government was busy dismantling the formal structures for effective revenue generation in both the public and private sectors, and selling off at a discount even some of the country's highly priced foreign assets to party supporters and foreign friends. The logic of the political class seemed to have been that the international community should be responsible for the welfare of the average Sierra Leonean, while government leaders, business groups and their supporters helped themselves to the country's rich resources. Patrimonialism was never threatened by such arrangements. Indeed, they strengthened it, as chief patrons or rulers passed on the burdens of national social provisioning and development to foreign aid agencies. Those who were outside of the so-called patrimonial system never stood a chance of benefiting from it. It is, indeed, unclear how marginal youth and Richards's excluded intellectuals could have benefited or suffered losses from the patrimonial system if they were not part of the patrimonial networks. From all accounts, these disadvantaged groups and other broad sections of the society suffered from the consequences of the crisis of the state and the deepening of the gains of patrimonialism – not from the crisis of patrimonialism.

Part of Richards's problem is the rather fuzzy way in which he applies the concept of patrimonialism to the Sierra Leone – indeed African – state. The African state has been poorly theorised in the works of most Africanists who have used the concept of neo-patrimonialism as a short cut to describe everything that the state in Africa does. As Thandika Mkandawire, once noted, Africanists who rely on the concept of neo-patrimonialism to describe the African state will have to explain why patrimonialism produced high rates of economic growth in most African countries in the 1960s and part of the 1970s, but dismal growth rates in the 1980s. Did patrimonialism suddenly emerge as a problem in the 1980s and 1990s? And why did patrimonialism allow one party and military regimes to flourish in much of Africa in the 1960s and 1970s, and not in the 1990s? The point, of course, is that the constant recourse to the concept of neo-patrimonialism could hide what is really very fuzzy thinking or lack of knowledge about the behaviour of African states and their actual dynamics. Those who use the concept of patrimonialism to explain the African crisis should, at least, be able to concretely identify the patrimonial groups – both the patrons and the clients – and changes in the volume and patterns of resource distribution among group members for their explanation to be credible.

Authoritarian rule, patrimonialism and the politics of war

Patrimonial arrangements constituted only one aspect of the problem of the Sierra Leone state. A fuller understanding of the political environment that created the conditions for the war requires analysis of other factors. Four such factors are worth mentioning. The first is the uncompromising and systematic centralisation of power under the governing All People's Congress, which gained power in 1968, following its victory in the elections of 1967 and a brief period of military rule. Despite much resistance from opposition political parties, the press and civic groups, full centralisation was achieved in 1978 when the APC made itself the sole political party in the country. The second factor was the equally systematic effort to destroy all forms of civic opposition – the labour unions, student unions, and the press – through repression, intimidation, and co-optation. Exit options, such as foreign migration, which grew in leaps and bounds in the 1970s and 1980s, reinforced the conditions for the shrinking of the civic arena and helped to reduce the political pressure on the government.

The third factor is the concentration of power in the capital and the neglect, or indeed, truncation, of development in rural areas. The concentration of power in the capital made it relatively easy for the ruling party and government to effectively deal with individual dissent or organised opposition. As part of the project to concentrate power in the capital, the district councils that provided a semblance of decentralised rule during colonialism and the first few years of independence were dismantled; and paramount chiefs became pawns of the government, which proceeded to make and unmake chiefs without regard for traditional procedures or democratic principles. Indeed, the only rule that governed decisions about who should be made chief was loyalty to the ruling party.

The fourth factor is the selective, but deliberate and undisciplined use of state violence to defend the APC order at specific conjunctures when it was challenged. A violence-prone para-military force, the Internal Security Unit (later State Security Division) was created; and politicians used the services of 'lumpen' or marginal elements of society to deal with party opponents and opposition civic groups. The language of violence as an instrument of political competition was freely used and justified in public speeches by leading members of the political leadership. The end result was a highly repressive, anti-developmental political system, which rewarded sycophancy (or what Sierra Leoneans like to refer to as *lay belleh*), and punished honesty, hard work, patriotism and independent thought. Abdullah and Ishmail Rashid, a student activist in the 1980s, have shown that it is the political regime that came out of these processes, in the context of a shrinking state system and blocked opportunities, that provided the conditions for the birth of revolutionary dissident activities and, ultimately, the formation of the RUF (this volume).

If Richards had focused on these issues, some of which he recognised but described rather sketchily in only two pages (Ibid: 40–42), it might have been possible for him to tell a different and more interesting story, and save some of his material on environmental and population issues for other intellectual pursuits. Indeed, the failure to pay sufficient attention to the country's political history, culture and dynamics meant that critical issues that relate to the politics of the war itself were only barely mentioned or totally ignored. Significant insights about the politics of the war had become public knowledge by the time the book was ready for the press in January 1996, which was subsequently revised after the May 1996 Sierra Leone electronic mail discussion group – Leonenet – debate on his article, 'Rebellion in Sierra Leone and Liberia' (See Oliver Furley, 1995).

Readers would have liked to learn something about the structure, social background, values and strategies of the official military and how they relate to, and conflict with, those of the RUF. It is well known, for instance, that the military recruited a large number of 'lumpens' or 'rarray boys' to prosecute the war against the RUF without checking their work records or social backgrounds. The army rapidly expanded in size by about five fold during this period. Both the RUF and the military basically recruited individuals with similar social backgrounds to fight the war. And the drug culture was central to the social practices of both soldiers and rebels in the war front. This may explain why innocent civilians became the main victims of both warring parties. It would have been interesting to pursue the view that part of the barbarism that the RUF displayed in the field was a response to similar methods of war practices from soldiers in the frontline. Also related to the issue of the politics of the war is the question of how the war spread beyond the border zones to engulf practically every region of the country. Richards should have examined the political and military logic that facilitated this transformation.

It is important to note that there was a very passionate debate in the country when the RUF rebellion engulfed the whole country. It was widely believed that some sections of the army colluded with the RUF to achieve this goal. Several military officers were even implicated by the military government and imprisoned for such acts of sabotage (Koroma, 1997). By 1994, the military regime that was warmly welcomed by Sierra Leoneans for overthrowing the rotten APC government had lost much of its support as people came to associate it with the problems of the war. Indeed, a very important national conference at Bintumani Conference Centre in Freetown in July 1994, in which the military government solicited the views of all paramount chiefs about how to end the war, demonstrated the wide gulf that had emerged between the state and traditional rulers, including, possibly, their subjects: paramount chiefs from the war zones made categorical demands to withdraw the soldiers from the war front as they were absolutely convinced that soldiers or *sobels* (soldiers-turned-rebels), as some of them came to be called, were partly responsible for the atrocities in the war.

This popular perception of the war process, as Muana tells us, was significant in the formation and growth of the *kamajoisia* militia movement as an antidote to the terror of both the RUF and the soldiers (Muana, Ibid). It was also significant in understanding why the military regime was unable to pressure the chiefs in the war zone and the rest of the population to extend its stay in power in the events leading to the elections of February 1996. Most of these issues have been widely discussed by home-based Sierra Leoneans and covered extensively in the national press, but Richards does not seem to take the national press seriously, perhaps because of his belief that at times it contains more opinion than factually based news' (Ibid:113). He discussed the national press in only one short paragraph in the chapter on youth and the media, even though it is obvious that large sections of the youth population read these papers regularly as a source of news, opinions, entertainment, and education – in several ways, perhaps, using the national print media in the same 'skeptical but constructive way' that Richards talks about in his discussion of films and videos. Richards makes no reference to any discussion or reporting of the war in the national newspapers in his very extensive bibliography.

It is also well known that the RUF war fed, or ignited, deep-seated local conflicts in the war zones. It has been reported that 'rebels' sometimes selected which houses to burn and who to first kill, based on information supplied by willing or coerced local residents seeking to settle scores with their opponents in the local communities, whose politics had been influenced by the strategies of the ruling national political party. Richards briefly discussed one clear instance of this dynamic, the *Ndogboyosoi* revolt in Pujehun, which he labelled 'rebellion from below', but treated it as one among several interpretations of the war, rather than as a key aspect of the process of war itself. One would have liked to see how the tendency to use the war to settle local scores was articulated in such well-known cases as the RUF's brief take-over of, for instance, Koidu, Kailahun, Pujehun, Kabala, Yele, Mile 91 and Masingbi. A discussion of local political institutions and processes would have made more sense than the selective and superficial treatment of aspects of traditional local culture, which Richards even detaches from the politics of local communities.

Youth, violence and war

Richards is correct in singling out the deepening crisis of youth and its exclusion from the social mainstream as important factors in explaining the early
appeal of the RUF among certain strata of youth, and why the movement has
been able to retain a core membership of loyal cadre, despite the serious
setbacks it has suffered in the war. The political statement of the RUF, drawn
up by expelled radical university students, appealed to the concerns of youth
and other disadvantaged groups in popular struggles to dismantle the corrupt
APC regime and institute a just and democratic polity that would protect the
basic needs of Sierra Leoneans. Those who hammered out the programme
may have been partly influenced by Gaddafi's Green Book ideology, but it is
doubtful that Gaddafi's text was that important in shaping the world view or
programme of the movement itself. The ideas it propounds are drawn from a
range of populist discourses that were current among many Left-wing uni-
versity-based groups in the 1970s and 1980s. Richards's attempt to read Green
Book ideology into every RUF action demonstrates a poor grasp of student
politics and actual RUF field practices.

Sierra Leone does have a phenomenal youth crisis and Richards's book
demonstrates this very vividly. Indeed, much of the narrative revolves around
the problems and perceptions of youth as they relate to issues of livelihood,
employment, education, media messages, the environment, and general survival strategies in the forest economy. Richards provides very useful insights
when he discusses youth problems in border areas that he has previously
worked on, which relate to his research project on ecology, culture and social
systems. The three detailed individual testimonies in chapter four throw much
light on the dilemmas of young people on the margins of society, and the role
which violence has played in the history of forest communities. This violence, as each one of the narratives maintains, has always been driven by
external forces or 'big men', anxious to exploit and destroy the forest's rich
resources – such as the conversion of humans into slaves in the Atlantic
trade, the depletion of the rain forest by timber merchants and colonial officials interested in the region's high quality mahogany tree products, the near
annihilation of elephants whose tusks were in great demand in Europe to
make ivory keyboards for the pianos that adorned the homes of Victorian
families, and the networks of unequal exchange that currently tie young mi-
grant diamond diggers to powerful patrons in the urban areas.

However, in his efforts to give substance and flavour to his narrative,
Richards displays a basic weakness in his method of work: he is too quick to
establish connections and to indulge in unguarded speculation, often on the
basis of very limited information or isolated experiences that may not have
been properly investigated. This tends to do much damage to the credibility

of the issues on which he seems to have much firmer information. Several illustrations will help to substantiate this point. In his treatment of the history of the Liberia-Sierra Leone border region, the status and social reach of the nineteenth century ruler of Luawa, Kai Londo, featured prominently as a major source of perennial instability in the region.

Richards concludes on the basis of the evidence of just one individual from Liberia, who complained to him about the colonial border policy of the British, which split village communities and strengthened the power of Kai Londo's successors against groups in Liberia, that there was a strong call for a Greater Liberia among bush fighters that would encompass part of the old Luawa polity in Sierra Leone. This call is then said to serve as an 'advance for the NPFL, or RUF, or both' armed groups (Ibid: 48), implying that the invasion of Eastern Sierra Leone in 1991 by the RUF and NPFL, which started the war, may have had something to do with this demand for the creation of a Greater Liberia. What started as a nice little story that was adapted from Arthur Abraham's study of nineteenth century politics on the border zone of Liberia and Sierra Leone turned out instead to be an effort to force conceptions of Greater Liberia on the Sierra Leone war. Richards is not bothered about the extent to which this appeal for Greater Liberia resonates among the majority of youth on both sides of the border and whether, in fact, it forms an important part of the strategies of both the RUF and the NPFL.

Another instance of hasty connections relates to the popular film, First Blood, and its likely effects on the behaviour of youth in Sierra Leone. The film is said by Richards to speak 'eloquently to young people in Sierra Leone fearing a collapse of patrimonial support in an era of state recession' (Ibid: 58). Such a conclusion is drawn even though Richards provides no evidence that the young people who watched the film were part of the patrimonial system that he bemoans. And Rambo, the key character in the film, is likened to another Sierra Leonean 'youth trickster of Mende tradition', Musa Wo, who is said to be a 'harbinger of fruitful innovation' in Mendeland, and whose stories are said to caution elders not to forget the 'energy and cunning' of the young. Richards then concludes that based on this experience of youth creativity that the destructive act of war by the 'young tricksters' of the RUF is 'to establish a national debate about a new and fairer patrimonialism' (Ibid: 59). There are many more of such types of unfounded speculation, which are likely to raise the eyebrows of readers who are familiar with the Sierra Leone scene.

The chapter on youth exposure to modern media addresses interesting issues on films, video and violence, but Richards equates the opinions of the bulk of the youth who have not been exposed to war with those of war combatants, whose views on the uses and abuses of video are clearly not sought in the survey. The fact that the former may creatively use film and video for peaceful imaginative and social pursuits does not mean, as Richards believes, that rebels do not 'feed Rambo films to their young conscripts as incitement to mindless violence' (Ibid:114). Richards fails to make a distinction between youths in war and youths in peace, and the likely effects of violent films on their different social experiences.

It is important to stress the point that the vast majority of Sierra Leone's youth are not war-prone. Most young people are linked to wider social structures that bind them to broadly shared community values and family-based systems of accountability. These social values and systems may have experienced considerable strain as a result of economic crisis, state contraction and war, but they have played a significant role in denying the RUF the bulk of the support it would have enjoyed from this group. The question Richards does not ask is why the majority of youth, including those in desperately poor situations, have not been attracted to the RUF's rhetoric of revolutionary change. My guess is that they have seen or heard about much of the RUF's violence to know that the RUF's project does not offer the path to stable youth salvation.

The vast majority of Sierra Leone's youth are anti-RUF. They sustain life as traders, artisans, farmers, apprentices, labourers, workers, tailors, dancers, dramatists, domestics and office helpers, in the now over-crowded cities and small rural towns. They are to be distinguished from youths with loosely structured relations of work and family life: lumpens who, as Abdullah's study suggests, are the driving force of the RUF project, even if other types of youth may have been coerced or recruited into the movement. Richards does not pay special attention to this category of youth as the foundation of the RUF movement.

Furthermore, one would be wary to embrace his conclusion, on the basis of an opinion survey whose methodology is not even explained, that the youth have a capacity 'to devise imaginative solutions to the challenges posed by the global epidemic of drugs and violence' (Ibid: 114), and that 'videos of violence may not be such a cause for alarm as some Western commentators choose to think' (Ibid: 104). Richards does not state what these imaginative solutions are, since his concern is to debunk the New Barbarism thesis. It is as if owning up to some drawbacks in youth behaviour would strengthen the case for New Barbarism. It ought to be stressed that lumpens abuse drugs and are prone to random violence in pursuit of objectives. And other non-lumpen categories of youth who are affected by drugs and excessive exposure to violent films may experience, and at the same time pose, serious social problems. These problems are not unique to Sierra Leone's, or Africa's, youth: they cut across most countries in the world, including in Western societies where they may have reached epidemic proportions. It does not help the search for solutions to these global problems to deny the fact that they constitute a problem for Sierra Leone's youth.

War–Peace transitions

Let me now examine Richards's recommendations on conflict resolution and peace-building initiatives. Richards puts much emphasis on the need to assist the efforts of 'citizen action' in rebuilding Sierra Leone's society, and cites cases where local efforts at peace building are already manifesting themselves in the Bo region. Peace, as he correctly states, has to come from within, and from the efforts of local people. This is based on the view that international assistance may not be very forthcoming to provide the kinds of resources that would make the project of post-war reconstruction less painful. Even when such assistance is provided, he warns that it should be used strategically and not liberally: it should come in the form of 'smart relief', which should shift the focus of relief from bulk food items to 'knowledge-intensive assistance', such as the provision of seed systems, genetic information and farmer intervention; this should be supported by systems of broadcasting to facilitate constructive debates in local areas about war-peace transitions.

Relying on Alex de Waal's and Mike Duffield's works on famines and the shortcomings of international agencies in providing relief in famine-prone and war-torn countries, Richards argues that the current international obsession with 'high profile' relief may weaken the emerging peace-enhancing 'attack trade' regime in war-affected regions: 'attack trade' regimes are trade deals which local people strike with combatants as a survival and commercial strategy that is suited to environments of protracted insurgency. In any case, he believes that by concentrating resources in particular areas, high profile relief has a potential to attract rebel attention and prolong wars. Richards's alternative is to make 'attack traders' contractors for the supply of relief items to refugee feeding programmes. It does not occur to him that 'attack trade' has a strong potential to endlessly feed wars, and legitimise war itself as a way of life in the regions where such trade occurs – the cases of Colombia, Afghanistan, Cambodia, Liberia and Angola, where 'attack trade' has turned war into huge commercial ventures escape his attention.

Richards identifies three Sierra Leonean traditions that he believes will help to contain the war and promote peace-building efforts. The first is what he calls the 'creolisation' of the Upper Guinea Forest region, of which Sierra Leone is a part. He highlights two types of creolisation: the creolisation that is a product of the Atlantic slave trade, which saw the resettlement of large numbers of Africans from different ethnic and regional backgrounds in Freetown, and which gave rise to Krio as a lingua franca in Sierra Leone; the other type of creolisation relates to what he refers to as the pre-colonial, largely sixteenth century, process of the 'Mandigoization' of the forest communities – leading to the adoption of a simplified 'trade version' of Manika as lingua franca, even suggesting a Manika root for the Krio language. Creolisation, he asserts, promotes cultural convergence and accommodation, checks conflicts, and provides the necessary cultural resources for the management of peace and stability. The concept of creolisation is an emerging fad among Western anthropologists and linguists, who have been anxious to move the debate on African social formations away from the old concept of 'tribe' that has been shown to have no empirical validity to one that now recognises the inter-penetration of cultures and languages. Richards latches on to this debate without adequate work on its implications for the Sierra Leone experience, and draws very contentious conclusions about the peace-yielding properties of creolisation.

It is obviously the case that the Krio language is the lingua franca of Sierra Leone. It serves as an important medium of communication among the country's youth. The language itself has been highly enriched by a number of Sierra Leonean and other African languages. Having a common language that most people understand may help to promote social integration but it does not necessarily prevent or solve conflicts. If use of a common language were a significant constraint to war, the world would not have witnessed the genocidal carnage in Rwanda, Burundi and Bosnia, as the warring communities in those countries speak the same language. What Richards fails to analyse are the complex layers of social relations and contradictions that structure the behaviour of those who use the Krio language. The emergence of Krio as a lingua franca has not eliminated other forms of ethnic identities and associations. Indeed, because of the wide use of the language, there are now several versions of Krio, which tend to reflect the ethnic origins and social or class status of the users. Besides, as a result of the systematic politicisation of ethnicity, beginning from the decolonisation period, the 'natural' process of 'Krioisation', which was previously associated with exposure to Western thought and practice, has considerably slowed down, if it has not been actually reversed.

Today, in Freetown, in addition to a large number of youth who still speak their ethnic languages in addition to Krio, there are many young people whose parents come from the hinterland who speak no other language than Krio (they are probably a much larger group now than those who use the language as a mark of their identity) but who do not identify themselves as Krio. If ethnicity has not been politicised, the youth who speak only Krio should have automatically identified themselves as Krio, since they share fairly common values and aspirations with those who identify themselves as such. Instead, the former identify themselves on the basis of their parents' identities even though they may not understand the institutions and values that are associated with such parental identities.

An urban culture has emerged that is a product of the experiences of the various groups (literally all the nationalities) that have shaped the everyday dynamics of the city. This culture cannot be reduced to that of any one nationality, or even the old type of Krio ethnicity. Instead, it embraces several aspects of these other types, as users incorporate or borrow whatever that is found useful for urban social integration and communication. This urban culture continues to co-exist with the relatively separate cultures, traditions and languages of the other ethnic groups in the city. While there is a high level of social integration, particularly among the youth, politics tends to be strongly influenced by the pulls of ethnicity as opposed to the pulls of 'creolisation' or even of the new urban culture.

We encounter similar problems when we examine Richards's thesis on 'Mandingoization' as creolisation. Here, Richards tries to force ideas on the Sierra Leone social reality that are largely relevant to other countries' cultural and linguistic experiences. It is true that the Mandingo language and culture have had positive effects on several communities and languages in West Africa, including in Sierra Leone. Mandingo competes with Fula as the language that is spoken in most countries in the region. Fula, however, failed to develop as lingua franca in any West African country, and is spoken largely by individuals who identify themselves as Fula. Fula was even overwhelmed and absorbed by the Hausa language in Nigeria despite the fact that it was Fulani intellectuals and religious militants who sacked the traditional Hausa states and established the Sokoto Caliphate in 1804, which incorporated Hausaland and other contiguous areas. It is useful to note also that even though variants of the Mandingo language are a trade-based lingua franca in several West African countries, Hausa is still the most widely spoken language in the region – claiming, perhaps, about 50 million or so speakers; and that there may even be more Yoruba (perhaps 20 or more million) and Igbo speakers (at least 15 million) than Mandingo speakers.

The version of Mandingo, Dioula, that Richards correctly cites, as a trade language in parts of the sub-region, is not used as lingua franca in Sierra Leone. Even though Mandingo and Mende, which is the lingua franca of the East and South of Sierra Leone, are part of the Mande group of languages, Mende and Madingo are not mutually intelligible. Only Mandingo, Kono, Koranko and Vai are mutually intelligible. The regional reach of Mandingo, popularised by traders, Islamic teachers, praise singers and musical entertainers, has meant that many of the languages of Sierra Leone are flavoured with Mandingo words. The word for a rich person in a non-related language, Temne, for instance, is *yolla*, possibly derived from the Madingo word, *dioula*, meaning trader.

There has been a high level of cross fertilisation of cultures and ideas among the various ethnic groups in the country. But Mandingo can hardly be said to be the dominant influence in this process of social integration. Instead, it would seem that most groups have benefited from a long process of mutually beneficial cultural exchanges. Because of the strong hold of Mende in the South and East, and Temne in the North, Dioula could not serve the same purposes in Sierra Leone as it did, for instance, in Côte d'Ivoire and parts of Liberia. Instead, Mandingo traders, teachers, artisans and musicians were absorbed into the expansive cultures of the Temnes and Mendes. This process of incorporating individuals into the cultures of dominant nationalities is not unique to the Upper Guinea Forest region. It is a world-wide process in the formation of nations. Indeed, all African countries today have one or a few local languages that have emerged as lingua franca.

The same experience that Richards describes as creolisation holds for the development of, for instance, Arabic in the Middle East, Swahili in East Africa, English in the UK and in America, Spanish and Portuguese in Latin America, Italian in Italy, Lingala and Swahili in Zaire, Wolof in Senegal, Twi in Ghana, and Amharic in Ethiopia. In other words, the concept of 'creolisation' loses its heuristic value once it is shown that all modern societies in the world have multi-ethnic and multi-lingual origins. This reality of shared history has not eliminated the scourge of war from our planet. Rather than creolisation being a crucial factor in checking the violence in Sierra Leone, it is rather the shared national experience of, and refusal to be intimidated by, RUF brutality that has kept the country together. We have also been lucky that the RUF movement was inspired by a radical youth vision of pan-Africanism and national unity – not ethnic divisions. Lumpens, we should also note, are generally not moved by ethnicity unless if they are employed by politicians to settle ethnic scores. On top of this must be added the rapid rate of regime turnover, which made it difficult for some of the ethnic interests that were already building up around state leaders to consolidate their grip on power, and colour the popular discourses on the war.

The second tradition, which Richards thinks will enhance the prospects for peace, is that of the initiation of young men and women into Bondo/Sande and Poro secret societies. He argues that these societies could play useful roles in civil defence and act as forums for debate on issues of war and peace, and training of youth in post-war reconstruction activities. Useful as these suggestions may be, Richards does not show how they could be achieved for a youth population that he has already projected as holding strong 'modernist' views and aspirations about society. Furthermore, while Richards recognises the positive values of these societies, adherents may find it disturbing to relate to the connections that he draws between the initiation rituals of these societies and the seizure of young people in forest areas for initiation into the RUF movement. He believes that both the RUF's communities' initiation activities form part of the same process of initiation of young people in 'bush schools' to 'adult ways'. He ignores the crucial distinction between traditional forms of initiation, which are forms of socialisation that enjoy community support, and the RUF type which is plainly terroristic, and which may have the consequences of destroying community institutions and values.

Richards's third traditional resource for peace building is 'cannibalism', which he thinks acts as an antidote to, or a 'moral critique' of, patrimonialism. He extracts sets of supernatural beliefs that are common in traditional societies to discuss how weaker clients can use ideas of 'cannibalism' to challenge the power of patrons or 'big men' in society. Cannibalism refers to a deeply held belief in most traditional communities that certain types of people have supernatural powers to turn into animals – say leopards, baboons or crocodiles – to bewitch or 'eat' people whom they do not like. Richards assumes that this belief is restricted only to patron-client commercial relations, and that it is only patrons who have the power to change into animals to bewitch clients. He also assumes that the wider society that loses from the modern patrimonial rule can invoke the traditional moral critique of cannibalism, thereby denting their legitimacy and capacity to rule.

The reality is that these beliefs cover all facets of social relations; and society has developed ways of dealing with them – such as employing the services of traditional experts such as 'diviners, 'murray man', and 'medicine men' to expose the activities of those who possess such qualities; and personal or family-based initiatives involving use of 'medicines', 'lassmami', and traditional power-enhancing devices such as amulets to repel such evil forces in the spirit world. However, it is difficult to see how the so-called 'cannibalism' method could act as a check on present day patrimonialism, especially when modern-day patrons know that these ideas lack empirical foundations, and when they have the means to employ the services of 'medicine men' or 'murray man' to counter the power of the so-called 'cannibals', or accusations of cannibalism. Reading this kind of stuff from someone who thinks that the crisis of patrimonialism is the most important cause of the war, creates the impression that Richards does not actually understand the society that he writes about.

Conclusion

Patrimonialism exists in varying degrees in all societies, irrespective of the character of their economic systems, levels of development, or political culture. In other words, personal ties, contacts, or networks, constitute inherent aspects of social relations, and influence the behaviour of public institutions. High levels of bureaucratisation can act as an important check on such personal ties and relations, but it does not eliminate them. The problem basically arises when formal bureaucratic rules become subordinated to 'patrimonial' arrangements or vested interests, making it difficult for those who are cut off from, or do not want to be included in, the 'patrimonial' networks to benefit from the services of the state, and hold leaders accountable to their policies. Something of the nature of this problem took root in Sierra Leone under the long rule of the APC, whose leaders abused the formal rules of governance and converted a large proportion of the country's resources into private or informal property regimes, which they then controlled or profited from. Sierra Leoneans paid a heavy price for the triumph of this informalised, inefficient, and authoritarian order.

The challenge in post-war reconstruction, it seems, is not to aim for a 'patrimonial-free' polity – which is clearly unachievable – but to ensure that vested interests, or patrimonial groups, where they emerge, are transparently regulated and held accountable to their public behaviour; and that the state system is structured in ways that can allow it to meet the minimum demands of groups who entirely depend upon it for such things as education, health, clean water, electricity, jobs and incomes. Issues of decentralisation; rural, grass roots development; the empowerment of local-level civic initiatives; the restoration and defence of healthy political competition; the protection of civil liberties and community values; and the de-linking of the state's coercive institutions from its past culture of violence should form important aspects of the strategies for a stable and equitable post-war society.

Notes

1   The book *Fighting for the Rain Forest* has gone through several reprints since it was first published in 1996. The author has however refused to engage or even acknowledge the works of Sierra Leonean scholars critical of his scholarship. See *Africa Development* 22, 3&4 1997, special issue 'Lumpen Culture and Political Violence: The Sierra Leone Civil War'.

2   Note the radical decline of GDP in the 1990s. No doubt, the war and the disruption of formal productive activities may have contributed to this decline. It is possible, however, that much of the unofficial economic transactions, which gained prominence even before the war, may have been unrecorded.

2

Bush Path to Destruction:
The Origin and Character of the
Revolutionary United Front (RUF/SL)

Ibrahim Abdullah

We recruited 54 boys, mostly from Bugisu, and started training them at Nachingwea. Unfortunately, once again, these boys had not been well selected. They had mostly been working in towns like Nairobi and had a *kiyaye* (lumpen proletariat) culture. They began misbehaving in the Frelimo camp and soon after their training, the Tanzanian government dispersed them.

I took personal charge of the Montepuez group and stayed with the boys during the training months in Mozambique because I feared that some of the recruits might be undisciplined *bayaye*, like those of 1973, and they might have caused us problems. With my presence in the camp, however, we were able to suppress most of their negative tendencies and attitudes.

Yoweri Museveni (*Sowing the Mustard Seed*, 1997: 85, 90)

When the Revolutionary United Front/Sierra Leone (RUF/SL) entered Kailahun District on 23 March 1991, few people took them seriously or even realised that a protracted and senseless war was in the making. The corrupt and inept government in Freetown was quick to label the movement as the handy work of Charles Taylor; the incursion a spill over from the Liberian civil war. This erroneous representation of the movement and the war was echoed by the media, both local and foreign; it later appeared in one scholarly investigation as 'the border war', and in another as an attempt by Charles Taylor to 'do a RENAMO' on Sierra Leone (Fyle, 1994; Zack-Williams and Riley, 1993). Twelve months after the initial attack in Kailahun, a group of young army officers from the warfront trooped to Freetown, the seat of government, and seized power from the corrupt politicians amidst popular support. Calling itself the National Provisional Ruling Council (NPRC), the new regime declared its intention to end the war, revamp the economy, and put the nation on the path to multi-party democracy.

What is the relationship between these two events? What is the link between the 'Revolution' (*coup d'état*) in Freetown and the 'Revolutionary' movement in the hinterland? What did the coup plotters, most of whom were in their 20s, share with those who had started the insurrection that gave them the opportunity to launch their 'revolution' in the city? Why did both movements borrow the same 'revolutionary' script? I provide answers to some of these questions by examining lumpen culture and youth resistance in Sierra Leone, for it is this oppositional culture that connects the 'revolution' in the hinterland (RUF) and the one in the city (NPRC), the seat of political power. Both were products of a rebellious youth culture in search of a radical alternative (though without a concrete emancipatory programme) to the bankrupt All Peoples Congress (APC) regime. To understand the historical and sociological processes, which gave birth to RUF, with which this chapter is concerned, it is necessary to situate the investigation within the context of Sierra Leone's political culture, especially the glaring absence of a radical post-colonial alternative. It is this absence, I argue, which paved the way for the bush path to destruction.

A radical tradition/alternative?

The demise of the militant Youth League inaugurated by Sierra Leone's legendary Pan-Africanist cum revolutionary in 1939 did not presage the end of radical labour/political agitation ((Denzer, 1977; Abdullah, 1995). Rather, it closed the formal avenues for radical politics through a series of concessions, in the form of constitutional arrangements, which eventually led to independence. Eliphas Mukunoweshuro has admirably mapped out the contours of this process of negotiation in his study of decolonisation in Sierra Leone (1993; Kilson, 1966; Cartwright, 1970). The sanitisation of politics, which was its outcome, did not adversely affect the labour movement. Labour activists such as Marcus Grant and Henry Georgestone who were inspired by the Youth League tradition of continuous agitation became influential in shaping the process of remaking the working class inaugurated by the colonial office and the labour department once Wallace-Johnson had been imprisoned and the organisation proscribed. The battle over an independent working class organisation and movement was the most important factor, which shaped post-war politics and labour agitation in the mines and in the city of Freetown. The incorporation and subsequent co-optation of prominent labour leaders Akinola Wright and Siaka Stevens into positions of authority in the era of decolonisation, did not blunt the radical edge of labour politics. In 1950, strikes and riots rocked the iron ore mines, while in 1952 diamond miners in

Yengema demanded a wage raise and shut down the mines for two weeks. In February 1955, Marcus Grant with the active support of Wallace-Johnson, defied the colonial state and called a general strike, which paralysed the city, and forced colonial officials and employers to concede workers' demand for a raise and the right to bargain directly with their employers (Abdullah, 1997).

The Youth league tradition was therefore alive in the 1950s; but it did not assume a national dimension nor did it emerge as a coherent and organised force in post-colonial politics. Arguably, it was partly because of the defeat of the Youth League and partly because of Wallace-Johnson's exit to Ghana that radical politics or a leftist tradition was shunted out of Sierra Leone's political culture. Attempts to revive this radical tradition with a working class party, the Sierra Leone Labour Party, were abandoned after the party was defeated in the 1957 elections.[1] Elsewhere in West Africa, notably Ghana, Nigeria, and Senegal, a radical tradition was kept alive in the labour movement and in national politics. What therefore marked Sierra Leone's post-independence politics was not its tolerance of a leftist tradition in the labour movement or in national politics, but its conservative orientation and uncritical support for the West. The APCs pretence at reviving the Youth League tradition was betrayed by its ethnic composition and empty socialist rhetoric.[2] It was only after the party made an impressive start in the 1962 general elections, and then swept the polls in the 1964 city council elections, that it was able to establish its credentials as a viable opposition. Siaka Stevens' trade union career and the party's predominantly working and the lower-middle- class leadership, lent credence to its claim to radicalism. This was in sharp contrast to the Sierra Leone Peoples Party (SLPP), which was dominated by the upper and middle class professionals, and their 'traditional' allies, the Paramount Chiefs (Cartwright, 1970).

But the APC government after 1968 was markedly different from the party in opposition or when it controlled the Freetown City Council. Once it had successfully reduced the number of SLPP members in the House of Representatives through fraudulent and not so fraudulent election petitions, in which the judiciary fully acquiesced, the party quickly began to dismantle the national coalition cabinet that was instituted in 1968. This move signalled the beginning of the APC's consolidation of power, and opened the road to a one-party dictatorship (Alpha Lavalie, 1985). From 1970, when the first attempt to unseat the government was made by Brigadier John Bangura and others, for which Foday Sankoh, the future RUF leader was jailed, to the alleged coup attempt involving Mohammed Sorie Forna and fourteen others, to the fraudulent elections of 1973 and 1977, the APC party did all it could to stifle the opposition and consolidate power. By 1978 when the one-party state was declared, the SLPP had been disabled by the arrest and detention of its members. The atmosphere of violence against any form of organised opposition or dissent, and the simultaneous centralisation of power in the hands of the party and the Pa, as President Stevens was normally referred to, transformed the state and by implication politics into an affair for and by APC members and supporters (APC: *The Rising Sun,* 1982). This centralisation of politics made access to resources impossible for non-members; it made membership of the party a *sine qua non* to get by; exclusion literally meant death by attrition (Kandeh, 1992; Zack-Williams, 1990). The end result of this process of extreme centralisation was the sidelining of state bureaucracy, the emasculation of civil groups, and the emergence of complex informal networks through which the affair of state was conducted. Informalisation meant direct access to party officials. It was within this context that university students and youth emerged as the informal opposition to the corrupt and decadent APC.

Uprising discourses: The making of an informal opposition

The search for an alternative political space to the SLPP, not necessarily a radical one, did not emanate from the youth. Nor did they make any systematic or independent contribution, based on their own agenda, towards the defeat of the SLPP. The immediate post -colonial period, from independence in 1961 to 1968, was characterised by a tussle for power between the two organised political machines: the SLPP and the APC. If the youths were involved their role was simply one of foot soldiers. Their marginalisation was expressed in the form of party youth wings; an arm of the party always peripheral to where real power was located. Their performance could therefore be read as a ritual; it always began with a crisis situation, and their mobilisation as thugs to do the dirty work. Once the project was complete, they fall back to the wings, waiting for another assignment. This reading of the political role of youth does not mean that those who joined the so-called youth wing were all thugs. But their role was strictly limited to 'action oriented tasks', such as the arson at Ginger Hall in Freetown in 1970, and the assault on students at Fourah Bay College (FBC) in 1977, with occasional trips to communists countries. On both occasions it was the unimaginative and politically ambitious members in the party's youth wing who organised lumpen youth (thugs) to do the dirty work. It was only in the 1970s that the party gave those who were still in the fold a rightful place in the sun.[3]

An interesting angle to ponder is why youth. An obvious historical parallel is Wallace-Johnson's Youth League. Was this performance of youth a throw back to the Youth League era of the 1930s? Siaka Stevens' admiration and respect for Wallace-Johnson is well known. Was this therefore a conscious attempt to re-enact that tradition by revisiting the Youth League days? These questions on historical memory and performance are tantalising not least because Wallace-Johnson's activities were youth centred: employed as well as unemployed. And he had argued in the heydays of Youth League radicalism in the 1930s that the youth of Sierra Leone would one day assume the mantle of radical leadership and redeem 'the Athens of West Africa' in the eyes of the Black World and of humanity (Denzer, 1977). Was this therefore the Wallacian dream come true or was it a caricature? I would argue that the youth project which started unfolding under the APC in the 1960s, and which inevitably culminated in the emergence of the RUF/NPRC, does not constitute a re-enactment of the Wallacian script because it lacked the discipline and the maturity that Wallace-Johnson was known to constantly emphasise in his writings and speeches. Yet it raises an interesting historical question: the role of historical memory (ies) in the construction/reconstruction of a radical project.

By Lumpens, I refer to the largely unemployed and unemployable youths, mostly male, who live by their wits or who have one foot in what is generally referred to as the informal or underground economy. They are prone to criminal behaviour, petty theft, drugs, drunkeness and gross indiscipline. It is precisely this culture, with its anti-social characteristics, which Yoweri Museveni so eloquently describes in his autobiography (Museveni, 1996). This youth culture, which became visible in the post 1945 period, had its genealogy in the so-called rarray boy culture.[3] It is a male-specific oppositional culture that easily lends itself to violence. In Nigeria, they are referred to as *yan banga* and *jaguda* boys (or the now popular area boys) respectively; in Algeria, they are called *hittiste*; in Uganda they are generally refered to as *bayaye*; and in Zambia they are *Kaponye* – they are to be found in every city in Africa (El-Kenz, 1996; Truilizi, 1996; Museveni, 1997). Their role in post-colonial politics, especially their discourse on empowerment and marginality, is only now beginning to attract scholarly attention.

In Sierra Leone, the first generation *rarray* boys acted as thugs for the politicians, a role they played partly because of their defective education (Abdullah, 2002). Mostly unlettered, they were predominantly second-generation residents in the city, whose abode, the *pote*, (historically a popular peri-urban rendezvous for unemployed youths), was also a cultural/leisure space constructed around the *odelay* (masquerade).[4] They were known for their anti-social culture: gambling, drugs (initially marijuana now crack cocaine), petty theft, and violence. Their periodic carnivals on public holidays are always under the watchful eyes of the police. Their revelry and riotous conduct alienated them from the city inhabitants: they were seen as a good-for-nothing bunch, best avoided.

This representation of lumpen culture began to change in the early 1970s, particularly when middle-class youths and other respectable bunch became key players in this urban popular culture. The character and composition of the *pote* also began to change as *odelays* emerged as a more reputable and respectable pillar of the urban cultural landscape. Yet this change was replete with the contradictory tendencies inherent in lumpens as a social category. Thus whereas politicians were interested in taming and co-opting this culture to ensure a ready supply of thugs to do their dirty work, the entry of middle-class youth and others into the *pote* as participants in the periodic carnivals, transformed the culture as well as the nature of the *pote* from an area for social misfit into one of political socialisation and counter-cultural activities. A majority of the middle- class youth elements was still in high school but participated in the drug culture, and gradually acquired the mannerisms, language and iconography of the emerging popular culture. Others dropped out of school entirely, following the footsteps of the original *rarray boys*. The entry of this new crop transformed the social composition of the *pote*. This change coincided with the coming of reggae music and a decided turn to the political.

The influence of music was at first local: it was the rhythm of local rock musicians, drug and political talk. It started in 1971 with Purple Haze, a musical group in the city of Freetown, then came Super Combo from Bo, followed by Afric Jessips, Suberb Seven from Liberia, and Sabanoh '75. The reggae music of Bob Marley, Peter Tosh, Burney Wailer and Jimmy Cliff, and the confrontational political lyrics of Fela Anikulapo-Kuti's Afro-beat, added another dimension to the repertoire of youth rebelliousness and non-conformity. Liberation struggles against settler colonialism also contributed to the development of this new oppositional culture. The *pote*, like the English pub, became an arena for discussions centred on what was popularly referred to as *de sistem*. Foday Sankoh, the RUF leader echoed this 1970s discourse in an interview: 'I said when I come out (from prison) I will organize the system' (Interview, Concord Times, Dec. 1996,9). System 'dread' became a slogan and a rallying call for alienated youths in the *potes*, who were mostly unemployed. The popularity of marijuana, the drug of choice, brought diverse groups to the *pote*, so that *pote* language gradually began to filter into mainstream society. Lumpen youth culture was suddenly at the cutting edge in the development of the Krio language, the vocabulary expanding to incorporate *pote* terms from gambling, petty theft, and hustling. The transformation from *rarray* boy to *savis man* (street wise) – as they subsequently became known – was complete with a new language and an iconography of resistance in which FBC students played a pivotal role. This transformation was concretized in a linkage between town and gown.

Ismail Rashid (this volume) has explored the connections between this new lumpen culture and FBC students. His discussion underscores the importance of 'organic intellectuals', those who were in the forefront articulating some form of change, as a distinguishing feature of this linkage. In the 1970s the group included many high school dropouts and some unfortunate

O and A level holders mostly unemployed. Though some later went to the university, most joined the city's expanding army of the unemployed who lingered mostly in *potes* and the numerous working-class pubs in the city. This group was conversant with the political philosophy of some distinguished Africans, they knew in outline the history of the slave trade and the dehumanisation of the African that it entailed. They could make connections between the colonial past and the post-colonial present and generally espouse some form of Pan-Africanism. *Pote* discourse was spiced with generous quotes from Marcus Garvey, Bob Marley, Kwame Nkrumah, Wallace-Johnson, and at times Haile Selassie. Some of these *pote* types had read a little bit of Kwame Nkrumah and Frantz Fanon, a bit of Che Guavara and Fidel Castro, and some undigested Marx and Lenin.[5]

The 1977 student demonstrations were organised and led by students who were participants in this rebellious culture.[6] This was not the first time that students were involved in national politics. FBC students were involved in the APC inspired agitation against the introduction of a one-party system under Sir Albert Margai. When the APC came to power in 1968, the populist Alfred Akibo-Betts sponsored the establishment of an APC youth league on campus. But like the lumpens before them, the students did not enter the political arena as independent actors; they were brought in as foot soldiers in the service of a mythical common agenda; 1977 was therefore the first time that FBC students as a body intervened in the political arena as an informal opposition with a clear cut agenda: to push for reform in the political and economic sphere. The initiative was taken by radical students who did not anticipate the consequences of their actions. The demonstrations were extremely popular, and exposed the fragility of the APC regime. The president was forced to grant some concessions: a general election was called three months later. In spite of its limited gains the demonstration was successful: it revealed the potential of organised protest by students.

By the 1980s, university students, particularly those at FBC, were a respectable bunch in the *pote*; they had become an important reference group for their unfortunate brothers. Their role in the 1977 demonstrations enhanced their status vis-a-vis other groups. In the *pote's* code of honour, essentially an extension of the general clientelist relationship in the society, due regard was given to the *pote* frequenting *savis man* who was also a student at FBC. Their unfortunate brothers listened to them as they preached, smoked and philosophised in the safe confines of the *pote*. It was within this milieu that the change from *savis man* to *man dem* took place; signifying a move from the individual to the collective. The camaraderie had come full circle; one love and brotherhood was the slogan of this new group of youths, evident in the popular support the 1977 demonstrations received from this youth constituency. From this vantage point the series of student protests in the 1980s become intelligible. The students, who were immersed in the rebellious youth culture, became the most articulate group to oppose the APC. They used the platform of student politics to launch an attack on APC rule and to call for radical change.

It was therefore not surprising that the APC government became involved in students politics by attempting to sponsor candidates. The move to draft noted radicals on campus did not succeed but it revealed the polarised nature of student politics as the nation entered the turbulent 1980s. The economic downturn in the early 1980s, partly fuelled by the lavish hosting of the 1980 OAU conference, and the dwindling mining revenues exacerbated by rampant smuggling, affected the provision of scholarships for students as well as expenditure on health and other social services. For the 1974/75 fiscal year, the expenditure on education totalled 15.6 percent of government expenditure; this was reduced to 8.5 percent in the 1988/89 fiscal year. Similarly, expenditure on health and housing dropped from 6.6 percent and 4.8 percent in the same period to about 2.9 percent and 0.3 percent respectively (National Accounts: 1970–71 to 1974–75 & 1983–84 to 1988–89). Since the state was the largest employer of labour, the downward economic trend affected the general employment situation. Thus whereas the number of pupils in secondary schools registered a phenomenal increase from 16,414 in 1969 to 95,709 in 1990, there were only about 6,000 in paid employment in 1985 (Koroma, 1997). By 1990, it had become impossible even for university graduates to secure jobs in the public sector, and this at a time when the private sector was downsizing.

In this grim economic context, the so-called informal sector, the natural abode of the lumpenproletariat, ballooned as a result of the continued influx of an army of unemployed secondary school leavers, dropouts and university graduates. This army of the unemployed continued to shape subaltern discourse in the *potes*, so that the muted discussions about revolution in 1977 gave way to open talk about revolution. How this revolution was to be prosecuted was never systematically discussed, nor were other options explored. But the talk about revolution, vague and distorted as it was, remained alive in the discourse of rebellious youths. Thus the language shifted from *man dem* to comrade, and finally to brothers and sisters, symptomatic of an ideological change particularly amongst the *pote* revolutionaries in the numerous study groups in Freetown, Bo, Kenema, and Koidu. This change was evident in the political groups which had emerged at FBC campus in the early 1980s. Anti-imperialists slogans were now appropriated as part of this youth iconography.

Meanwhile student-administration relations on FBC campus deteriorated. A student demonstration in January 1984 resulted in a three-month lock out. A commission of inquiry set up to look into the frequent complaints of students and conditions in the campus was favourable to students.[7] By 1985 the college administration was determined to discipline students and keep state interference to a minimum. The unprecedented appointment of an ex-Police Chief, Jenkin Smith, as warden of students, reflected the change of policy. It was in this context that a radical student union leadership emerged. The Mass Awareness and Participation (MAP) student union President Alie Kabba was elected unopposed, while he was in Libya attending the annual *Green Book* celebration. The MAP was a loose coalition of radicals: it included members of the *Green Book* study group, the Gardeners' Club, PANAFU, and the Socialist club. Its incendiary rhetoric, bordering on adventurism, alarmed the college administration. The new government did not follow in the footsteps of previous student leaderships who only commented on national issues during crisis situations; they took the initiative, partly as a result of the popular youth culture of which it was part, to link up with youths in the city. Their publicity campaign spawned numerous anti-government flyers and graffiti on campus and the city. A 'peoples' tribunal adjudicated between students; it served as check on anti-social behaviour. It was a popular government based on an imaginary 'peoples' power. These activities, along with rumours that the student leadership was been sponsored by the Libyans, did not endear them to the administration.

What remains unclear in the muddled accounts of several participants is the source of the wild campaign of disinformation about Libyan sponsorship and involvement in student politics.[8] Perhaps, Alie Kabba's trip to Libya prompted the charge about Libyan sponsorship. But the trip was neither clandestine nor was Kabba the only student who travelled with the Sierra Leonean delegation. There were two faculty members on the delegation: Cleo Hanciles and Moses Dumbuya. Whatever the case, the charge of Libyan involvement was serious enough to provoke another student lockout.

The events which led to the expulsion and suspension of some 41 students was connected to the allege Libyan linkage of the student leadership. The students were accused of holding on to their keys during the lent semester break because they intend to camp Libyan mercenaries in their hostels. Neither the college administration nor the government investigated the charge. What the college administration did was to invite the notorious State Security Defence (SSD) gendarme on campus to literally 'flush' students from their hostels. When the college reopened, the administration was faced with a militant demonstration which subsequently engulfed the city. In the ensuing melee, the principal's car was set on fire. Three faculty members – Olu Gordon, Jimmy Kandeh and Cleo Hanciles – judged friendly to the students lost their jobs. Olu Gordon and Cleo Hanciles were founding members and patrons of PANAFU. The student union president, Alie kabba, and four other students – Haroun Boima, Olutumi Mark, Samuel Foyoh and Kai Banja – were arrested and detained for two months.

They were later arraigned and then released for allegedly torching the principal's car.

The action of the student radicals could be described as infantile. They were neither politically mature nor sufficiently well disciplined to realise the shortcomings of whatever leverage they imagined they might have on the administration or the state. They naively thought that mere rhetoric would deliver their puerile call for people's power. Compared with the 1977 leadership, the 1985 leadership was more organised though politically immature. They could not grasp the inherent limitation of student politics and the dead end of confrontational politics.[9] Elsewhere in West Africa, notably Nigeria and Ghana, this confrontational stance had taught students a bitter political lesson. The unpopularity of the regime was a factor, which shaped student militancy: the students enjoyed tremendous support on campus and in Freetown. But the utterances of Alie Kabba, the union president, were according to some his closest advisers, too politically immature. The interview he granted to the BBC about the change ('Mount Aureol will not be going to the State House this time; the State House will have to come up') was, in the words of one of his closest comrades 'a stupid mistake' (Interview with radical Students, October, 1996). Their expulsion from FBC ended a phase in the making of an informal youth opposition. Henceforth, the baton passed to the lumpen youths and their organic intellectuals in the numerous study groups and revolutionary cells in Freetown, Bo, Kenema and Koidu.

Why did student radicals, obviously backward in comparison to their counterparts in Nigeria and Ghana, embrace bland Pan-Africanism and Libya's *Green Book* ideology? Why did Ghadaffi's *Green Book* 'take root' in Sierra Leone and not in other West African countries? During this period, students in Nigeria and Ghana supported the anti-imperialist stance of Colonel Ghadaffi and applauded Libya's uncompromising position on Africa's liberation and Third World independence. But they did not embrace the Colonel's message partly because they were wedded to Marxian/dependency political economy analysis and, partly because they were critical of Ghadaffi's 'Third Universal Theory'.[10] That radical students in Nigeria did not theorise the role of students as vanguard of the revolution was partly because of the existence of a recognised radical fringe in national politics and a radical labour movement. Their position on the Nigerian 'revolution' was always articulated from the vantage point of an alliance of progressive forces. The disastrous attempt by Isaac Boro, a student leader in the 1960s, had seemingly foreclosed this option for student radicals in Nigeria.

The poverty of the student movement in Sierra Leone with regard to ideology, and the lack of a post-colonial radical tradition, were probably the principal factors in explaining the attractiveness of Ghadaffi's *Green Book* (Interview with student radicals, Oct.–Dec., 1996).[11] Their failure to critique

Ghadaffi's ideas indicates their level of political consciousness. They did not debate Ghadaffi's populist ideas and could not make the obvious connections between the *Green Book* and Libya's foreign policy. No attempt was made even to understand the Colonel's support for Idi Amin or his claim to Chadian territory (Ogunbadejo, 1986; Simons, 1996). This lack of critical ideas explains why Pan-Africanism was uncritically appropriated, and why bland revolutionary Pan-Africanism became an option. Pan-Africanism was therefore the ideational context within which the movement unfolded; Libya, the midwife of the destruction to come.

Ghana and Libya: The external connection

The expelled student union president was not the first president to visit Libya. Abdul Gbla was the first student union president to visit the Libyan Arab Jama'riyya in 1983. But Gbla's visit was not clandestine; he was invited to participate in their annual revolutionary celebration. He went with two other students – Abdul Gabisi, Nurudeen Wilson – and two faculty members: Cleo Hanciles and Moses Dumbuya. Gbla received an executive treatment; he had a session with the Colonel and was specifically asked to stay after the celebrations. He however declined the offer because of fear of getting involved with the Libyans (Interview with Gbla, Former Student President,1981–82; Oct.–Nov. 1996).

The Libyans entered Sierra Leone in the mid-1970s and began to make inroads into civil society by using religious as well as non-religious channels to establish a presence. They gave generous grants for the annual pilgrimage to Makkah; established links with the powerful and crafty diamond dealer J.S. Mohammed who arranged a state visit for Siaka Stevens; provided a printing press for *The Tablet* newspaper the main opposition tabloid; and sponsored *Green Book* study groups at FBC. They generally maintained a low profile, and gradually worked their way into State House. Their alleged bankrolling of the 1980 OAU conference in Freetown remains unsubstantiated.[12]

If the ex-student leader was not the first student president to visit Libya, how did he establish the link, which eventually led to the training of Sierra Leoneans in Tajura in 1987 and 1988? It is quite possible, based on interviews with student radicals who knew Alie kabba, that he had visited Libya before 1985; his occasional disappearing acts lend credence to such beliefs. Why did the expelled students (who were allegedly provided with a generous grant to pursue their studies) choose Ghana, not Nigeria or Liberia, the two other English speaking countries in the region to pursue their studies?[13] The choice of Ghana may not be unconnected with Jerry Rawlings' support for Libya, and therefore an ideal place to pursue their revolutionary objectives. From the standpoint of the Libyans, the expelled students were in exile to prosecute the 'revolution'.

When Kabba and others were released from prison their first port of call was Conakry, Guinea. From Conakry, they travelled to Ghana. It was a Peoples Bureau official, as the Libyan embassies are known, who instructed them to proceed to Ghana were they subsequently gained admission to Legon University (Interview with some of the expelled students, Oct.–Dec., 1996). As noted above, the choice of Ghana is significant. During this period the Libyans were busy trying to set up their African revolutionary army to pursue the Colonel's dream of controlling the Azou Strip in Chad. Ghana had a regime sympathetic to Libya, and Jerry Rawlings' 'revolutionary' pretensions also endeared him to the Libyans. Libyan foreign policy was crafted in the 1980s in furtherance of a specific goal: 'revolution'. Everything about Libyan foreign policy in West Africa in the 1980s therefore revolved around this idea. It was this aspect of Libyan foreign policy which interested them in individuals like Alie Kabba, and before him, Charles Taylor and the confused Kukoi Samba Sanyang (known as Dr. Manning), who proclaimed a dictatorship of the proletariat in the Gambia in 1981 (Tarr, 1993; Ellis, 1995; Interview with student radicals).

The Libyan connection brought in some money which made it possible for the expelled students in Ghana to sponsor for four others who joined them the following year, bringing the number to eight. Kabba was known to frequent the Peoples Bureau in Accra, made numerous trips to Libya, and occasionally to Guinea. It was during this period that he met Charles Taylor of the NPFL who had been imprisoned in the United States and Ghana, Kukoi Samba Sanyang, and other so-called revolutionaries who crisscrossed the Ghana–Burkina-Faso–Libya 'revolutionary triangle' (Ibid). Kabba's relationship with these types validated his 'revolutionary' credentials. This was important because what is known about Libyan connections with revolutionary organisations in Africa suggests that they always operate through a contact person, through whom they channel funds and issue directives about 'revolutionary assignments'. This was the type of relationship they had with the several Chadian factions they supported in the 1970s and 1980s; with Museveni's National Resistance Movement (NRM); and Kwame Toure's All African Peoples Revolutionary Party (AAPRP). The onus of communicating with the organisation therefore rests with the individual, in this case Kabba. What the Libyans did not understand, or rather did not want to understand, was the fact that the ex-student leader had no constituency outside FBC campus. Perhaps because the Libyans had never experienced or made a social revolution, they were incapable of distinguishing between inflammatory student rhetoric and a revolutionary movement in the making. When he was given a 'revolutionary assignment' to attack US targets in Freetown, Kabba could not get the job done: he tried to subcontract the job to PANAFU by promising monetary support but was told to go away. And when it was time to deliver recruits for military training in Libya in 1987, Kabba and his group in Ghana had no alternative but to turn to Freetown.[14]

When the recruitment exercise commenced there was no program of action, nor was there any guideline on the procedure and mechanism for recruitment. The students in Ghana espoused no concrete political philosophy which would have provided a theoretical guide for their commitment to arms struggle, nor did they operate through any formal political structure or organisation. They remained, throughout their stay in Ghana, an informal political group linked together by their common experience of expulsion and their commitment to radical change. There was therefore no common ideological platform nor an agreed political programme besides acquiring military training. The period from April 1985 (when students were expelled from FBC) to July–August 1987 (when Sierra Leoneans started leaving for military training) saw a shift in the composition of the radical groups in the city of Freetown and elsewhere. Student unionism had been proscribed at FBC in 1985 so that the centre of operation for the radicals became the city of Freetown, Bo, and Kenema and to a lesser extent Koidu. This shift catapulted those radicals operating in 'revolutionary' cells in the forefront of the movement for radical change. It was therefore to these groups, especially PANAFU, that the students in Ghana turned for recruits when they were ready to embark on the bush path to destruction.

The expelled students and others who saw themselves as 'revolutionaries' were not the first to initiate a call to arms, nor were they the first to emphasise the need for military training. The APC had established training camps in Guinea under the command of then Col. John Bangura in 1967. After the 1977 student demonstrations the insurgency alternative was freely discussed in radical circles. Other victims of APC repression, notably in Pujehun District in the early 1980s, had expressed interest in arming themselves as a form of protection against state sponsored terrorism.[15] What the student group and their allies appropriated was therefore the collective property of the growing army of potential insurgents. Armed struggle had become part of the folklore of the revolution-to-be. The major difference is that it would not be an ex-military officer who would co-ordinate the new call to arms. By a curious irony it turned out to be an ex-corporal in the signal unit, Foday Sankoh, who had been convicted for his involvement in an attempted coup, who would champion this ancient call to arms and pursue it to its logical conclusion: the overthrow of *de sistem*.

When the call for recruits came from Accra in June 1987, a special session of the PANAFU congress reluctantly tabled the issue. The majority decided against an adventuristic enterprise in the name of revolution. This led to a split in the union between those who supported the move to go to Libya and those who were against. Those in favour were in the minority, and were eventually expelled from the union. Among these were Abu Kanu, a founding member of Future Shock club and a graduate of Njala University College, and Rashid Mansaray, an activist from Freetown east end, who had allegedly left the country in 1986 to join the MPLA in the fight against UNITA in Angola, only to be told to return home and pursue the struggle in his own country. Abu Kanu, Rashid Mansaray and others left Freetown in July 1987, via Conakry and Accra, for Tajura, Libya. Another group which included Foday Sankoh left in August 1987. Sankoh's group included recruits from Freetown and the hinterland. A third group consisting mostly of high school students arrived in January 1988. It was not the case that politically conscious individuals were specifically targeted. Once PANAFU had rejected the idea of participating as an organisation, the project became an individual enterprise for any man (no attempt was made to recruit women) who felt the urge to acquire insurgency training in the service of the 'revolution'. This inevitably opened the way for the recruitment of lumpens. It is therefore no coincidence that only three of those who went to Libya had any form of employment.[21] Richards' belief in an excluded intellectual group in the RUF is unfounded.

There was no concrete program about what was to be done once the military training was over, nor was there any debate about the program of action to be adopted. The only available document – *The Basic Document of the Revolutionary United Front of Sierra Leone (RUF/SL): The Second Liberation of Africa* copiously quoted in the RUF propaganda booklet *Footpaths to Democracy: Towards a New Sierra Leone*, vol. one – was essentially a critique of the neo-colonial regime. It was originally a PANAFU call for a popular democratic front (PDF), involving a return to multiparty democracy, even distribution of resources, reform of education and an end to mercantilist rule of the Lebanese comprador bourgeoisie over the economy, which was subsequently redrafted and edited by Abu Kanu and Rashid Mansaray to reflect the armed phase of the 'revolution'. Parts of it were butchered to appear as Foday Sankoh's words. But the document had nothing to do with Sankoh or the RUF; it predated the formation of the RUF, and was appropriated by Sankoh and his vanguard after they entered Kailahun in 1991[22]. The document was produced in Ghana before the departure for military training in Libya.

Perhaps, the tragedy of the 'revolution' has to do with the fact that those who recruited Foday Sankoh underestimated his capacity to think and act politically. Sankoh was recruited by a PANAFU member, Victor Ebiyemi Reider, a high school drop-out who was active in Freetown 'revolutionary' circles in the late 1970s.[23] Ebiyemi left for the hinterland after a key member of his group, Said Kamara, departed for Cuba around 1980, and organized a 'revolutionary' cell in the diamond area where he discovered Sankoh.[24] This eclectic and half-backed *pote* 'revolutionary' became Sankoh's teacher and 'revolutionary' guide throughout the period leading to their departure for Libya in July 1987.[25] Sankoh became associated with his group, attended meetings and started, for the first time, to acquaint himself with pan-Africanism. But Sankoh was not interested in reading, he was an action-oriented man who was impatient with the slow process of acquiring knowledge and understanding of the situation which a revolutionary project entails. Put in another way, Sankoh was a militarist.[26] Before this period his world view did not go beyond the Sierra Leonean border; his ideas remained that of an angry man who had an axe to grind because of his imprisonment. His critique of what was popularly referred to, as *de sistem* was very much party and personality centred. Yet, he was willing to listen and eager to learn. His age and his involvement with youths, some of whom could have been his children, earned him some respect and sympathy – Hence Pa Foday or Papay. There is evidence that Sankoh did not abandon the possibility of seizing power through another military coup. His idea of revolution, if he had any before this period, was to seize power by any conceivable means. So when the call to Tripoli came from Accra, Sankoh willingly joined the crowd. What the others did not realise was that they were paving the way for Sankoh who had waited for just this kind of opportunity.[27]

Kabba's control of the purse, his clandestine and not so clandestine connections with people's bureau officials in Accra, and his unbridled ambition to be the spokesperson of the 'revolution', had begun to sow discord within the group in Ghana as early as 1986. It was however impossible to put up any organised opposition because the recruits were scattered in various camps, and only Kabba knew where all the groups were. When Kabba subsequently installed a 'revolutionary' high command, supposedly to direct the Sierra Leonean contingent, it was stoutly opposed by the majority of the recruits. The charge that he wanted to establish himself as the spokesperson of the movement was echoed; others simply repeated what they had been told about his undemocratic practices; while others made it clear they were not interested in pursuing the project any longer. Attempts to get kabba to account for money he supposedly got for the whole recruitment project proved impossible. In the end the motley collection of 'revolutionaries' who went to Tajura, about thirty-five, some say fifty, left Libya frustrated and divided.[28] Some decided to forget about the experience; others decided to pursue the goal of 'revolution'. For the expelled students from Ghana, this was the end of the project. But 'It is here,' Kabba pleaded, 'that we should locate the vacuum that made it possible for the wrong individuals to lead the journey to what turned out to be anything similar to the democratic programme we had earlier envisioned.' [29] It was the 'wrong individuals', lumpens in my view, who therefore took the next step in the bush path to destruction.

The making of a lumpen movement

All those who went to Libya, and who later became involved in the RUF, including Sankoh, returned to Sierra Leone before the launching of the armed struggle. Attempts were made to recruit and train cadres in the Yele area; this was however abandoned because it was considered risky. Up to this point Sankoh had not emerged as the leader of the movement; there was no organisation, it was a loose collection of individuals who had returned from military training in Tajura. 'At the beginning, there was no leadership. All of us were all (sic) organisers',[30] Sankoh revealed in an interview. Among those who returned to Sierra Leone determined to pursue the 'revolution' were Foday Sankoh, Abu Kanu and Rashid Mansaray. They formed a closed-knit group in the city, met periodically to discuss strategy, and embarked upon another recruitment drive. This time, they decided to leave Freetown and settle in the hinterland, a move that opened the link between the RUF-to-be and the NPFL in Liberia. From the time they left Libya in 1988 to the period when they entered Sierra Leone as armed combatants, this trio travelled extensively in Sierra Leone and Liberia exploring avenues through which they could further their 'revolutionary' objectives.

Sankoh met Charles Taylor in Libya in 1988, who then invited him to join the NPFL. This account does appear credible because the NPFL was originally constituted as a pan- African movement with membership open to all Africans. The Gambian, Kukoi Samba was a founding member and vice-president of the NPFL. Sankoh was later invited to visit the Po military camp in Burkina Faso, where the bulk of the NPFL fighters were trained. It was at Po that Sankoh came into contact with the mercurial NPLF commander Prince Yomi Johnson (Yomi Johnson, *The Guardian*, Lagos, 17 June 1999). Like General Thomas Quiwonkpa before him, Taylor visited Sierra Leone in 1988 to explore the possibility of using Pujehun as a launching base for his 'revolution'. Travelling on a Burkinabe passport, he was arrested, detained, and subsequently deported.

By mid-1989 a deal had been struck: Foday Sankoh and his group would help Charles Taylor 'liberate' Liberia, after which he would provide them with a base to launch their armed struggle. After this informal alliance the *Basic Document* was amended to reflect the change. The historical relevance of the name – Revolutionary United Front/Sierra Leone – remains intriguing. Wallace-Johnson's West African Youth League was always the West African Youth League/ Sierra Leone. Whether this was inspired by the pan-African ideal or whether it was a leaf from the Wallacian script is not clear. Yet it remains an aspect of the pan-Africanist image with which the RUF wants to be identified. There is no direct evidence that Sierra Leoneans took part in the initial NPFL attack on Nimba County in December 1989, though by November

1990, some members of this group, notably Kanu and Mansaray, had seen action as NPFL combatants. Sankoh, Kanu, and Mansaray were in Freetown up to a week before the initial RUF attack in March 1991 to convince those who had gone to Libya to join the RUF. Their activities alarmed some PANAFU members who threatened to report their presence to the police.[31]

From the time they left Libya to the period when they entered Kailahun, the group did not organise an election, nor was there a central committee. The loose organisation was headed by a collective leadership of three: Sankoh, Mansaray and Kanu. It was generally agreed that Sankoh would be the spokesperson for the group. When on 23 March 1991 the Revolutionary United Front entered Bomaru in Kailahun District it was Sankoh who announced to the world what the RUF was all about. By then *The Basic Document* had become the RUF manifesto, with Sankoh as leader.

The insurgency force from Liberia was composed of three distinct groups: those who had acquired military training in Libya (predominantly urban lumpens) and had seen action with the NPFL as combatants; a second group of Sierra Leoneans, resident in Liberia, mostly lumpens and criminals recently released from jail; and a third group of hard- core NPFL fighters from Liberia on loan to the RUF. Contrary to Richards' account, the Sierra Leoneans recruited in Liberia were not 'political exiles and economic refugees' but lumpens and criminals in Liberia (Paul Richards, 1996: 4; Interviews with Sierra Leoneans who returned after the NPFL attack on Monrovia, Oct. 1996; *Footpath to Democracy*, 7)[32]. The late Capt. Papa Kamara, one of the RUF's ablest commanders, and the late field commander Sam Bockarie aka Maskita were both recruited in Monrovia and Abidjan respectively. Kamara was a high-school drop out who later became an APC thug and was involved in criminal activities before drifting to Liberia. Bockarie left high school in form three, and had a stint as an illicit diamond miner in Kono before moving to Monrovia and then Abidjan, where he was recruited by Sankoh. Jonathan Kposowa who was the RUF Adjutant-General was serving time in a prison in Monrovia; he was released to join the RUF.[33] This social composition of the invading force is significant in understanding the character of the RUF and the bush path to destruction.

The character of the Revolutionary United Front

How revolutionary is a revolutionary movement which slaughters and terrorises the very people it claims to be liberating? What yardstick do we use to judge a movement which claims to be revolutionary without revolutionaries? To understand the character of the RUF, we need to look at the social composition of the ruffians, their policies, actions, statements, and programmes, if any. We need to go beyond their rhetoric and examine the contradictions in their pronouncements and actions; the silences, and the (mis) representations, about themselves and their programme. The wanton destruction of life, the hacking of limbs and the slitting of pregnant women was so disturbing that Foday Sankoh was compelled to make a special plea: 'Yes, we have committed atrocities. One day we shall stand before the people and ask for forgiveness' (Amnesty International, *Sierra Leone: Towards a Future Founded on Human Rights*, 25 September 1996: 25). In whose name were those atrocities committed?

The Revolutionary United Front is a peculiar organisation. It does not share any of the essential characteristics of ideology, organisation and discipline which mark revolutionary movements in Africa or elsewhere, except for the use of force to attain power. The RUF is strikingly similar to RENAMO which was formed as a counter-revolutionary force to sabotage the Mozambican revolution, and whose bandido activities did not cease when the leaders were compelled to reinvent themselves as liberation fighters and democrats (Young, 1990). Unlike RENAMO, the RUF started as a 'revolutionary' movement. What connects the two is the wanton violence on women and children, the systematic destruction of the economy, and the general terror in the countryside.

Though Richards does come to grips with the role of youth in the drama surrounding the war and its continuation, his heavy reliance on resources of the forest (he should instead have concentrated on the trees) to explain the war totally neglects the centrality and dynamics of rebellious youth culture in shaping the process leading to the rebellion and war. His assessment of the movement leaves too many substantive issues unanswered. His comparison with the Shining Path also neglects the historical contexts within which the two movements evolved. The Shining Path was formed by radical intellectuals inspired by Mao. There were no radical or excluded intellectuals in the RUF, nor did the movement establish any meaningful relationship with the peasantry based on the acceptance of a common program produced within the context of a revolutionary dialogue. The RUF had a chronic lack of cadres imbued with any revolutionary ideology. Its lumpen base made it impossible for the movement to attract support from any social group. It is not surprising that the only movement with revolutionary pretensions comparable to the RUF was the NPFL: they were products of the same cultural milieu; their membership was recruited from the same social group; and they employed the same tactics – indiscriminate use of drugs, forced induction and violence – to further their goal of capturing power. The torture and eventual murder of Sergeant Doe by the former NPFL commander Yomi Johnson, the mutilation, murder and rape of innocent women and children by the RUF, are acts that are incompatible with a revolutionary project. These 'revolutionary' acts, I would argue, were committed again and again precisely because of

the social composition of these movements and the lack of a concrete programme of societal transformation. A lumpen social movement breeds a
lumpen revolution.

The RUF's *Footpaths to Democracy: Toward a New Sierra Leone* contains words
and phrases lifted from Mao Zedong and Amilcar Cabral. Hurriedly drafted
in London and tossed back to the Zogoda (the RUF headquarters in the
Sierra Leone rain forest) for approval, it was subsequently reformatted complete with the RUF anthem and generous quotes from the head of ideology,
Foday Sankoh.[34] 'We moved deeper into the comforting bosom of our mother
earth – the forest'....'The forest welcomed us and gave us succour and
sustenance'...'Why we continue to fight' are taken from Mao and Cabral. If
the RUF cadres or leadership had read Mao and Cabral, however, they would
have related to the peasantry in a different manner. If they had read Cabral
they would not have recruited lumpens. Cabral had cautioned, based on the
PAIGC experience in Guinea', against the recruitment of lumpens in revolutionary organisations. It is tempting to attribute this to Frantz Fanon who is
quoted on the first page of *Footpaths to Democracy*. But this would be reading
too much.[35]

There is, I would argue, no revolutionary theory which guided the practice
of the movement. If there was any theory, and certainly not a revolutionary
one, it evolved on an *ad hoc* basis as a result of their experiences in the forest.
The RUF document acknowledges this:

> Initially we fought a semi-conventional war relying heavily on vehicles for mobility.
> This method proved fatal against the combined fire power of Nigeria, Guinea and
> Ghana....Frankly, we were beaten and on the run....We dispersed into smaller units....We
> now relied on light weapons and on our feet, brains and knowledge of the country-
> side (*Footpaths to Democracy*, 10–11).

If the RUF leadership were immersed in any revolutionary theory and practice, it would have come to grips with the basics in guerrilla warfare, and thus
avoid a 'semi-conventional war'. A semi-conventional war in a context were
people are not politically organised could only lead to collective self-destruc-
tion. The RUF might have acquired its fighting skills on the battlefield, but it
did not learn how to relate to the people in the area under its control. Instead
of implementing a revolutionary program, it embarked on a campaign of
terror in the countryside. This aspect of the RUF explains why the peasantry,
the natural ally of most revolutionary movements in the so-called Third World,
deserted the movement. It is also not surprising that in the predominantly
rural Mende southeast, the major theatre of war, the RUF cadres were collec-
tively referred to as the *Njiahungbia Ngonga*, meaning riff raffs/lumpens/un-
ruly youths (Muana, 1997). The bulk of the RUF battle front commanders
are lumpens from the rural southeast.

Richards emphasis on the communitarian principles which the RUF alleg-edly established in the enclaves under its control have nothing to do with *Green Book* ideology. Such populist's pronouncements as 'Every member of the community has rights to basic needs (food, housing, health, and trans-port)' are consistent with the demands of movements like the RUF seeking to sell themselves as popular movements, but not in themselves constitute revo-lutionary practice (Richards, 96:34). They should be seen as populist propa-ganda rather than influences from the *Green Book*. If the RUF had any ideol-ogy, it was definitely not shaped by the *Green Book*. Its populist rhetoric backed by some ad hoc measures, such as the change from semi-conventional to guerrilla warfare, were designed as survival tactics to win support from the very public it terrorises. Richards' erroneous assumption that the *Green Book* was influential in shaping the views of student radicals led him to look for *Green Book* signs that were markedly absent in the RUF. Ironically none of the student radicals whom Richards claimed were influenced by the *Green Book* joined the RUF.

When the RUF first entered Sierra Leone in 1991, the movement was divided into two sections: vanguards and special forces. The former were further sub-divided into two: those who trained in Libya in 1987/88 and lumpen/criminals recruited in Liberia. The first group included Sankoh him-self, Abu kanu and Rashid Mansaray. Vanguard members sat on the war coun-cil, which was constituted before they entered the country in 1991, and were in charge of administrative day-to-day affairs, including intelligence in the areas under their control. The Special Forces were those NPFL fighters on loan to the RUF. They were a law unto themselves and only Sankoh could control their excesses. The erstwhile commander-in-chief Mohammed Tarawalie (Zino), was also with this group. Foday Sankoh was the head of ideology. After the NPFL Special Forces were recalled in 1993, the movement was reconstituted along military lines with the establishment of battle-group and battle-front commanders. The battle-group commanders were directly in charge of operations; they coordinated and commanded all battle front com-manders in their sectors and were also members of the war council. The battle-front commanders were mostly lieutenants and captains directly re-sponsible to the battle-group commanders. Below them were the standbys, mainly captives and conscripts, followed by the under age combatants.

If the initial wanton violence against innocent civilians, which, the RUF concedes, 'became a nightmarish experience for our civil population' (mainly women and children), was attributed to the special forces on loan from the NPFL, why did the violence continue after they left? (*Footpath to Democracy*, 8). An explanation has to be sought in the composition of the movement, its lack of discipline, its indiscriminate use of drugs of all sorts, and the absence of a concrete programme besides vague populist formulation about foreigners and rural development.

The first major crack within the RUF was connected with the indiscriminate violence and terror against civilians in areas under their control. In August 1992 Abu Kanu (Commander BK) was executed by firing squad for failure to follow instructions (FFI) and conniving with the enemy. The following November, Rashid Mansaray, another leading vanguard commander, was executed for technical sabotage – failure to defend a strategic position against the enemy. He was tried in front of the last two-storey building on the Koindu-Kailahun road and shot by firing squad (Interview with Foday Sankoh, Lome, Togo, June, 1999). These trumped up charges against the two other members of the original troika were masterminded by Sankoh to get them out of the way. They were the only top-ranking members who were with Foday Sankoh before the formation of the RUF; they were popular with the cadres and could have contested the position of leadership had there been a general congress or a popular assembly. They were also among the two leading strategists in the movement.

There is evidence that neither Kanu nor Mansaray were happy with the random violence that RUF forces were committing in the name of the 'revolution'. An ex-PANAFU member in the army reported that the area under Kanu's control was generally peaceful and well organised; he reached out to explain what the RUF was about to the peasants, and was not engaged in unnecessary violence against civilians. Rashid Mansaray's opposition to the indiscriminate killing of innocent civilians was one of the reasons why he was executed (Interview with PANAFU members, Oct. 1996). This was confirmed by his second in command who served as provost to I.H.Deen-Jalloh, the former head of RUF intelligence. Stories about the slitting of pregnant women and the raping of young girls, some of who were forcibly taken as 'wives', were common (Interview with under-aged girls captured, abused and molested by the RUF; Oct. 1996). Once the movement had established some presence with the help of Charles Taylor, and Sankoh had acquired some modicum of respectability with his newfound pan-Africanist credentials, he no longer needed these vanguards anymore. Those who subsequently became key players in the movement did not know Papay, as Sankoh was called, before 1991, or the prehistory of the RUF. Philip Palmer, Faiaya Musa, I.H. Deen-Jalloh, Gibril Massaquoi, Dr. Barrie, Sam Bockarie, Morris Kallon, and Issa Sesay joined the movement after they returned from Libya or after they attacked and occupied Bomaru in 1991.

Youth culture, revolution, and violence

The involvement of lumpen youths in political violence is not particularly new. This group provided some of the fighting force for the Mulele rebellion in the Congo in the 1960s, the MPLA and FRELIMO in Angola and Mozambique, ZANU and ZAPU in Zimbabwe, the fighters of Guokouni Waddei and Hissen Habré in Chad, the UPC in the Cameroons, the warlords in Liberia and the Revolutionary United Front (Tungamirai,1995). They are to be found weilding AK 47s and rocket-propelled grenades in the numerous militia groups in Congo-Brazzaville (Ninja, Zulu and Cobra), and the Democratic Republic of the Congo (DRC), and among the different militias in Somalia. Whereas the 'classical' liberation movements had policy guidelines with respect to the recruitment and training of lumpens, the new movements, with the sole exception of Museveni's NRM, are more concerned with having people who could wield weapons in the name of 'revolution' (Museveni, 1997; Mamdani, 1986-7). The lack of discipline and of a clear-cut ideology helps to explain why the RUF tolerated all sorts of terror and anarchy in the name of revolution. Another important difference was the influx of more teenagers as lumpens; a true reflection of Africa's economy in this age of structural adjustment. This new development significantly narrowed the age differential between the leadership of these movements and the rank and file. In the case of the RUF, with the exception of Foday Sankoh and a few others who were not in the original group, the bulk of the leadership and membership are below thirty-five. This is also true of the NPFL in Liberia.

In his perceptive analyses of the social structure in Guinea-Bissau, Amilcar Cabral laid bare the considerations which informed the recruitment efforts of the PAIGC in Guinea, and identified this particular group as the crucial link between the urban-rural networks so important to the success of the PAIGC. But Cabral, as usual, was careful not to generalise; he mapped out the specificity of the situation in Guine, he did not provide a blue print for activists (Cabral, 1969). Museveni had approached the issue from the standpoint of culture, while Cabral had emphasised their social dislocation as problematic. Both Museveni and Cabral identified the same group, which Frantz Fanon had singled out as the only revolutionary force in the continent: the lumpenproletariat. But Fanon's analysis ran counter to orthodox Marxists who had nothing but contempt for lumpens; an idea which stems directly from Marx's obsession with proletarian consciousness and revolution (Fanon, 1961). This line of enquiry was pursued by some British-based Africanists in the 1970s. They argued that the lumpenproletariat were incapable of taking political action on their own because they always end up fighting the battles of others in the political realm (Cohen and Michael, 1973).

But the so-called second independence struggle tells a different story, at least in the Sierra Leonean context. The Revolutionary United Front was not only a product of lumpen culture but its membership was also lumpen. They took political action and proclaimed a 'revolution', which reflected the true character of their lumpen base. The movement did not possess the revolutionary drive or the maturity to undertake a concrete analysis of the situation which comes with a revolutionary project. It had no revolutionary intellectuals, and the radical students who originally spearheaded the call to arms were not involved in the project. Lacking an alternative source of arms, since the Soviet Union is no more, they had to depend on exploiting the resources available in their area of operation to pursue their 'revolution'. Their failure to win the sympathy of the very people they claim to be fighting for compelled them to recruit their army from lumpens and juveniles, two vulnerable groups to whom their bush path to destruction appeared more appealing. It is this lack of a clear cut programme, the wanton use of violence for violence sake, and the absence of a well articulated ideology, which disqualifies such second independence movements as a vehicle for progressive change in Africa.

Notes

1   Marcus Grant and the other executive members of the Labour Party subsequently joined the victorious Sierra Leone Peoples Party (SLPP).

2   The party's red flag and socialist rhetoric were seen as symbols of its radical orientation.

3   Rarray boy is a pejorative term for 'underclass' youth. It is also used in Nigeria with reference to rebellious youth culture. I have used the term lumpen instead of *rarray* boy.

4   The *pote* shares a lot in common with the shebeens in Southern Africa. See Michael O. West,'"Equal rights for all civilized men": Elite Africans and the quest for "European" liquor in colonial Zimbabwe, 1924–1961', *International Review of Social History*, 37,1992.

5   Kwame Nkrumah's *Class Struggle in Africa* and Fidel Castro's *History Will Absolve Me* were popular texts.

6   In the interview refereed to above Foday Sankoh claimed to have been involved in the 1977 student demonstrations. There is no evidence to support this spurious claim.

7   The Kutubu Commission report was never published.

8   The newspaper accounts are silent on these issues.

9   'Students do not make revolutions' was a popular saying during and after the 1977 demonstrations.

10 The following works were influential: Claude Ake, *Revolutionary Pressures,* London, 1978; Dan Nabudere, *The Political Economy of Imperialism,* London, 1978; and some of the exchanges published in the Dar-Es-Salaam journal *Utafiti* in the late 1970s. For a good summary of the debates on the Nigerian left see Narasingha P. Sil, 'Nigerian Intellectuals and Socialism: Retrospect and Prospect', *Journal of Modern African Studies,* 31,3,1993.

11 Some of the radical students interviewed attribute this to youthful adventure; others thought it was the money.

12 Paul Richards, *Fighting for the Rain Forest,* alleges that the Libyans paid part of the cost for hosting the 1980 OAU Conference in Sierra Leone.

13 The four expelled students enrolled at Legon University reportedly received $6,000 each from the United Nations.

14 It was after Kabba graduated from Legon in 1987 that the recruitment of Sierra Leoneans for military training started.

15 The Ndorgborwosu rebellion was the first rural uprising against the APC.

16 There was one high school teacher, an engineer, and Sankoh, who was a photographer.

17 The document became part of the propaganda material of the RUF to be when Abu Kanu and Rashid Mansaray teamed up with Sankoh after their return to Sierra Leone in 1988. For excerpts from this document see *Footpaths to Democracy: Towards a New Sierra Leone,* vol. (no date). Alie Kabba has claimed authorship of this document.

18 Victor Ebiyemi Reider, Sankoh's ideology teacher, is now a Member of Parliament representing the ruling SLPP.

19 Reider and Sankoh spent some time at Sankoh's home town, Massam in the Tonkolili district, from whence they moved to full scale mining in the Nongowa Chiefdom, Kenema district in the early 1980s. Interview with Reider, January, 2000. See TRC interview of Gibril Massaquoi a key RUF member. Reider's submission to the TRC is silent on these and other issues. He deliberately 'forgot' to mention that he went to Libya for military training in 1987.

20 In the *Concord Times* interview Sankoh incorrectly claimed to have started a study group in Bo. This is not correct.

21 He also claimed that he wanted to use PANAFU in 1986 but ' they were only concerned about South Africa and the rest of the world, forgetting that we have our own local problems'. This is also doubtful because it was through PANAFU that Sankoh was able to make the trip to Libya. See Concord interview.

22 Interview with PANAFU members and those who went to Libya in 1987/88. In his attempt to write his own story Sankoh claimed he left for military training in 1986. Again, this is incorrect.

23 Sankoh alleges that 150 youths were trained outside Sierra Leone. This figure is a gross exaggeration. Perhaps he was referring to those who were trained in Liberia. According to him "we were eleven at first and I later sent about 150 men". The

number of Sierra Leoneans who went to Libya between 1987/88 was not more than fifty.

24 Ali Kabba, Leonenet, 18 December 1996.

25 Sankoh was referring to 1986 when in fact this is true of the period after 1988. See *Concord* interview.

26 Rashid Mansaray reportedly bought all the available maps in the government bookstore. Interview with some PANAFU members and those who were in Libya.

27 See TRC interview of Jonathan Kposowa the RUF Adjutant-General who was released from prison by Charles Taylor to join the RUF.

28 Ibid.

29 This is a propaganda document hurriedly put together by Addai Sebo of the International Alert, the conflict resolution group based in London. The second volume is yet to be published.

30 The quotation 'Each generation must out of relative obscurity discover its mission, fulfils it or betrays it' is taken Frantz Fanon's *Wretched of the Earth*, the chapter 'On National Culture'.

3

Student Radicals, Lumpen Youth, and the Origins of Revolutionary Groups in Sierra Leone, 1977–1996

Ismail Rashid

For ten years Sierra Leone experienced one of the most brutal wars in the modern world. Three groups, the Revolutionary United Front (RUF), the National Provisional Ruling Council (NPRC) and the Armed Forces Ruling Council (AFRC) have played pivotal roles in initiating or sustaining this war. All represented themselves as 'revolutionary' forces but ended in victimizing different regions and segments of the Sierra Leonean society. The RUF, the most vicious of the three, targeted children, women, youth, the elderly, farmers, miners, urban workers, teachers, traders and politicians. What are the origins of these groups, which all lack coherent political programmes, disciplined leadership cadres, or mass support base? What animates their different versions of 'revolution?' How can their behaviour and actions be explained?

The different scholars and pundits, who have investigated the conflict, interpret it variously as the consequence of social atavism, youth delinquency and environmental depletion (Kaplan, 1992, 1995: 32–69 & 401–409); a 'crisis of modernity', fuelled by rural disaffection and orchestrated by 'excluded intellectuals' (Richards, 1996); Charles Taylor's revanchism and an extension of the Liberian civil war (Fyle, 1994; Zack Williams and Riley, 1993); the collapse of the Cold War system, weak state structures and warlordism (Reno, 1995 & 1998). While some of these interpretations, like those offered by Kaplan and Richards rightly locate the youth as a central element in the crisis, their analyses of the origins and character of this youth factor are partly flawed (Abdullah, 1997; 1998; Bangura, 1997). The Liberian interpretation locates the external supporters of Foday Sankoh and timing of the insurgency; it does not explain the character of the RUF or the entrenchment of the insurgency in Sierra Leone. Similarly, Reno's Cold War and state-centric analysis reveal much about the role of international forces and state actors in creating the context for the crisis, it shows little concern for non-state and subaltern forces.

This chapter builds on Abdullah's claim that an investigation of the history and sociology of urban youth culture and politics in the 1970s and 1980s is more likely to yield more insight into the character of the conflict and its main architects than other interpretations (this volume). The architecture of that youth culture, and the ways in which it impinged on national politics, are crucial in understanding the events that led to the rise of the RUF and the general character of the movement. To illuminate this point, this chapter focuses primarily on radical students at FBC, a critical fraction of the youth population in the 1970s and 1980s. It looks at their antecedents, character, politics, and their relationship with the Freetown lumpen youth. The interaction between radical students and the urban youth significantly influenced the political orientation of the latter. Between 1977 and 1992, it was the radical students and urban youth who took a leading role in directly, and militantly, challenging the authority and the legitimacy of the All Peoples Congress (APC) party government. It was the attempts at repressing student politics by government and university authorities in the mid-1980s that ultimately led to the events, which gave birth to the RUF, and insurgency among the youth.

African students: A legacy of political radicalism

As in many other areas in the world, student and youth militancy in Africa has a along and checkered history. The annals of African anti-colonialism, nationalism, and post-colonial struggle for political reform and democracy would be incomplete without acknowledging the dynamic role of student and youths. From the 1920s and 1930s, African students abroad actively contributed to anti-colonial reform and nationalist organizations. Some of these students were influenced by Marxism and had strong affiliations with European labour, communist and socialist organizations. The role of the West African Students Union (WASU) and West African National Secretariat (WANS) in promoting nationalist, anti-colonialist and pan-Africanist ideas in Britain and its colonies is well documented. Many members of WASU later became part of the post-colonial ruling elite in the late 1950s and 1960s (UNESCO, 1994; Adi, 1998 & 2000).

The tradition of student involvement in politics continued after the attainment of independence by African countries. Throughout the 1960s and 1970s, a new generation of students in Southern Africa, Senegal, Ethiopia, Ghana, Nigeria, Sudan and Congo, like students in other parts of the world, attempted to reform their campus and national environments. They used petitions, negotiations, strikes and demonstrations to end the vestiges of European colonialism; change government policies and structures; and reform the curricula and character of their universities. Given their disparate goals, levels of commitment and organization, and often limited alliances with other forces in the wider society, and the forces arraigned against them, student impact were generally limited (Emerson, 1969; Hanna, 1975; UNESCO, 1994). These university-inspired actions spawned a minority group of Marxist-oriented professors and students, who saw themselves as the vanguard opposition to the political establishment. They theorised about the neocolonial and underdeveloped nature of their countries, and the ineptitude, corruption and dictatorial excesses of their governments. In their statements and writings, they advocated revolutionary change and socialism. In their political actions, they sought to forge alliances with working-class organizations (*Review of African Political Economy*, 1985: 1–14).

The situation in Sierra Leone was completely different. Despite a history of pan-Africanism and militant colonialism, radical politics was not a major feature of the university culture until the late 1970s and 1980s. In its demographic composition and evolution, the Sierra Leone colony was not only an abolitionist and imperialist enterprise, it was a pan-Africanist project. The colony produced or attracted vocal proponents of Pan-Africanism like Holy Johnson, Orishatukeh Faduma and Edward W. Blyden. In the first three decades of the twentieth century, branches of the Aborigines Rights Protection Society, the Universal Negro Improvement Association (UNIA) and the National Congress of British West Africa (NCBWA) flourished in Freetown. But, it was I.T.A. Wallace-Johnson, very much influenced by communism, who moulded this tradition into a radical anti-imperialist alternative. His West African Youth League (WAYL), with its vocal mouthpiece, *The African Standard*, brought together workers, youths and other popular groups in the Western Area. The British colonial administration reacted swiftly: it destroyed the political potency of the league and inaugurated a transfer of power to a more conservative political faction (Abdullah, 1995: 195–221; Denzer, 1973: 413–452 and 563–580).[1]

In the euphoria of the post-independence period, pan-Africanist ideas filtered into the Fourah Bay College (FBC) and was manifested in a short-lived student group the Pan-Africanist Nkrumahist Student Organization (PANSO). Enamoured by the ideas of Kwame Nkrumah and Sekou Toure, members of PANSO condemned neocolonialism, expressed their support for the different liberation movements and endorsed the radical call for continental unity. They appropriated the popular slogans of the Convention Peoples Party of Kwame Nkrumah and the Parti Démocratique du Guinée

(PDG) of Sekou Toure and, following Nkrumah, produced a student paper, *The Spark*. In 1965, when the White minority regime led by Ian Smith unilaterally declared independence, PANSO members joined other students to protest against the settler regime. And when Nkrumah was overthrown and exiled in Guinea, the group wrote and visited him in 1966. Yet PANSO could hardly be compared to the leftist tendency, which had emerged in the other African universities. As one member put it, 'we were more interested in the philosophical content than in the radical politics of Pan-Africanism'. PANSO was not directly involve in national politics and the ethnic acrimony generated by 1967/8 national elections drove a wedge among the members, so that by 1969 the group was dead as an organization.[2]

The FBC radicals

Unlike PANSO, the radical students of the 1970s were militant and more directly involved in national politics. Radical students espoused a mixture of anti-establishmentarianism (University and Central Government), non-conformism, populism and reformism. They distinguished themselves from other students, whom they regarded as 'ballheads;' a moniker for social conformism and political conservatism. Housed mainly in the humanities and social science faculties, these students came to constitute the 'active minority', which many suggest, is essential for the provision of leadership, direction and organization for campus-inspired political actions (Hanna, Hanna & Sauer, 1975: 71-102). Solidly liberal, college radical wanted to purge the system of its obnoxious aspects; make it more plural and responsive to social and economic problems. By the 1980s, a new tendency emerged among the radicals; this tendency was markedly leftist with slogans that were 'populist', 'socialist' and 'pan-Africanist'. These students did not only oppose the system; they advocated its replacement with alternative models. Nkrumah's united socialist Africa, Castro's Cuba, Gaddafi's Libya and Kim Il Sung's Korea featured among some of the desired models. This was new in the history of student radicalism; it mirrored developments in Ghana, Nigeria and Ethiopia. The evolution of these ideas is crucial to understanding the crisis of the 1990s.

PANSO and radicals aside, FBC campus, the primary terrain of student politics, had a legacy embroidered with religious conservatism, elitism and political passivism. The college started out as a Church Missionary Society (CMS) sponsored theological institution in 1827 in Cline Town, near the Freetown harbour. Its initial mission was to produce clergymen (Sumner, 1963). In 1876 it became a degree granting institution affiliated to the University of Durham. Until the 1950s, the majority of its students were foreign students and only a small fraction came from the tiny Freetown Krio elite.

Of the 357 degree students enrolled in 1954, only 49 were Sierra Leoneans. By 1985, the student population numbered over 1,500. The student enrolment pattern and curriculum began to change during the period of decolonization when the British colonial administration suddenly discovered that natives were human beings. By the 1960s, more Krio and students from the hinterland were finding their way into the institution (Sumner 1963, Hargreaves, 1985). In 1972, Fourah College was formally amalgamated with Njala University College (NUC) to constitute the University of Sierra Leone. It was these changes in orientation that made possible for PANSO to emerge in 1960s.[3]

Government supervision and funding, especially in the 1970s, exposed the college to the problems faced by the state. As government fiscal position worsened in the 1970s and 1980s, the college found it difficult to fulfill its academic mission or provide decent facilities for the student population. In a similar fashion, it was forced to confront the problems of the larger Freetown community (Hargreaves, 1985). Many of its constituents including students, faculty and workers came from the city. Yet, the linkages between town and gown were not always apparent given the detached and elevated location of the campus on Mount Aureol. 'Mount Olympus', as it is fondly called by it younger denizens, provided a fairly autonomous and common space for student organizations, ideas and politics.

The post-independence ethnic, cultural and social diversity of the student populace was reflected in the plethora of clubs hosted by College. They included alumni associations, district unions, fraternities and sororities, faculty groups and social clubs. The radical tendency was expressed in two of these social clubs, Gardeners and Auradicals, both founded in the early 1970s. Membership of both clubs ranged from 30 to 50 students in the 1970s and 1980s. New members were recruited from those students who displayed a 'positive' attitude and anti-system posture. Gardeners, the more militant, met in the college's Botanical Gardens to discuss campus and national problems. Amidst its 'politicization' sessions, its members freely smoked marijuana, the ultimate symbol of its social non-conformism. In the late 1970s, it produced an annual magazine, *Frontline*, with a logo sporting a blood drenched fist clasping a barbed wire.[4] The magazine covered several aspects of campus life, but what made it different from other campus publications was its anti-government (or anti-Siaka Stevens) and anti-Lebanese (specifically anti-Jamil Sahid Mohamed) lampoons and cartoons.[5] The most politically active and vocal students usually came from the ranks of these radical clubs in the 1970s.

Radical clubs exerted considerable influence on campus politics. Campus political competition centred on controlling the leadership of the Fourah Bay College Student Union (FBC-SU) and National Union of Sierra Leone

Students (NUSS). Both unions dealt with issues pertaining to student welfare on campus and provided the bridge between students, university administration and the central government. Since student leadership was elected annually policies tended to be discontinuous. Political competition was vibrant as radicals and their supporters battled with '*fixity*,' a voting block of largely matured students who tended to vote for conservative and more moderate candidates. *Fixity* was also ethnic politics. No single group dominated campus politics. The pendulum swung from one to the other depending on the configuration of forces and the relevant issues of the day. Student politics was the sum of the contradictory and complementary interests and personalities that defined it. Upwardly mobile, largely dependent, and from diverse backgrounds, students in their politics espoused a mixture of idealistic, pragmatic and opportunistic tendencies. Defending the masses, a popular refrain amongst students, was sometimes inextricably linked with protecting their privileges and future prospects.

Student radicals provided the vital link between students on campus and the lumpens in the city, and the merging of socially acceptable and unacceptable youth practices. College radicals participated in the coded linguistic and cultural practices of the marginalised urban youths; they were generally of the same generation and shared similar sociological characteristics. They frequented *potes* – places in the city that formed the cultural and organizational foci of the city's lumpen youth – to fraternize, politicize, discuss social problems and smoke marijuana with them. In their structure and settings, the meetings of Gardeners Club of FBC (and their counterpart, Future Shock of Njala University College) mirrored the urban *potes*. Also, student radicals intermittently converted their dormitory rooms into mini-*potes*, sometimes attracting lumpens on campus. In short, the *pote* as a formation became a place for the pursuit of unacceptable social activities, a forum for political discussion and exchange of ideas, and a meeting point for student's radicals and the urban lumpen youth.

The Freetown lumpen youth

Lumpenproletariat has been utilized in this essay for want of a more appropriate collective term to describe a conglomerate with diverse social and ethnic origins. It is therefore used in its crude Marxist sense to represent those strata of the society that cannot fully employ or sell its labour power because of capitalist transformation, restructuring or retrenchment.[6] Whether labeled *raray-boys, savis-man' dreg man* or *liner*, the emergence of the Freetown lumpen population was a function of the colonial political economy at the end of the 19th and beginning of the twentieth century. Escaped and freed rural slaves and peasants drifted into the city in search of employment settling largely in peri-urban enclaves. Their numbers grew steadily with the poor performance of the Sierra Leone economy. The opening of iron ore and diamonds mines in the 1930s failed to stem the drift. Worried about crime, vagrancy and destitution, the colonial government, supported by the Freetown elite, passed a plethora of legislation and took actions to tribalize, control, stop and reverse rural urban drift (Harrell-Bond et al., 1978: 30–40 and 135–141). These efforts however, failed. Lumpens remained in the city providing irregular casual labour. In Krio middle class perception, the city's lumpen population became associated with all that was decadent in the society: sloth, petty crime, gambling, prostitution, drugs and violence.

By 1961, lumpens had emerged as a relatively coherent social group with identifiable cultural forms, dress habits, language and life style. They knotted the bottom of their shirts and sprinkled their Krio with slang and could be found in the sea-side areas in the city like Mo Wharf, Sawpit, Customs Bay, Magazine and Kanikay. These areas hosted brothels as well as *Potes*. *Potes* were fixed and temporary spaces set up by this underclass for smoking marijuana, gambling and planning cultural activities. Among their major cultural activities were the odelay masquerade processions and lantern parades (Nunley, 1987). *Odelay* processions, which were organized during public holidays, included a *billah* man (the masquerade guide), *ode* (the decorated masquerade), musicians and revellers. Lantern parades were usually held at the end of the Ramadhan month of fasting. By the late 1960s, *odelay* and lantern societies had proliferated in the city, reflecting not only the demographic expansion of the group, but also the participation of working-class elements in these cultural forms. Tolerance by the city's populace came grudgingly since the Krio middle class regarded *odelays* as corrupt versions of their older hunting societies.

Violence among lumpens spawned the mystique and terror that came to be associated with some of their better-known members. Abayomi Alhadi (alias Highway), Bra Bankie, Bra Langbo Sugbala, the John brothers, Bunting and Clinton, and Bra Karay became legends of violence in their life time. In the 1960s and early 1970s, this group provided a pool of hired thugs for politicians of All Peoples Congress (APC) party. Mobilized largely through networks created by S.I. Koroma, they terrorized APC's opponents during the 1962, 1967, 1973 and 1977 elections. They were so effective in the 1973 elections that the opposition SLPP withdrew from the elections. As the wider populace became disenchanted with APC's rule and terror tactics, these older lumpens lost all public sympathy.

The demography, character and culture of the urban lumpen population changed significantly in the 1970s and 1980s. The post-independence youth who had benefited from the expansion of primary and secondary educational facilities came of age. The 1985 National Census estimated the youth population, aged between 14 and 35 years, at about 1,028,590 or 29.4 percent of the total population (estimated at 3,518,378). In Freetown, their number was 168,763 or 35 percent of the city's population (estimated at 469,776) (Makannah 1995, 2–6, 66–85). The majority of this population faced bleak educational prospects; access was limited to few vocational and tertiary educational institutions. The limited labor market could not absorb them, and to make matters worse, the public and private sectors were downsizing. Youth unemployment was as much a problem of the neocolonial structure of the economy as it was of the type of formal education given to the youth. Its colonialist emphasis on producing a bureaucratic and professional class meant that they were largely lacking in the vocational and technical skills. This new lumpen population was different: it included a significant youth element with middle and lower-middle class backgrounds. Being literate, they were more aware of the country's problems and more critical of its political leadership. With their unfulfilled higher aspirations, they tended to be strongly anti-establishment and rebellious towards authority. This shift in generation and attitudes coincided with and was reinforced by changing local and global popular cultural context within which they operated.

The new culture separated the colonial generation from the post-colonial generation in music, dress, attitude and behaviour. Iconoclastic and avant-garde, the emerging cultural landscape supported soul, rock n' roll, disco, reggae, Afro-beat, drugs, Afro, mini-skirts, bell-bottoms and platform shoes – cultural staples consumed by youths internationally. In addition, the Sierra Leone youth danced to Super-combo, Afro-National, Sonny Okosuns, Fela Anikulapo Kuti, Osibisa, Bob Marley, Bunny Wailer and Peter Tosh. John Collins in his reflections on West African popular music aptly describes the moment as one of 'creative explosion'; a moment, which witnessed the cross-fertilization of rhythms from African and other cultures (Collins, 1985). Although older lumpens also partook in the emergent culture, its most active consumers were the younger lumpens who were more literate and politically conscious. Yet, these younger lumpens saw *potes* not only as centres for the pursuit of unacceptable social practices, but also places of radical political discussions. They continued to participate in the *odelay* festivals but attempted to create more politically oriented organizations. The All Youth Organizations (AYO-WIZZ) formed in 1975 attempted to bring together members of the different groups for more progressive ends. It was this younger group of lumpens who interacted with the student radicals in the *potes*.

The global and domestic economic crisis of the 1970s reinforced the disenchantment and militancy within the youth culture. The global oil-shocks of 1973/4 accentuated the structural and fiscal problems in the primary commodity-based export economies like that of Sierra Leone (Parfitt and Riley 1989:126-147). The yearly budget deficits from 1975 hovered between 50 and 60 million Leones. The price of oil related products and other imported commodities increased while production and prices of primary commodities fell. Unprofitability forced the closure of the iron ore mines at Marampa in 1978. Official output of diamonds declined (partly due to rampant smuggling) although the relatively high prices provided the government with some financial relief.[7] The decline in the diamond production was a consequence of the depletion of resources and the development of 'parallel' economy by Lebanese entrepreneurs and their political allies. Overall, export revenues fell while import expenditure increased. In many African countries, including Sierra Leone, this translated into major fiscal and budget deficit.

The fiscal crisis was a function not only of international forces but also of domestic politics and the structure of the post-colonial economy. The APC had assumed power in a post-colonial state rife with economic and political problems. The terms of trade and government revenues from export of primary products were already deteriorating before the global oil crisis. The leadership of the party and the government had to contend with opposing political forces outside and within its ranks. To consolidate his leadership, Siaka Stevens eliminated and excluded potential rivals from the political process, and replaced 'true political competition with a struggle for his favor' (Reno, 1995: 111, Hayward 1989: 165-180). He deprived local politicians of access to resources and alternate sources of power by promoting Lebanese entrepreneurs at their expense, especially in diamond business.

The most visible aspect of Steven's strategy was the intimate public and private relationship that emerged between the President and the Afro-Lebanese business tycoon, Jamil Sahid Muhammad. Stevens used Jamil to invest his wealth in private commercial investment and foreign banks, and to bankroll the state when it needed urgent financial relief. The latter strategy may have added to the veneer of political stability but it exacerbated institutional decay and public corruption. By 1977, what Parfitt and Riley described as 'the debilitating effect on the development of personalized or neo-patrimonial rule and policies' had become evident (Parfitt and Riley 1989: 127). The state was in serious crisis.

In radical student politics, and indeed, in popular youth perception, Siaka Stevens and Jamil Sahid became both the metaphor and the embodiment of the country's crisis. The relationship between the two men represented the negative fusion of private and public immorality and corruption. The more Stevens utilized his links with Jamil Sahid to resolve food, fuel and salary problems, the more negatively the public perceived the relationship. It was, therefore, not surprising that student and youth dissent against the state and its ruling elite took the form of direct protest against these men and their relationship.

The Politics of confrontation, 1977–1982

The deteriorating economic conditions and growing youth militancy provided the context and the catalyst for the most significant intrusion into national politics by students since the 1960s.[8] The stage was set by the visit of President Kenneth Kaunda of Zambia in January 1977 to brief the Sierra Leone government about the Liberation Movement in Zimbabwe. Zimbabwean students, supported by FBC students, demonstrated in support of their country's struggle. After this, ideas on a demonstration on national issues gained ground among radical students. They chose the 1977 university convocation ceremony to express their discontent against the national leadership of Siaka Stevens. Their protest started innocuously. Stevens, the Vice-Chancellor, and members of his government had assumed their usual pride of place at the convocation without incident. Towards the end of the ceremony and in the middle of his speech, a group of 'radical' students plucked out their concealed condemnatory placards and hurled invectives at him – on corruption, brutality and larceny. According to George Roberts, the spark for the protest was a rumour that Stevens had appropriated $40 million from the national treasury. Surprised and humiliated by the incident, Stevens hurriedly exited from the Campus without completing his speech (Roberts 1982:252–254).

In retaliation, government supporters unleashed 'a counter-demonstration' two days later. About 500 thugs drawn largely, but not exclusively, from the APC Youth League descended on campus with banners supporting the president and his party: 'Siaka Stevens is unshakeable'; 'abolish all aid to the University'; 'APC Forever' (*West Africa*, February 7, 1997). Kemoh Fadika, a seasoned APC youth, led the 'counter-demonstration'. He allegedly occupied and converted the principal's office into a command post for the operation.[9] Students were brutalized and extensive damage wrought on campus property. Armed units of the Cuban-trained paramilitary Internal Security Units [ISU, later called Special Security Division (SSD)], personally controlled by Stevens, followed on the trail of the thugs, allegedly to control the situation. They joined in the operation and arrested a number of lecturers and student leaders. Hindolo Trye, the student union president was later picked up at Lumley, a suburb on the outskrit of Freetown, and taken to the Criminal Investigation Department (CID) headquarters at Pademba Road.

As news of the 'counter-demonstration' spread, FBC students and other students mobilized pupils and students in various parts of the city with word that the government has closed the college. On February 2, 1977, chanting 'No College, No School', thousands of secondary school students converged at the Cotton Tree and the CID in the city centre where Hindolo Trye was held. Trye, sporting a red sowetan cap, gave a clenched fist salute to the crowd. The ISU unsuccessfully attempted to disperse the crowd with tear-gas. The demonstration continued to the east end of the city where it degenerated into looting and vandalism when lumpen elements joined. By the end of the day, 40 people lay dead and many others wounded. In the succeeding days, lumpens and students in Bo, Kenema and Kono took up the protest. They burnt native administration and government buildings as well as private houses *(West Africa,* February 28; March 1977). The government declared a State of Emergency. Enforcing the emergency produced regular street battles between the police and militant youths. The practice of violently engaging state security forces during protests became part of rebellious youth culture.

Although lecturers, trade unionists and the general public sympathized with students and youth actions, no organization came out unequivocally in their support.[10] As the crisis took on a national character, what had been a spontaneous anti-Stevens demonstration became a more coherent political challenge with the release of a list of student resolutions on February 8, 1977. The resolutions called for 'free and fair elections', lowering of the voting age to 18, reduction in electoral constituencies and cabinet posts, abolition of the position of deputy minister, reduction in defence spending and the 'disarmament of the Internal Security Unit (I.S.U.)'. One resolution stressed, 'non-Africans have too much say in our economy, especially Lebanese and Indians'. Their demands were democratic and nationalistic and echoed the sentiments of many Sierra Leoneans.[11] The opposition SLPP, which clearly benefited from student actions, produced their own statement two months after the event.

With the stability of the state threatened, the shaken Stevens' regime conceded to elections in May 1977 and lowered the voting age to 18. It ignored the other demands. Before then, the student Union President, Hindolo Trye, appealed for calm and understanding, and agreed to cooperate with the government over national radio *(West Africa,* February 21, 1977: 391, *West Africa,* February 28, 1977: 398). Conducted under a state of emergency in June 1977, the elections were neither free nor fair. The Party unleashed its now seasoned 'thugs' and the ISU. Amid widespread violence, harassment, killing and destruction of rural settlements, only a mere 15 opposition SLPP candidates squeaked through to parliament. The majority of APC candidates, including some university lecturers, went unopposed. These lecturers who became politicians and later, government ministers include Abdul Karim Koroma, Abdulai Conteh and Joe Jackson. *Unopposed, dem pick am, he day insae dae,* (Unopposed, s/he has been chosen, s/he is in) became the popular refrain of broadcasts, and a source of popular parody (Daramy 1993: 203).

The autocratic state under Stevens had rallied from the brink of crisis. The students, lumpens and the opposition SLPP offered no serious political alternative. The president had rallied the disaffected sections of the elite by playing up the insecurity and instability created by political confrontations. The parliament, dominated by APC cronies, denied the SLPP 'official oppo-sition' status (*West Africa*, July 11, 1977:1448, *West Africa*, August 1, 1977: 1607). Instead, Stevens and his APC pushed through the One-Party Consti-tution in a fraudulent referendum in 1978. SLPP members had the choice of either crossing over to the ruling APC or vacating their seats. Only one SLPP member, Mana Kpaka, chose to vacate his seat. Evident in this process of political re-consolidation and state revitalization was the co-option of a number of lecturers who had criticized the government's actions against stu-dents in January 1977 and its 'invasion' of the campus.

The 1977 student intrusion into politics had limited gains. If anything, it served to revive a government under crisis but also opened up the possibility of sustained and organised opposition outside formal structures. A tradition of anti-system or anti-government confrontation was inaugurated. Institu-tionalized in 'All Thugs Day' as January 31 came to be known on FBC cam-pus, it served as a rallying point for radicals (Fyle, 1994: 139). Radical student leaders became radical journalists with the launching of the *Tablet* newspa-per. The editor, Pios Foray, received a hero's applause after successfully de-fending himself in parliament against contempt by Brigadier J.S. Momoh.[12] Attempts to launch a political movement that would transcend the limits of student and lumpen oppositional politics failed. The Movement for Progress in Africa [MOPA], modelled after MOJA in Liberia and the Gambia, which was set up, was quickly banned by the government (*Awareness Magazine*, 1980).[13]

The crisis revealed the ambivalent relationship between students and lumpens; both subaltern categories. On one hand, the group of politically motivated and mobilized party thugs challenged and attempted to repress students' rights to protest, and in the process discredited themselves in the eyes of younger lumpens and students. On the other hand, a younger gen-eration of youth and school children gave critical support to the students' demands. Many of them would join the ranks of student radicals and lumpens in the blighted climate of the 1980s. The confrontation further emphasized the hiatus between the 'older' and 'younger' lumpen culture. The politics of collaboration was giving way to the politics of confrontation. The terror and mystique cultivated around the older lumpens began to wear thin after 1977. Many of them retreated from active thuggery. For its subsequent terror cam-paigns, the APC relied more heavily on the lumpen youth from the hinterland. Like the older group, the younger urban lumpens continued to be a fixture in politics especially during elections. Unlike them, however, they had no set loyalties to the APC or the political system. They regard elections as opportunities to '*chap*' (make a fast buck) and had no hesitation in joining students in their continued confrontations with the state. This ambivalence notwithstanding, it was evident that rebellious youth culture was being transformed into a 'culture of resistance', analogous to the one which Nkomo identifies in the South African 'ethnic universities' in the 1970s and 1980s (Nkomo, 1984: 151–152).

Politics of opportunism, revolution and repression, 1982–1992

Instead of concentrating on resolving the endemic social and economic problems, Stevens used his consolidated position to pursue his ambition of becoming a 'respectable African elder statesman'; he hosted a lavish OAU conference in 1980 at tremendous cost to the country. But student antagonism persisted; a campus strike against the conference was ignored by state officials (*Tablet*, February 20, 1980). A 1981 student demonstration resulted in the torching of the official car of the Mayoress of Freetown, Dr. June Holst-Roness who had accompanied the visiting Mayor of Hull to the campus. Stevens blamed the Mayoress for the incident.

Siaka Stevens' moment in the African spotlight pushed the country into deeper insolvency and fanned the flames of further social discontent. The 1980s were marked by government struggle with a growing foreign debt, recurrent budget deficits, decline in agricultural and mineral exports, smuggling and foreign exchange problems (Hayward, 1989: 174–177) Institutional corruption became pervasive as the cost of living rose steeply. 'Vouchergate' the first in the line of many official embezzlement scandals, broke out in 1982 (Kpundeh, 1995: 62–63). Meanwhile, chronic fuel, power and rice shortages plagued the urban centres. Youth unemployment continued to increase. When the Sierra Leone Labour Congress (SLLC) struck for better wages and conditions of service in 1981, their leadership was intimidated and the strike beaten. The anti- government *Tablet* newspaper had their offices raided by APC party thugs, their printing facilities destroyed, and key members of the press chased out of the country. Student response to both the strike and destruction of the *Tablet* printing press was muted. Students attention now turned to the deteriorating conditions on FBC campus, and this produced opportunism among the student leadership. In seeking to improve living conditions on campus, student leaders entered into an uneasy alliance with Alfred Akibo-Betts, an APC youth-leaguer, with an established reputation as a thug.[14] As a parliamentary assistant in the Finance Ministry, Akibo reinvented himself as an 'anti-corruption crusader' and successfully insinuated himself into campus politics. When the APC wanted to restrain Akibo during the 1982 General Elections, students defended and campaigned for him in the

Freetown Central 1 constituency. His opposition, Wilsworth 'Ajoti' Morgan, another youth-leaguer, with considerable lumpen followership received a rough ride from students. The government later cancelled the elections. The alliance with Akibo divided the campus radicals. The anti-Akibo radicals, recalled his days of thuggery and maintained uncompromisingly that he was still a part of the corrupt APC system. Pro-Akibo radicals, including Abdul Gbla, the 1981/1982 FBC-SU president, were expelled from the Gardeners' Club.

The fracture among the radicals coincided with the rise of a left tendency. Starting in 1982, new radical groups – Green Book Study Club, the Pan-African Union and the Socialist club – gained prominence on campus. Although these clubs had shared membership with the Gardeners and Auradicals, they were decidedly different in ideological orientation. They began to eschew the drug culture and advocate a serious ideological engagement on campus. The Green Book Club promoted ideas of revolutionary mass participation in 'Popular Congresses and Committees'.[15] The Pan-African Union (PANAFU) dawned the mantle of the radical West African Youth League advocating 'total unity, liberation and development of Africa under a just and egalitarian system' (*Pan-African Union Information Brochure*, 1992).[16] They organized seminars, meetings and rallies on campus. There was a noticeable change in language: *man dem* the comradely salutation gave way to *com* and *brothers* and *sisters*.[17] The youth culture of resistance was now assuming a 'revolutionary' posture with more coherent organizational forms.

International political shifts helped galvanize these developments. Libya, under pressure from the US and France, developed an aggressive 'anti-imperialist' foreign policy in West Africa. Through its People's Bureau, it sponsored Green Book Study Clubs and demonstrated a willingness to give military training to young militants, if necessary (St. John, 1987; El Khawas, 1986). The struggle against Apartheid in South Africa also intensified. Images of youth confronting the South African police, the popular 'Free Mandela' campaign, and the Namibian liberation struggle were disseminated widely among the lumpen youth and students, through the media and efforts of exiled students from African National Congress (ANC), Pan Africanist Congress of Azania (PAC) and South West African Peoples Organization (SWAPO) in Sierra Leone.

In this context, the crisis, which had started in the 1970s, deepened. The state contracted considerably and seemed on the verge of collapsing.[18] The APC government and the state institutions increasingly became incapable of responding to the recurrent budget deficits, currency devaluation, commodity shortages, and rampant corruption. The army, the SSD, and the unions, which had hitherto been on tight leashes, showed signs of restiveness. The army and SSD clashed in the city after an incident at a football match at the National Stadium. The Sierra Leone Teachers' Union (SLTU) and Sierra Leone Labor Congress (SLLC) asked again and again for higher salaries and better conditions of service. Siaka Stevens, who had previously been able to ma-noeuvre his way through the contentious forces, began to show acute weak-ness. His vulnerability became apparent in the reaction to his equivocation on going for a life-presidency or departing from politics (*West Africa,* January 28, 1985). Serious internal squabbles surfaced among members of the APC party over his continuity in office and succession.

Despite the rumblings in different sections of the population, it was the radical students and urban youth who directly challenged Siaka Stevens and scuttled his political plans. The hint of life-presidency led to a major student demonstration and urban riot on January 12, 1984. Over 2,000 college stu-dents and urban youth took to the streets carrying placards, which condemned the president's plans for life presidency. The demonstrators stormed the City Hall and disrupted the ongoing APC party congress. There was widespread looting in the east end of the city and the police arrested and detained two students. Daniel Kamara, the 1983\4 Student Union president, spearheaded the action. Four months earlier, he had marched Arthur Porter, the Vice-Chancellor, and Eldred Jones, the FBC principal and key college administra-tors to the state house to demand an improvement in student living condi-tions. Rattled by the disruption of the APC congress and fed up with the recurrent demonstrations, Stevens shut down FBC for three months and instituted a commission of enquiry headed by Justice Kutubu.[19] The Com-mission investigated, and found not only evidence of poor conditions on campus but also serious administrative mismanagement. Testifying, Eldred Jones, principal of FBC catalogued 'chronic problems of poor library facili-ties, overcrowding in hostels and classrooms, shortage of chairs in lecture rooms and poor food' (*For Di People,* January, 1984). The government never released the report. Instead, it became leverage to get the FBC administra-tion to rein in the students. The administration tried to do so by changing registration procedures. It insisted that all students should sign an agreement of 'good conduct' before being accepted into the University. The 'agreement forms' were objects of much derision and ridicule when they were first intro-duced in 1984.

Yet they became useful instruments for tackling and then repressing the 1985/1986 student union leadership and the radical left on campus. In March 1985, the Mass Awareness and Participation [MAP] Student Union leader-ship under Alie Kabba was elected unopposed with strong support from the campus radicals. Members of the Union leadership included Green Book, Gardeners and Pan-African Union members. The MAP government had made no secret of its intention to translate the current radical left ideologies on campus into practice. The move led to a propaganda offensive with 'populist' and 'anti-government' posters on FBC campus and the city. When a student was caught stealing, a people's tribunal was set up, and he was summarily disciplined. Alarmed by the militancy of the new student leadership, the vice-principal, C.P. Foray, refused to speak to them when they marched to his residence to complain about water and food. The administration and students were on a collision course.

K. Koso-Thomas, the newly appointed Vice-Chancellor of University of Sierra Leone, of which FBC was a constituent college, became embroiled in the attempt to contain the new FBC Students Union leadership. The students gave him the opportunity when they collected dormitory keys at the end of the Easter term to prevent a lockout the following term – a clear infringement on the province of then unpopular Student Warden, Jenkins Smith. Rumours were quickly disseminated that the students intended using their hostels as barracks for encamping Libyan mercenaries. Using this as an excuse, the Vice Chancellor and Principal, Eldred Jones, called on the SSD to remove the students who were staying on campus for the Easter break. The SSD raided the campus brutalizing and forcibly removing students staying on campus. The incident led to a city-wide demonstration. By the time the college reopened for the Epiphany term in April 1985, the University administrators had declared 41 students, including the student leadership and 2 female students 'ineligible' to re-register (*West Africa*, May 6, 1985: 911, *West Africa*, May 20, 1985: 1021). Student protests against the decision of the university led to a campus demonstration, which ended in the burning of a Mercedes Benz car belonging to the vice-principal, Cyril Foray.

The confrontation continued in the city where students were supported by lumpen youths. Cars were smashed, government buildings ransacked, and shops looted. The university eventually suspended and expelled a total of 41 students. Three young lecturers, Olu Gordon, Jimmy Kandeh and Gilbert Cleo Hanciles were sacked.[20] Hanciles and Gordon were members of the Pan-African Union; all three were deemed friendly with students. Alie Kabba, the FBC-SU president and four other students were arrested and detained for two months for allegedly torching the vice-principal's car.[21] The case was later thrown out of court. The campus purges were well timed, coming a few weeks before the APC convention to choose a new Party leader and president. To ensure a smooth transition, the APC needed to repress troublesome constituencies.[22]

Stevens engineered a successful and peaceful transfer of power to his protege, Major-General Joseph Saidu Momoh, the head of the army. The transfer of power to Momoh represented an attempt by the dominant politi-

cal elite to revitalize the collapsing state and extend the life of the APC regime. The change was greeted with popular euphoria. His military credentials
and his warped and undigested notion of constructive nationalism seemed
to have impressed the uninformed public. Momoh promised to instill discipline in public life and improve the lot of Sierra Leoneans. To strengthen his
power base, he solicited support from lumpen youth. The Paddle Odelay
Society granted him the honour of leading their masquerade in 1985. But
this optimism soon gave way to cynicism as Momoh proved unable to enforce national discipline, reverse the general institutional decay, or stem the
creeping economic decline. The reach and capacity of the state contracted.
Official corruption magnified as *Squandergate* succeeded *Vouchergate* (Kpundeh,
1995: 63). The economy, with its high inflation, devaluation, power outage,
rice and fuel scarcity, hung around the necks of Momoh and his cabal like
albatrosses. The president's attempt to create his own informal networks of
power by bringing in Israeli businessmen and other foreign interests to invest
in the economy turned sour. The two Israeli businessmen, Shaptai
Kalmanowitch and Nir Guaz, had to be expelled from the country (Reno,
1995: 155–176). Youth and students had initially protested the presence of
these men in Sierra Leone labeling them agents of the Apartheid regime. By
the end of 1986, the youths that Momoh had tried to woo turned against
him. Members of the Paddle Odelay Society heaped unprintable invectives
on his person during their annual masquerade festival. The president resorted
to the 'ethnicization' of power and became dependent on a small cabal from
his ethnic group, the Limba. James Bambay Kamara, the Inspector General
of Police and a leading member of Ekutay, as this group was known, acquired considerable power in the process. The president himself called on
other Sierra Leoneans to organise ethnically!

After a three-year ban, the Student Union of FBC was revived again in
1989. It resumed the radical tradition of anti-government confrontation. In
1991, it called for multi-party politics, immediate dissolution of the Momoh
government and the establishment of an interim administration to oversee
elections (Interviews with Students, 1995). A major demonstration planned
to back up the resolutions had to be called off because of the massive deployment of security forces on the way leading to the college, and on the
advice of journalists, politicians and Pan-African Union members.[23] The revived student leadership continued to act within the radical anti-establishment culture of campus politics but it was clear that the leftist tendency was
on the retreat.

Beleaguered by a crumbling economy, a divided party and attacks from
different constituencies, the Momoh regime conceded to multi-party politics
and elections in 1991. As elections grew nearer, there were indications that

the government intended to rig the elections. This was when the Revolutionary United Front [RUF] under the leadership of Foday Sankoh, struck. With the help of Charles Taylor of the National Patriotic Front of Liberia (NPFL) he attacked Bomaru, Kailahun District, Eastern Province on March 21, 1991, with the goal of ending 22 years of APC rule. Momoh sent the army to combat Foday Sankoh and the RUF. Most of the soldiers who bore the brunt of the fighting were young soldiers recently drafted into the army. Even as insurrection weakened the decrepit state, its minders continued their corrupting ways. On April 29, 1992, a group of young unpaid and disgruntled soldiers stormed the capital city and toppled the Momoh regime. They instituted the National Provisional Ruling Council [NPRC], a regime of largely twenty-year-olds under the leadership of Captain Valentine Strasser.

RUF, NPRC and the radical youth tradition 1991–1996

The RUF attack of 1991 and the NPRC coup d'état of 1992 were direct results of youth and student political actions, and government reactions of the 1980s. The 1985 expulsion and the three-year moratorium on student politics temporarily restored social peace on the FBC campus; yet they were also the key events, which were instrumental in producing the RUF and the NPRC. Pushed into the city, PANAFU, had greater opportunities to mobilize the youth than when it was confined to the College campus. The group established a working relationship with the different lumpen youth organizations that had emerged in the late 1970s and 1980 including the Mandela Youth Organization and Freetong Players. PANAFU also reached out and established cordial working relations with the unions and the radical press (*For Di People*). In 1991, PANAFU was instrumental in setting up the Mass Democratic Alliance (MDA), which incorporated many cultural and political groups. In short, the PANAFU continued to build on the left tradition of the campus radicals. Hundreds of lumpen youth, including those who became members of the NPRC and the RUF around the country attended the meetings and rallies organized by PANAFU.[24] The majority of these youth never became committed members of the group but they did soak up its popular revolutionary slogans. As an organization, PANAFU was never able to develop the capacity to organize the youth into a solid political force against the state. And it is doubtful whether the organization would have had such an impact on the youth had it not been forced to relocate to the city.

The second major consequence of the expulsions was that some of the student leadership went into exile in Ghana where they continued their political activities. They opened direct links with Libya and worked on creating a movement to oppose the APC government in Sierra Leone. In Accra and in Tripoli, the group met and established contacts with other West Africa revolutionaries including Charles Taylor of Liberia and Kukoi Samba Sanyang of Gambia. They then began recruiting youth through their Lumpen youth networks in Sierra Leone for military training in Libya in 1987 (Abdullah this volume; Abdullah, 1998). The vanguard of this nascent political project was to be an organization called the Popular Democratic Front (PDF). The aims, goals and political programme of the organization were outlined in a document prepared in 1987. But the attempts to build an exile political organization with a possible military wing were short-lived. By 1988, the exiled student group had disintegrated under the weight of their political bickering and competing personal ambitions. Even so, the groundwork for the emergence of the RUF had already been laid. One of the odd recruits for the training programme was a cashiered corporal and former political prisoner called Foday Sankoh. Not a youth himself, he witnessed first hand the potential of youth militancy in his wanderings in the countryside in Sierra Leone and in the PANAFU meetings he attended (Abdullah, 1998; Interview with Foday Sankoh, Lome, 1999). He seized the opportunity offered by this training programme to advance his personal and political ambition. He quickly capitalized on the contradictions among the exiled student leadership to utilise their contacts with the Libyans, their links with other 'West African revolutionaries', and their political project. It was just a matter of time before he turned all of them against the Sierra Leonean state (Ibid).

The NRPC may have differed from the RUF in its tactics of capturing state power. Yet its origins, political slogans, iconography, and overall behaviour were very much similar to the RUF. Like the RUF, the leadership and the political ideas of the NPRC were formed in the maelstrom of the urban youth culture and politics of the 1980s. Ben Hirsch, the slain architect of the takeover, was in constant touch with FBC radicals then resident in the Southern and Eastern provinces. Two of the six original coup makers, Tom Nyuma and Komba Mondeh were members of PANAFU and had participated in student protests before joining the army in the late 1980s. It was therefore not surprising that the NPRC fished for support from the urban Lumpen and students to consolidate its grip on power. On the day of the coup d'état, the national radio hummed 'non-stop rap and reggae music' (Opala, 1994: 197). Students and youth took over the city and demonstrated in support of the new military regime (Interview with Students). The leadership of FBC Student Union was vociferous in its support of the regime.[25] Lumpen youths also rallied in support of the regime. These early demonstrations and declarations of support were critical in galvanizing popular acceptance for the new regime. In an explosion of civic pride and 'revolutionary zeal' they gave the city of Freetown a face-lift; murals sprang up in the city centre, pavements were repaired and potholes filled, all in the name of the 'revolution'. These actions by youths and students gave the regime the 'revolutionary aura' it needed (Opala, 1994: 197). It is easy to understand why the lumpen youths and student radicals would identify with the new NPRC regime. Apart from their age, they shared the same political and cultural roots and aspirations.[26]

Like the RUF, the NPRC incorporated elements from the culture of resistance and revolution cultivated by students and lumpen youth in their early political phraseology and ideology. 'Binding One Love' became a popular catch phrase for revolutionary solidarity and support.[27] Slogans like 'Mass Awareness and Participation [MAP]' and 'Mobilization for Reconstruction' were taken right out of the student experience of 1985 and used to rally youths and students. The sum of these efforts was an eclectic collection of catch phrases and statements, which wore thin as the NPRC stayed longer in power and the initial euphoria died. The regime co-opted radicals in their regime. Hindolo Trye, former student leader and 'hero' of the 1977 demonstrations and Kandeh Yumkella, president of Njala Student Union in 1979/80 were given ministerial appointments *(Awareness Magazine*, 1980). Student radicals of the 1980s also provided propaganda for the regime. Mahdieu Savage, a.k.a Karl Marx, was member of the NPRC public relations committee and editor of the *Liberty Voice*, the ideological mouthpiece of the regime. Martin Mondeh became the editor of *Daily Mail*, the official national newspaper. The task of mobilizing the youth and students fell to the National Social Mobilization Secretariat [NASMOS]. Hassan 'Priest' Sesay, another student radical, became one of its coordinators. Without a clear ideology, direction and leadership, NASMOS achieved little. Many other 'radicals' were co-opted in different capacities at State House and other areas of the government bureaucracy. Some of them were included in the personal staff of the NPRC members.

In spite of its co-option of student radicals and attempt to appear ideological, the NPRC did not represent a significant divergence from the regime it replaced. The soldiers revealed their lumpen instincts in their desire to get rich quick, the use of drugs, disrespect for ordinary citizens and excessive womanizing. They failed woefully in all aspects of their 'revolution'. In spite of its promise to end the war swiftly, it continued fighting the RUF throughout its four years in power until it became mired in the very corruption that it avowed to curtail *(Focus on Sierra Leone*, November 30, 1996). Lastly, it conceded elections and allowed a transition to civilian rule in March 1996, only after popular opinion and the international community gave it no choice. When elements in the 'reformed' NPRC attempted to disrupt the elections, it was the youth who defied them and ensured that the election proceeded.[28] The ranks of the unemployed swelled as a consequence of the war and the regime's uncritical implementation of the IMF conditionalities, which included massive retrenchment of government workers, floatation of the Leone and the privatization of government corporations. In the end, a regime that had promised 'revolution' for the youth delivered little.

The informal alliance between the NPRC and the youths (students and lumpens) in general turned out to be a brief marriage of convenience. Although the regime gave buses to the students, campus conditions remained abysmal. When the romance turned sour both university campuses became subjected to frequent closure. In 1994, the NPRC set up a Commission of Enquiry, headed by Professor Kwame, Vice-Chancellor of University of Science and Technology, Ghana to investigate the continuing disturbances and the conditions on campus. It forwarded a programme for a multi-billion Leone refurbishment of campus buildings and academic facilities. Significantly, it also recommended the recall of lecturers and students who had been dismissed or expelled from the University. But the report remained on the shelf of the NPRC chairman until 1996 when they were booted out of power.

Conclusion

In assuming the role of an informal opposition against a corrupt system, the student radicals inadvertently unleashed those forces that led to the formation of the RUF, NPRC and later the AFRC. They were not the first to introduce lumpen youth into the political arena; the APC had already done that in the 1960s. What student radicals did was to help reshape the role and agency of these youths through generational contiguity, cultural interaction and radical politics. The failure of the corrupt and decrepit APC to respond meaningfully to demands for systemic change, and their inability to resolve the endemic crisis of the 1970s and 1980s, ensured the inevitability of the tragedy of 1990s. The RUF and NPRC represented, to a certain extent, an empowerment of sections of lumpen youth population, and their radical student allies. The short-lived AFRC Council of Johnny Paul Koroma, and its Peoples Army, which united elements from the RUF and the NPRC, highlighted the profound commonalties within this broad social group (See Lansana Gberie this volume). Their social behaviour and politics during the 1990s contained all the inherent ambiguities of that culture: social indiscipline, nonconformism, anti-establishmentarianism, violence, revolutionary sloganeering and confrontational politics.

That the NPRC, RUF and AFRC failed to deliver the 'revolution' and instead produced profound tragedy for Sierra Leone should therefore not be surprising. The revolutionary discourse they appropriated had no deep coherent ideological or programmatic content; the leftist radical student faction, who had aspired to be the vanguard of progressive change in Sierra Leone, never developed the necessary capacity to play that role. Like most student groups, this faction was disparate in its composition, ambivalent in character, and unstable in political commitment. Even with the solidarity and commitment, which comes from a more sustained experience of working and struggling together, it is doubtful whether it could have built a credible national political organization on its own. Unlike their counterparts in Latin America and other parts of Africa, the Sierra Leone student radicals only seriously attempted to forges alliances with labor, civil groups and the press after they had been pushed out of the campus environment. The student radicals and their faculty allies never had the time to reflect critically on, and shape, the different left ideologies into a credible alternative political programme for Sierra Leone. By the late 1980s, the radicals had lost whatever initiative they had to the forces that they had inadvertently helped awakened. The events of the 1970s and 1980s clearly reflect the potency, as well as the glaring limitations, of radical student/youth politics.

Notes

1   Radical Left politics in Sierra Leone had a tradition dating as far back as I.T.A Wallace-Johnson and the West African Youth League (WAYL). By 1970s, it had all but disappeared.

2   This information was based on an interview with Arthur Abraham, who is currently a professor of history at Virginia State University, and an active member of PANSO.

3   Interview, Professor Arthur Abrahams.

4   Contrary to Paul Richards' assertion, Southern African Liberation struggles exercised a far much stronger influence on Gardeners than 'Libya'. Gardeners were not a 'Libyan inspired' cell but a group that grew out of the youth and student culture of the 1970s. See footnote 18 in Paul Richards, 'Rebellion in Liberia and Sierra Leone', *Conflict in Africa*, p. 168.

5   Much like an *eminence grise*, Jamil Sahid Mohamed, a well-known 'Afro-Lebanese' business magnate, wielded considerable power and influence over Siaka Stevens and his government.

6   I am grateful to Ibrahim Abdullah for sharing his ideas/notes on his project on the Lumpen and unemployed in Freetown.

7   In 1976, diamond exports declined from 731,900 to 481,400 carats while no iron ore was exported in 1976, after the export of 1.3 million in the previous year. Food exports were about 15-20 percent of the import bill showing the large dependence on the mining sector. *West Africa*, February 21, 1977.

8   Students made significant forays into national politics in the 1960s. They participated in the debate on One-Partyism during Albert Margai's premiership. They booed and stoned Albert Margai in protest against corruption in 1966. *Awareness Magazine*, 1980. They also pressured the National Redemption Council [NRC] of Juxon Smith to hand over power to a democratic government in 1969 and were

reportedly, the 'major inspiration behind Sierra Leone's strong stand against UDI in Rhodesia'. *Times*. August 23, 1974; *Times*, July 19 , 1974.

9   Kemoh Fadika, popularly known as Waju-Waju, happened to be have been the 'billah man' for Liner Odelay. He was made deputy ambassador to Nigeria in 1978.

10 The Senior Staff Association of Fourah Bay College issued a statement condemning government 'invasion of the campus' but did not openly endorse the student protest. The Sierra Leone Labor Congress criticized the counter-demonstration. It stated that 'The Sierra Leone Congress wished it to be understood that if no action is taken to release all students already detained it will sympathize with them'. Quoted from the Sierra Leone Labor Congress [SLLC] resolution in George O. Roberts, *The Anguish of Third World Independence*, pp. 255–256

11 College Students' Statement of February 8, 1977.

12 Pios Foray and Hindolo Trye later went to exile in the United States as a consequence of the APC's repressive tactics. They continued their journalistic activities by publishing the short-lived *Tablet International* and *Tawakaltu* magazines. Paul Kamara, who set up For di People, in the early 1980s, after graduation, continued this tradition of radicals launching anti-government newspapers. *For Di People* maintained a strong pro-students stance in the 1980s and 1990s.

13 Movement for Justice in Africa [MOJA] was an active anti-government force in Liberia and Gambia. Some of its leading members later participated in the AFRC government of Master-Sgt. Samuel Doe. Among the initiators of MOPA were Jimmy Kandeh, Jeff Bowlay Williams and G. Cleo-Hanciles. The movement was set up 'to combat injustice whenever it occurs on our continent, and we recognize the socialist movement to be a genuine force aim at removing .. all obstacles in our path of progress, implanted there by imperialist, colonialist and neo-colonialist regimes'.

14 As a parliamentary special assistant in the Ministry of Social Welfare, Akibo-Betts and a group of thugs had stormed a disco-dance organized by the Engineering Society of Fourah Bay College in 1978 and manhandled three students. *Tablet*, February 3, 1978.

15 This is one of the central political ideas of Gaddafi's revolutionary theory. See Muamar Qathafi, *Green Book* (London: Martin Brien and O'Keefe Ltd, 1978).

16 It is the central tenet of the organization's ideology and it is clearly indicated in all their literature.

17 The term, 'com' short for comrade gained widely circulation. 'Brothers' and 'Sisters' was preferred by the Pan-Africanists and had a more restricted usage.

18 For a good discussion of the origins of the collapse of the Sierra Leone state see Jimmy D. Kandeh, 'Predatory Regime Continuity and the Demise of the Sierra Leonean State,' Canadian Association of African Studies, May 1–5, 1996, Montreal, Canada).

19 The College was reopened after the 1993/1994 FBC-SU president, Daniel Kamara, apologised to the president. Students mobbed and nearly beat him up for the apology. *For Di People*, March 1984.

20 All three petitioned the University. Jimmy Kandeh and Olu Gordon took the university to court for wrongful dismissal. Kandeh won. Gordon stopped pursuing the case after a while.

21 The students charged were Alie Kabba, Haroun Boima, Derek Bangura, Israel Jigba and Mohamed Barrie. *West Africa*, June 10, 1985.

22 See the March 4, 1985, April 29, 1985, May 6, 1985, May 20, 1985 issues of *West Africa* magazine to get a sense of the politics of transition in Sierra Leone at this time.

23 Model Junction is the intersection at the foot of Mount Aureol. By controlling this junction security forces can effectively check the movement of students into the centre of the city.

24 A few well-known members, Abu Kanu, Rashid Mansaray and Tom Nyuma of PANAFU did participate in the formation of the RUF and NPRC. Others like Ben Hirsch, Komba Mondeh and Mike Lamin claimed membership of the organization and participation in its activities.

25 See the video by Hilton Fyle, Sunrise in Paradise [1992]. Student leaders interviewed were vociferous in their support for the new military regime.

26 The alleged architect of the coup, late Lt. Ben Hirsch, frequented campus and interacted with the leadership of the student union in 1980s. Three of the six coup makers had strong links with the students in the early and mid 1980s. Lt. Tom Nyuma grew up on F.B.C. campus where his father worked and was a member of the Pan-African Union. Lt. Komba Mondeh's brother, Martin Mondeh was a campus radical and deeply involved in campus politics in 1984 to 1986. Lt. Karefa Kargbo dropped out of college in the late 1980s to join the army.

27 'One Love' comes from the lyrics of the Reggae musicians, Bob Marley and Peter Tosh.

28 Brigadier Julius Maada Bio replaced Captain Valentine Strasser on January 16, 1996 in palace coup. *The New Citizen*, January 18, 1996; *Vision*, January 18, 1996. For Youth and popular demonstrations against the regime's attempt to hold off elections, see *For Di People*, March 7, 1996.

4

Corruption and Political Insurgency in Sierra Leone

Sahr Kpundeh

Public offices in Freetown reopened this week after Col. Maxwell Khobe, commander of the ECOMOG task force called on all civil servants and heads of institutions to return to work. This brought to an end a civil disobedience campaign begun immediately after the coup by public servants who had preferred to stay off the job and remain unpaid rather than work for the junta. Jonathan Sandi, a computer operator at the Ministry of Trade, was among those who had stayed away. 'I believe in democracy and the will of the people. I thought it was morally wrong to work under the junta', he told IPS. Like most people here, he is happy that the AFRC has been overthrown. 'Even if I were to go without salaries for one year, I would continue working as long as it is under a democratic system', he says.

Electronic Mail & Guardian, 20 February 1998.

Introduction

Sierra Leone is a country with a corrupt and tumultuous past that has gone through a brutal rebel war waged against its government, its military and its citizens since 1991. Political and institutional instability and a poor record of good governance have defined the history of post-colonial Sierra Leone.[1] And although the country is endowed with substantial mineral wealth, marine resources, and a varied agricultural resource base, its social indicators are worse than countries with similar levels of per-capita income. The Gross Domestic Product (GDP) has steadily declined during the past ten years. In 2000, the UNDP rated it as having the lowest human development index in the world with an average life expectancy of 37.9 years, a GDP per capita of US$458, an adult literacy rate of 31 percent and a combined primary, secondary and tertiary gross enrollment ratio of 24 percent (Human Development Report, 2000). Such failure, arguably stems from a myriad of abuses and neglect ranging from a lack of accountability – both horizontal and vertical –

ethnically based adversarial politics, the politicization of the army, a civil war, and an absence of political will and commitment to curb pervasive systemic corruption.

The country suffers from a long history of systemic corruption. This entered the official record in 1967, with the Foster Commission of Inquiry, which the National Reformation Council (NRC) established to investigate mismanagement during the Sir Albert Margai Administration, 1964–67. The National Provisional Ruling Council (NPRC), also investigated financial irregularities during the preceding APC administrations of both Siaka Stevens and Joseph Momoh. From 1968–1985, Siaka Stevens led a government so notorious for malfeasance that in 1981 he declared a state of emergency due to serious financial irregularities. Civil servants allegedly misappropriated millions of leones (Kpundeh, 1995). The NPRC Administration also fell victim to governmental abuse and corruption, evidenced by the lifestyle of key members of its inner circle. They allegedly plundered more government wealth during their reign than the combined years of the Stevens and Momoh administrations. Tejan Kabbah's tenure in office has also been marred by corruption. Although each commission of inquiry has recommended the seizure and forfeiture of assets of former ministers, public servants and heads of parastatals, systemic malfeasance continues unabated.

This chapter analyzes the relationship between corruption and political insurgency in Sierra Leone. Using Paul Collier's conceptual distinction between greed and grievance as a motivation for political insurgency in Sierra Leone, I argue that although the insurgency arose because of a deep-seated *grievance* held by the RUF leaders and their 'backers' to rid Sierra Leone of the corrupt and incompetent APC government, *greed* was a major motivating factor for the insurgency because the RUF aspired to wealth through capturing the resources of the country extra-legally, and ultimately the machinery of government (Paul Collier, 1999). The chapter concludes that the issue of 'collective action', which ironically helped the RUF in prosecuting the war, may be the same approach needed to address the persistent problem of corruption, establish effective institutions of accountability, so as to improve the quality of governance in the country.

Corruption and political insurgency

The deepening systemic corruption since the 1980s, evidenced by the lack of accountability and transparency, produced the proximate causes of the rebel war: exclusionary politics, violations of rule of law, rural isolation leading to ethnic and regional grievances, extreme centralization, economic decline and high unemployment. The level of corruption under the various governments since 1980 – the APC, the current SLPP government, and successive military regimes – and the inability of these governments to address the problem contributed to deep-seated grievances which the RUF was able to utilize to wage a nasty rebellion.

The All People's Congress Party 1968–1992

The personalization of politics and the deepening of patronage links was used by the APC under both Siaka Stevens and Joseph Momoh as a way to construct hegemony and dominance. Their approach to governance contributed to deepening entrenched grievances resulting from party politics after the very close elections in 1967, and the resulting military rule in the country from 1967–68. In addition, the general lack of accountability and transparency in governance, exploitation of political institutions for power and wealth, general weakening of monitoring institutions, persistent economic decline, were some of the general characteristics of the system established by the APC while in power. One major consequence of the above problems was the fragility of the state which was used to promote the dominance of one group while alienating the majority of society.

Andreas Schedler argues that political accountability carries two basic connotations: *answerability*, the obligation of public officials to inform and explain; and *enforcement*, accounting agencies' capacity to impose sanctions on power-holders who have violated their public duties (Schedler, 1999: 14). A lack of *answerability* (which I interpret here to mean transparency) in Sierra Leone began in 1978 with the introduction of the one-party system. It closed the door to vertical accountability[2] in civil society. No structure existed to allow citizens to impact the political system either through electoral politics in the form of opposition party candidates or adversarial positions from special interests groups.

The SLPP was voted out of office in 1967 and in 1968, the APC came to power and instituted a one-party state ten years later, systematically repressing any opposition from civil society. Presidents Stevens and Momoh constantly pressured and intimidated civil society organizations or unions that opposed the government. University students who organized protests faced stiff resistance from the security agents that sometimes appeared on campuses with a show of force, violently chasing students and closing the university. For example, following a student uprising at the 1977 Annual University Convocation, security forces brutalized students and damaged campus property. Armed units of the Cuban-trained paramilitary International Security Unit (ISU, later called Special Security Division) joined the operation arresting several lecturers and student leaders (Rashid this volume). Similarly, in 1981, when the Sierra Leone Labour Congress (SLLC) struck for better wages and working conditions, government security effectively broke the strike by physically intimidating their leadership. An anti-government newspaper, the *Tablet*, had its printing facilities raided and destroyed by APC party thugs (ibid.). Additionally, few indications of vertical accountability were evident in the internal operations of the Stevens Administration as all his senior parastatal appointees, including his cabinet ministers, were directly answerable to him.

Horizontal accountability according to Schedler refers to 'all acts of accountability that take place between independent state agencies' (Schedler, 1999: 25). The political machinery in place during Stevens' reign which continued under Momoh had no room for horizontal accountability. The Executive branch of government was excessively powerful and the legislative and judicial branches took their marching orders from the State House. Constitutional amendments and laws were easily enacted at the pleasure of the President. For example, Stevens changed the constitution to allow Momoh to replace him as Head of State, without consulting those to whom the president is answerable and 'grand' corruption cases such as 'vouchergate' adjourned indefinitely by a non-functioning judiciary without any major conviction (Kpundeh, 1993). Once President Stevens had effectively eliminated any opposition to his one party dictatorship that established the machinery to enable him acquire and use power arbitrarily he was in a safe position to 'rule' not to 'govern'. Joseph Momoh, his hand-picked successor, continued this trend despite the country's descent into anarchy and corruption.

In addition, general weaknesses in the political system have created political as well as legal restraints. Patronage networks thrive under this system, transcending and subverting the institutions of governance and, ultimately, undermining public order and good governance. According to Jimmy Kandeh, the failure of the state in Sierra Leone paradoxically enhanced the role of political patrons and expanded opportunities for the predatory expropriation of public wealth in an increasingly volatile environment (Kandeh, 1999). State offices and public resources were converted into sources of private wealth among the elites, which included senior public officials who embezzled government funds and, in some cases, sold public property and diverted those funds to personal accounts. The numerous commissions of inquiry established during the NPRC regime revealed such gross abuses (Kpundeh, 1995, 1999).

There were also distributional grievances emanating from rural isolation, and ethnic and regional rivalries. Victor Davies, argues that Steven's regime aggravated isolation of rural Sierra Leone – home to 80 percent of the population and producing much of the country's wealth – through under-pricing of export produce by the Sierra Leone Produce Marketing Board, exchange rate overvaluation, subsidies on imported food that implicitly taxed rural agriculture while subsiding urban consumption, and complete deprivation of the rural areas of electricity, pipe-borne water, telecommunication facilities, a developed road network and other facilities (Victor Davies, 2000). The railway linking the rural areas to Freetown was dismantled in the late 1960s with no new network of roads connecting Freetown and the hinterland. Socioeconomic indicators provide further evidence of rural isolation. In 1990, access to safe water and sanitation was 83 and 59 percent respectively for the urban areas, compared with 22 and 35 percent for rural areas (Davies, 2000).

The lack of a participatory approach to governance through APC's rural isolation policy was also a contributing factor to the widespread corruption resulting in the deepening of grievance against the regime. A participatory approach to governance involves popular participation in the decision-making process, including identification of the problem, project design, implementation, distribution of benefits, and the evaluation of impact. This was far from being the case under both the Stevens and Momoh Administrations. The voice of the rural population was consistently ignored as political activity was concentrated mainly in Freetown. In 1972, the so-called Committee of Management replaced elected local government, eliminating any popular participation of those resident in the rural areas ('Position Paper on the Reactivation of Local Government and Decentralization in Sierra Leone', February, 1997). Centralization of the country's political and economic power essentially isolated and ostracized the more vulnerable groups in society. Yusuf Bangura describes these ruling elites as 'patrimonial groups', insensitive to the plight of those who operate outside the 'patrimonial networks', and therefore, have been badly affected or humiliated by the informalization of the country's resources and the astonishing contraction of the state (Bangura, 1999).

Local authorities were they existed consisted of political cronies or party sympathizers, serving the primary purpose of maintaining the status quo as opposed to genuine citizen participation and representation in the governance of their town or province. Decentralization under Stevens, and subsequently Momoh, was a ruse. These dictators captured state institutions and rewarded their supporters in the provinces with positions of authority void of any power. The provinces remain poor and without revenue as they are unable to raise funds or taxes to develop their communities. Put differently, the inability of the people to genuinely participate in the governance of their communities contributed to entrenched corruption and abject poverty in most of rural Sierra Leone. Growing numbers of people relocate to the capital cities in search of a better life, which unfortunately, cemented the dependency syndrome between rural and urban areas.

Victor Davies provides several reasons to illustrate how the rural isolation under the APC government of Stevens and Momoh contributed to the war.

First, it induced large-scale migration to towns by young people, who merely swelled the ranks of the unemployed and constituted a recruitment base for the rebel movement. Second, the chiefs appointed by Stevens were generally unpopular and repressive, alienating many subjects some of whom joined the rebel movement to seek revenge. Third, apathy towards the rural areas induced a nonchalant response to the war by government and the more influential Freetown public, who initially perceived it as a distant 'rural' war until major towns were hit. Furthermore, both government and the Freetown public generally tended to be complacent about the war as long as Freetown was 'safe'. Lastly, rural isolation provided a strong appeal for recruitment in the rural areas (Davies, 2000).

The National Provincial Ruling Council (NPRC) Regime, 1992–1996

Despite removing the APC from power on allegations of corruption and mismanagement, the NPRC regime also failed miserably in addressing the problem of corruption. And inspite of its self-declared mission to eradicate mismanagement and institutionalized malfeasance, the administration was plagued with accusations of corruption. Its own members ignored its policies aimed at infusing morality and discipline. Senior military personnel including Valentine Strasser lived in style comparable to non-before them. The regime looted diamonds from the country for their own personal gains. In late 1993, Strasser's government allegedly exported diamonds worth 435 million dollars to Sweden. The headline in the September 1993 edition of the Swedish newspaper *Sunday Express*, read: 'Sierra Leone's Great Redeemer Becomes a Millionaire Whilst the People Continue to Starve'. Strasser reportedly sold diamonds worth US$43 million in Antwerp, and bought a house in London. The report also painted an image of widespread corruption by Strasser's NPRC colleagues.

When Julius Maada Bio replaced Strasser in a 1996 palace coup, there was absolutely no change of policy in addressing the persistent allegations of corruption. Instead, the rumors continued and the military leaders did not take any measure to tackle the issue. Instead, they continued to benefit from huge misappropriations of military expenditures and in some cases, several of the NPRC members, notably Karefa Kargbo and Komba Kambo, allegedly kept government money allocated to procure weapons to prosecute the war for their personal use. This was primarily why the NPRC members attempted unsuccessfully to delay multi-party elections using the war as an excuse (See Abraham this volume). Julius Maada Bio allegedly stole huge sums of money and has bought several houses for family and friends. The frivolous lifestyle of the NPRC members living abroad, confirms some of the allegations of their corruption in office. For example, Karefa Kargbo has bought several houses for himself and his family members including expensive BMW and Mercedes Benz cars for relatives, including his wife, and an expensive private wedding at the Watergate Hotel in Washington D.C.

The Sierra Leone People's Party, 1996–Present

In April 1996, Sierra Leoneans democratically elected a government that, like its predecessors, claimed it wanted to fight corruption. Although President Tejan Kabbah appeared committed, he did not have a political base and consequently had to rely on the 'old hands' in his party to win the elections. In addition, Kabbah struck deals and entered into an alliance with other political parties, notably the People's Democratic Party (PDP), resulting in five ministerial positions, ambassadorial posts and parastatal board memberships to the PDP party. Kabbah also appointed John Karimu, the leader of the National Unity Party (NUP), and Aiah Koroma, the leader of the Democratic Centre Party (DCP) to his cabinet. While Kabbah boasted of a government of national unity, he created a bloated government of 45 ministers and deputy ministers.

Schedler argues that the exercise of accountability involves elements of monitoring and oversight, and this implies that accounting actors do more than simply 'call into question'. Accountable persons tell what they have done and why, and more important, accept the consequences for those actions, including any censure (Schedler, 1999). The capacity to punish and enforce Sierra Leone's corruption laws is abysmally poor. Like his predecessors, the SLPP administration under Tejan Kabbah has selectively enforced the law against corruption, and in most instances, as in the case of his former Minister of Agriculture Harry Will, the guilty culprits are slapped on the wrist and ordered to refund any diverted money. Although Harry Will was convicted for conspiracy to defraud the government, he was only fined Le500,000 or approximately US$250 (*Concord Times Newspaper*, Freetown June 1, 2000). It seems only the 'small fry' are vigorously prosecuted, and usually for petty corruption while the 'big fish' engaged in 'grand' corruption go untouched or are given small fines. Consequently, because these so-called 'big fish' are well connected, gross abuses of public offices, such as bribery, extortion, and embezzlement, have escalated and generated public skepticism about the government's commitment to reform.

The enforcement agencies established to prosecute corruption offenses are not free to carry out their mandate. For example, President Kabbah overturned the court's decision that would have imprisoned Abbas Bundu, a former presidential candidate and foreign minister. Instead, Bundu, convicted for selling Sierra Leonean passports to foreign national, was simply fined. Kabbah's explanation was quite simple: 'he was one of the brains in the country and it does not make sense for him to languish in jail' he was reported to have said! According to Jimmy Kandeh, 'Kabbah's amnestization of rogue politicians, his lame response to the problem of corruption and the fact that his cabinet consisted mainly of discredited politicians signaled continuity rather than rupture with the past' (Kandeh, 1999). This view is consistent with the popular perception of majority of Sierra Leoneans. A recent household survey, the *Sierra Leone Anti-Corruption Survey 2000* demonstrates that Sierra Leoneans think that lack of political will is a major constraint to the government in its bid to fight against corruption.[3]

The majority of respondents, 38.1 percent, indicate that lack of political will, and corruption in high places pose the greatest constraint to government's efforts to curb corruption. This was followed by the state of insecurity (24.1 percent), and vested interests/official collusion (21.8 percent). A sizable proportion of respondents, 13.3 percent, considers lack of cooperation from the public as the most serious constraint. The survey suggests the need for more robust action on the part of the in government its commitment to fight corruption.

Government's attempt to address corruption through new institutional mechanisms continue to evince either a lack of political will or how little is understood about the fight against corruption. For example, the recently published *Anti-Corruption Act 2000* requires the Commissioner to submit for consideration to the Attorney-General and Minister of Justice the findings of all investigations that in his opinion are liable to criminal proceedings (*Supplement to the Sierra Leone Gazette*, 81, 7). The Attorney-General will in turn examine the report and decide whether there are sufficient grounds to prosecute the public official concerned. In other words, the Act clearly states that no prosecution shall be instituted without the written consent of the Attorney-General and Minister of Justice (*Anti-Corruption Act 2000*). These provisions were clearly designed to continue to allow politics to have a great influence in the fight against corruption in the country. If one takes the history of the Kabbah Administration's interference in prosecuting high profile people engaged in corruption as any evidence of its commitment, then it is only fair to conclude that the Anti-Corruption Commission has been established to appease the donors. An oversight cum advisory committee comprising members of civil society to review the work of the Commission, as in the Hong Kong Operations Review Committee (ORC) would have been more effective in the battle against corruption (Heilbrunn and Stevens, 2000).

If such an oversight body were to be established and is effective, it might be able to help win the confidence of the citizenry in the work of the commission, which is currently very low, based on available data. Nearly 60 percent of the respondents in a recent anti-corruption survey said that they have no confidence that the Bureau and its officials will be able to successfully minimize corruption. This view was endorsed in all regions except the North where two-thirds of the population (66 percent) indicated some confidence in the work of the Bureau. However, more than a quarter of all respondents in all regions were not sure about reposing confidence in the Bureau, which may be explained by a lack of sufficient public education about their activities. In the West, about 16 percent declared no confidence in the Bureau. Perhaps, an independent review committee comprised of representative stakeholders that reviews cases and makes recommendations to the Attorney General will help to demonstrate the government's commitment to reform. Additionally, the Anti-Corruption Bill should be amended to give the Bureau some prosecutorial powers.

Data collected on people's perceptions about the government's reform movement helps to substantiate some of the points made earlier. The vast majority of these (926) respondents, (75 percent), believe that government's ineffective efforts in tackling corruption can be attributed to the failure to promptly prosecute or adequately punish culprits. Lack of accountability and transparency, political patronage, greed and selfishness are other reasons respondents identified as responsible for the government's ineffectiveness.

Citizens and the military are skeptical and are disillusioned with their country's governance because they experience its negative effects daily. For example, in several African countries, corruption translates into political instability and frequent regime changes. The overthrow of governments in Sierra Leone, Mobutu's Zaire, Moussa Traore's Mali, and Samuel Doe's Liberia are just a few examples of countries where high-level and systemic corruption directly contributed to the overthrow of regimes. More recently, the civil unrest in Sierra Leone has been associated with increasingly high levels of systemic corruption and the inability of the leadership to effectively respond to this persistent problem. In other words, the citizenry in Sierra Leone as in other African countries have continued to hold their leaders responsible for economic hardships in large part because of widespread abuse in official circles. In some countries, this abuse has forced civil society to take matters into its own hands and demand more transparent and accountable systems of government (Kpundeh, 1992). Foday Sankoh, the head of the Revolutionary United Front (RUF) made such claims when his rebel invasion was launched in 1991 to overthrow Joseph Saidu Momoh's All People's Congress. The next section explores the dynamics of corruption and the role it played in the rebel war.

RUF greed or APC misgovernance?

Although the discussions in the previous section highlight a pattern of poor governance in Sierra Leone leading to deep-seated grievance against the corrupt APC regimes, it is equally plausible to make the argument that 'greed' has also played a major role in precipitating armed conflict. To begin with the APC's non-inclusive approach created opportunities for the RUF recruitment efforts. Foday Sankoh and his group preached to people who were either excluded or had distanced themselves from the authoritarian and neo-patrimonial politics practiced by the APC. Political dissidents withdrew to the rural areas or left the country. Some former politicians publicly sympathized with the proclaimed reasons for the invasion while vehemently condemning the inhumane tactics. The war has led to the death of over 70,000 Sierra Leoneans, the displacement of more than two-thirds of the population of 4.5 million, the crude amputation of more than 10,000 people, and the destruction of the country's limited infrastructure (Lansana Gberie, 2000, *Africa Now* August/September).

Ibrahim Abdullah argues that it is important to understand the origins and character of the RUF for one to appreciate whether their claims of removing the corrupt APC was rhetoric or a genuine determination to help improve the quality of governance. 'The RUF is not only a product of lumpen culture, but its membership is also lumpen. It took political action and proclaimed a 'revolution' which reflect the true character of its lumpen base' (Abdullah, 1998; this volume). According to Lansana Gberie, the RUF 'was created from outside the country, trained and armed to invade and destabilize Sierra Leone. There were enough socially uprooted and unemployed young people in the country ready to seize the opportunity for loot and other profitable criminal activities under the cover of warfare' (Gberie, 2000: 14). Gberie further argues that the view that the RUF is an uprising of the rural poor against the corrupt, Freetown-based elite and their exploitative foreign backers, most of them based in the capital, a place from which resources have been taken and used to underwrite the predatory taste of the country's political and educated elite, may be reading too much into the RUF's handbook, entitled, *Footpath to Democracy.*

While I agree with this characterization of the RUF, I also believe authoritarian rule as well as the APC's record of poor governance from 1968 to the beginning of the war in 1991 created an environment of resentment and a public sentiment for change. Abdullah and Rashid (this volume) have demonstrated how the repressive regime of the APC blocked opportunities and provided the conditions for the birth of revolutionary dissident activities and, ultimately, the formation of the RUF. I agree that the APC regime was repressive and corrupt, and that the uprising may have begun as a response to corrupt and greedy politicians. However, RUF's brutality of innocent civilians has diverted and tainted the focus of the rebel's original intent. It is beyond the scope of this chapter to discuss whether their intentions are pure rhetoric. My comments are limited to the atmosphere that preceded the war and provided opportunities for RUF. As argued earlier, pervasive systemic corruption, repression, lack of tolerance and political competition, and the non-inclusive nature of the politics created fertile ground for RUF recruitment. People wanted a change. The citizenry did not benefit from the patronage machinery and, were therefore open to any alternative as evidenced by the 1992 coup.

On whether there is any link/relationship between bribery with corruption and the war, data from the *Sierra Leone Anti-Corruption Survey*, demonstrates the link between corruption and the civil war. More than half the respondents (53 percent) talked about linkages; about 28 percent, however, said there was no link, and nearly 20 percent had no opinion.

Available evidence suggests that the RUF has been a corrupt organization from its inception as the trafficking in diamonds was central to its survival as an effective fighting force. There is some evidence to support Gberie's contention that the war was 'about greed, loot, and pillage, and that the principal instigators are outside the country' (Gberie, 2000: 17). When the RUF struck in 1991, their force included a large number of mercenaries from Liberia and Burkina Faso, but their alleged freedom crusade quickly devolved into a campaign for resources; an excuse to loot and kill. This was what happened in the Pujehun and Kailahun areas, the two districts, where the rebellion initially took off.

If Sankoh's leadership and his actions as Chairman of the Commission for the Management of Strategic Resources are examples of a RUF administration, had he succeeded in his coup, then the country would have been totally bankrupt and governed by foreigners. Accusations that the RUF trafficked diamonds through Liberia to its President, Charles Taylor, the alleged mastermind of the original incursion, are well documented. Taylor has been described as the 'banker, the arms contractor', and effectively the shadow leader of the group. Others include Blaise Compaoré of Burkina Faso, and possibly Eyadema of Togo (Gberie, 2000: 17). When Sankoh became Head of the Commission for the Management of Strategic Resources, he did nothing to stop the flow of diamonds to Liberia. According to Minister of Information, Julius Spencer, when Sankoh's house was raided by protesters in May 2000, they not only found evidence that he was planning a coup for May 9, 2000, but also secret RUF documents on mining operations in Kono. An inventory of every diamond collected by an RUF officer between October 30, 1998, and July 31, 1999 was also among the documents found. It confirmed a nine-month haul of about 768 carats of white diamonds and 887 carats of industrial diamonds. The stones included a 17-carat orange, a 9-

carat white, and numerous others between one and six carats (*Vanity Fair*, 2000).

Under Sierra Leonean law, which Sankoh was charged with upholding, all mined diamonds must be weighed, classified, and assigned a value by the government's Gold and Diamond Office. If a licensed exporter wants to sell a 2.5 percent tax is paid to the government, after which the stones are boxed, sealed and stamped. The box is not supposed to be opened again until it reaches its destination. Members of the RUF did not follow the law. They simply smuggled diamonds through Sierra Leone's porous border with Liberia or by light airplane. Once in Liberia or Guinea, the stones are presented as domestic products and shipped to international markets in Antwerp and Tel Aviv.

For the past ten years, Sierra Leonean diamonds have flowed unchecked, first to Liberia and, then, to other countries. According to reports by the United States Geological Survey, the total output from all Liberian diamond mines is a paltry 100,000 to 150,000 carats a year. The Diamond High Council, however, reported that Liberian Diamond imports averaged six million carats per year, between 1994 and 1998 (*Vanity Fair, 2000*). Studies conducted by the non-profit group Partnership Africa Canada, and Robert Fowler, Canada's ambassador to the United Nations, suggests that an international diamond boycott of diamonds from conflict countries, so-called blood diamonds, would cripple insurgent movements like the UNITA in Angola and the RUF in Sierra Leone. An international campaign against the purchase of so-called blood diamond prompted De Beers, the world's leading diamond retailers, to back the call for punitive action against dealers trafficking in diamonds from conflict zones. The UN proposed a ban on the export of all Sierra Leonean diamonds that have not cleared customs in Freetown while the European Union cut off foreign aid to Liberia because of President Taylor's support of the RUF.

In his capacity as Chairman of the Strategic Resource Commission, Sankoh entered into agreements and awarded contracts to buy and sell diamonds to various international companies. Documents found in Sankoh's residence after the May shoot out, revealed that he entered into a contract in October 1999 with the BECA Group, an offshore company registered in Tortola, British Virgin Islands, giving them a monopoly on all gold and diamond mining in the rebel-controlled area of Sierra Leone. BECA was to run all mining operations in the RUF-controlled areas and handle all export and sale of diamonds on the international market. The RUF was to provide security and labour for the mining operations and facilitate the transportation of diamonds out of the country. BECA and the RUF would split all profits (*Vanity Fair*, 2000). The contract further specified that the agreement would become null and void as soon as the government of Sierra Leone activated the Commission for the Management of Strategic Resources, National Reconstruction and Development. Sankoh, of course, at that point would be chairman and a new contract would be negotiated between BECA and the Commission.

The above allegation, in addition to the RUF's efforts to control diamond mining, seems to support the popular perception that the RUF is a rogue and corrupt organization and their motive for war was purely driven by greed. Acquiring wealth through capturing the resources of the country extra-legally was but a short cut to ultimate control of the machinery of state. RUF had no legal mining rights in Sierra Leone. Inspite of Sankoh's position as chairman of the Strategic Resources Commission, the RUF as a movement/party had no legal mining right, nor was Sankoh authorized to solely negotiate any mineral contracts. Western businessmen could not have exploited the system, without the full cooperation of Sankoh's illegal diamond network. The RUF's so-called desire to rid the country of one-party dictatorship was a pretext designed to cover up its excessive greed. Sankoh's disagreement with the APC machinery was not over the organization and exercise of political power, but over who should have access to public offices and resources (Kandeh, 1999).

Conclusion

The above discussions highlight the role of corruption in Sierra Leone's political insurgency; and identify systemic weaknesses that inhibit reformers' ability to address the problem. The challenge for Sierra Leoneans is how to strengthen local institutions to ensure that accountability becomes a tenet of governance. The lack of political accountability, both vertical and horizontal, has resulted in missed opportunities to initiate political incentives that would help reform the system.

Civil society is not very active and involved in the country's governance. However, its overwhelming rejection of the AFRC coup in 1997 was an indication of its potential. Out of protest and fear, Sierra Leoneans put up a stout resistance to the ruling junta's orders to return to work. Only a strong civil society will enable structured political competition that can be instrumental in rehabilitating a system that lacks civil liberties, political freedoms and incentives. More important, a strong and vibrant civil society reinforces the political will needed for reform (Johnston, 1998; Kpundeh, 1998). Establishing civil society organizations as community oversight is encouraging and a homegrown strategy, which demonstrates ownership and improves sustainability.

Political will is a critical starting point to ensure the sustainability and effectiveness of anti-corruption strategies and programs. However, its presence cannot be assumed. Reformers face resistance from groups that benefit from corruption in any society, and coupled with their insecurity in office about how power changes hands, their political will to pursue reform is threatened. This is the case of the current President Tejan Kabbah, who is more interested in consolidating his political support than enforcing corruption laws. He interferes in the country's accountability mechanisms to ensure that he establishes a total grip on the system – very similar to the APC regime.

I have argued that the lack of inclusiveness was a factor in the road to insurgency. Encouraging collective action reform strategies by targeting additional support to programs that promote collaboration among various stakeholders should be an approach government pursues vigorously. It helps to win the confidence of skeptics. However, the adversarial relationship that exists between the government, civil society organizations, the press, and other stakeholders casts doubt on the government's efforts. Coalition building continues to be one of the foci in future reform strategies and encouraging this process is crucial to sustainability and strengthening political will.

Finally, inclusiveness, coalition building, civil society and political will all hinge on an effective decentralization program. A divided country is a constant threat to stability. Providing support to community-based programs with practical initiatives, especially at the municipal level, helps to develop an inclusive system. Community-based programs have a higher rate of success and include the neglected rural population in good governance. All citizens can articulate their needs, establish their priorities, and monitor service delivery effectively – one of the issues the RUF exploited to recruit its followers and, unfortunately, shaped the dynamics of its terror.

Notes

1 'Governance', within the context of this analysis refers to the use of political authority / exercise of control to manage resources for social and economic development. 'Good governance' entails the efficient and effective reciprocity between rulers and the ruled.

2 Vertical accountability according to Andreas Schedler describes a relationship between unequals: it refers to some powerful 'superior' actor holding some less powerful 'inferior' actor accountable – or vice versa.

3 For more detailed information, see the *Sierra Leone Anti-Corruption Survey, 2000*. Some of the data used in this paper is adapted from the above survey.

5

State Complicity as a Factor in Perpetuating the Sierra Leone Civil War

Arthur Abraham

Every state in the modern world has certain basic and fundamental duties it is expected to perform irrespective of what form of government it has or where it is located. The inability to carry out these basic duties/obligations, such as defending its territorial integrity or protecting the lives and property of its citizens, undermines the collective interests of the state. There is complicity when the state fails to act, or to prevent developments that might affect its collective interest and its citizens. Where it concerns state security, for example, the government may be in possession of accurate intelligence information, and yet fail to take appropriate or adequate, or sometimes any action whatsoever. This may be due to sheer stupidity, inertia, excessive bureaucracy or incompetence on the part of the head or any senior state official. But the fact remains that the state is culpable as long as in the end, the actions (or the failure to take actions) lead to deleterious effects on collective interests and its citizens. The difference between the kinds of actions, whether of commission or omission, can only be one of degree, as long as their outcomes are similar. In any of these circumstances, by failing deliberately or otherwise, to resolve or tackle the particular problem facing the state, the leaders automatically become part of the very problem. The concept of state complicity can be usefully employed to understand the intractability of the Sierra Leone civil war.

State complicity can be conceptualised as a continuum of culpability, with acts of commission as the high point, and acts of omission as the low point, with any combination of various proportions in-between the two. Of the three governments in Sierra Leone that battled the RUF, the NPRC stands out distinctly as belonging to the high point of complicity, followed by the Momoh and Kabbah governments. In the end, all three are culpable for failing to terminate the war when it was possible to do so. This chapter is concerned with the complex ways in which state complicity and the vitiated motives of three successive governments contributed to the survival and revival of a RUF on the run, causing much pain and suffering to the people of Sierra Leone.

Enter the NPRC: Sound and fury signifying nothing

In April, 1992, disgruntled young soldiers who had been sent to fight the RUF came to Freetown to protest about poor pay and conditions and ended up overthrowing the APC. The overthrow of the APC regime was immensely popular not because people welcomed the young and inexperienced officers but rather because they were fed up with more than two decades of one-party dictatorship. The coupists formed a government NPRC, under one of their peers, Captain V. E. M. Strasser, who 'was never part of the planning', but being a trusted colleague who was already Captain while the rest were Lieutenants, he was given the leadership by unanimous consent (Musa, 1995). Uncomfirmed reports at the time of the coup suggest that there was a secret collaboration between the RUF and the NPRC. According to the RUF document (RUF/SL, 1995), they had expected to be accommodated, since it was claimed that the NPRC coup-makers got their political education from the RUF. The RUF target, the rotten APC system having been removed, Sankoh thought it was time to bring peace, development and progress to the nation, and so he communicated the offer of a unilateral ceasefire by radio to the coup-makers and some senior officers, who knew him personally. Obviously, Sankoh expected to be one of the major players. The RUF explains that the NPRC reaction was positive until a visit to Ghana and Nigeria, after which, the NPRC decided to end the war militarily.

In actual fact however, the RUF wanted collaboration with the NPRC but wished to dictate the terms that would give it a political and military advantage to enable it to possibly seize power. The NPRC wanted to form a broad-based government, but Sankoh wanted exclusion of APC members and a radical purge of the civil service as well as withdrawal of all foreign troops. Fearing that this would provide Charles Taylor an opportunity to install Sankoh as President through a large-scale offensive, the NPRC suggested a compromise that would make the RUF disarm while foreign troops were withdrawn in phases. Taylor is believed to have advised that the plan be rejected as a foreign ploy to get rid of the RUF, which it did and revoked the ceasefire (Abdullah and Muana, 1998). Unable to obtain his wishes, Sankoh argued for a resumption of war on grounds that the NPRC was undemocratic because it did not represent the people; it was simply illegitimate, corrupt and repressive like the APC. Sankoh wanted a 'people's government' and disliked international organizations for their recognition of the NPRC (RUF/SL, 1995; NA, June 1995).

NPRC and RUF: Conflict, collaboration or 'Sobelization'?

The army grew five times its size in the first three years, and the NPRC put a lot of pressure on rebel positions. Then in mid-1992, a desperate RUF launched out recapturing some of its original positions and over-running the diamondiferous Kono District. Even so, the government kept up its offensive, and in April, 1993, captured Pendembu, the RUF's 'capital'. To most people, the end of the war was just now a matter of time. But unfortunately, it was not to be. According to Solomon Musa, NPRC Deputy Chairman who was removed in July 1993,

> it is sad to note that in less than a year in power, Captain Strasser and my other colleagues were already exhibiting the same tendencies of the former regime....nakedly accepting bribes, heavily involved in mining and at the same time, misusing defence funds...[and implicated in] the illegal sale of diamonds, money-laundering and frequent shopping sprees abroad (1995: 6).

Once in the diamond areas of Kono and Tongo, the officers got involved in large-scale mining, which sadly introduced diamonds into the war equation, causing a qualitative change in the matter of the official prosecution of the war. Thereafter, both parties to the conflict alternated military operations with alluvial diamond mining activities (Richards, 1996a). They actually institutionalised the practice, whereby one party would allow the other to mine for about two weeks without being disturbed until the other group announced its intention to start by specified warning gunshots. Copying from their superiors, the desire to make money spread very quickly among the ranks of a poorly paid army, giving rise to the extraordinary phenomenon of *sobels*, that is, soldiers by day, rebels at night. The people knew of this lycanthropic existence of the military, and the press took the liberty to announce it, but the government and army establishment disliked the accusations against sobels and fiercely defended the army.

As the NPRC and top military officers were busy enriching themselves, they turned a blind eye on the activities of the *sobels*. They attacked towns under the guise of rebels and looted property; they could 'sell game'(switch sides) by which government forces would withdraw from a town, leaving arms and ammunition for the rebels behind them. 'The rebels pick up the arms and extract loot...and then retreat. At this point, the government forces re-occupy the town and engage in their own looting, usually of property (which the rebels find hard to dispose of), as well as engaging in illegal mining' (Keen, 1995). With this kind of collaboration, the government soldiers kept an interest in creating the false impression that the rebels were very formidable. The RUF made great propaganda out of 'capturing arms' from government troops who ran away leaving them behind (RUF/SL, 1995: 13). But this, like major cases reported in the press, such as a withdrawal ordered from Pujehun District in 1992, were clear evidence of collaboration. Under no imminent threat, the commander ordered withdrawal, leaving behind huge quantities of ammunition, uniforms, and intelligence reports. According to military authorities, when troops withdraw under threat of enemy attack, they must fire into any ammunition they leave behind in order to explode them and prevent the enemy getting hold of them. There does not seem to have been any cases like this, where the government troops acted professionally on the countless occasions on which they withdrew from positions. Instead they left stockpiles of arms behind for the RUF.

Government soldiers could also use rebel tactics, pure and simple, or reach an accommodation with the RUF to exchange arms and uniforms for cash or diamonds. 'Sometimes, the method was to drive a supply truck into a pre-arranged ambush and abandon it' (Richards, 1996a). This way, the war would be prolonged, to the benefit of both sides. That is why the umpteen government announcements of the capture of myriad 'rebel bases' never led to an abatement of the war.

The government, already steeped in massive corruption, knew exactly what was happening, and condoned it although its squealer-spokesman, Karefa Kargbo, in a bare-faced and courageous falsehood, was 'confident' that the NPRC was 'honest' hoping '…history to show that we made a difference' (*West Africa*, 15–21 November 1993). Indeed we now know that the NPRC made a great difference – it mercilessly plundered what was left of the country and, through collaboration with the RUF, destroyed all central and local institutions, causing one of the greatest humanitarian disasters the world has seen. But to cover up, a number of 'rebel suspects' were not unusually incarcerated, but many of them got released (*West Africa*, 19–25 July 1993). The most publicised cases of attack on civilian targets were usually brought to trial on charges of aiding the enemy. The government admitted to the role of its troops in looting, but it down-played the true magnitude and significance of 'sobeldom', always assuring the nation that the 'situation is firmly under control' (*West Africa*, 26 September–2 October; 21–27 November 1994).

A celebrated case was that of Lt. Col. Chernor Malador Deen, Brigade Commander for the North, whose tenure saw a spate of RUF successes. He was arrested in August 1994, and charged with aiding and abetting the enemy. He was tried by a Court Martial, found guilty and sentenced to death in January, 1995. One newspaper said the whole episode was a plot by Deen's enemies, because Strasser had tipped him to become Force Commander (*Punch*, 19 February 1997). If this was so, why did Strasser not grant him pardon? On the other hand, he was not executed, but kept in jail, until President Kabbah granted him pardon 'in the interest of national reconciliation', in February 1997. It appears that the NPRC government liked Deen, but his activities exposed or embarrassed them. To have released him would just have confirmed what was public knowledge and which the NPRC denied – collaboration with the RUF. The best action in this dilemma was to leave him in jail.

This situation was further compounded by the probable multiplicity of 'rebel groups' involved in the war, about half a dozen or more (*West Africa*, 1-7 May 1995). Apart from the RUF, these included not only bandits who saw an opportunity presented by the anarchy to acquire some wealth for themselves, but disgruntled soldiers with various loyalties and motives, e.g., those recruited into the army by political means and were diehard supporters of the APC; troops loyal to individual senior army officers who were not happy with the NPRC sweeping the carpet from under their feet; supporters of dismissed senior officers; or those fearing that the war was ending, and wanted to acquire as much as they could before the game was over. All of these joined in the brigandage, which helped create the impression that the RUF was very powerful, even though the RUF knew nothing about the existence of some of them.

In actual fact, relative to the ambitious scale of its planned operations, the RUF was resource-poor. Hostage taking in 1995 was meant partly to bargain for 'logistics' – weapons, and in the case of the seven Catholic nuns, medicines, a generator, and a satellite telephone (*West Africa*, 20–26 February 1995). The RUF were able 'to project an image of great power' (Richards,1996a: 8) due to high levels of organizational efficiency, but which itself was meant to compensate for resource-poverty. Thus the RUF alone is not to blame for 'the continuing destruction of our country…the rebels have many different faces…there are rebels among us [soldiers], there are mercenaries among us, some of them our own people. The problem is not the RUF alone…' (Conteh, 1995). This was the honest view of someone who had been a Commander of the Army for a period during the war.

As early as the end of 1993, the NPRC was in a position to end the war (some say it actually did) by crushing the RUF as it had promised to do. There was a general perception that the war was at an end. In April, the army began a new offensive and captured Pendembu, the RUF 'capital'. The speed and determination of the army signalled the end of the war. Strasser echoed this national expectation, when during his first anniversary speech he stated, 'the conclusion of this brutal and savage war is in sight' (*West Africa*, 10–16 May 1993). However, it might have just occurred to Strasser that the end was coming too soon, and he would then be out of power. This probably explains why the district capital of Kailahun, only seventeen miles away, could not be captured for several months. In November, Kailahun and Koindu, the famous market town on the border with Guinea and Liberia, which had been under rebel control for the previous thirteen months, was recaptured, as well as nine other towns in Kailahun District. Strasser announced that, 'the rebel war is becoming a thing of the past' (*West Africa*, 22–28 November; 6–12 December 1993), but rather strangely, even though nearly the whole district had been liberated from the RUF, the civilian population was not allowed to return there.

Ex-Army Chief, Brigadier J.O.Y. Toure, who saw service as Brigade Commander in the east, confirmed this, lamenting that 'the war would have been history since 1993, but for the fateful command and orders of my then Commander-in-Chief, Captain Strasser' (*The Echo*, 20–24 August 1996). Johnny Paul Koroma, another veteran who was to head the AFRC military junta that removed the Kabbah government in 1997, echoed the views of Toure: 'the SLA [Sierra Leone Army] drove the RUF right back into Monrovia before Strasser gave them leeway in his unilateral ceasefire'(Personal Communication). Even the RUF rather shamefacedly, admits this fact: 'By late 1993, we had been forced to beat a hasty retreat…we were pushed to the border with Liberia. Frankly, we were beaten and were on the run…..' (RUF/SL, 1995:10-11).

But why did the war not end? Strasser declared a unilateral ceasefire on 1 December, without consulting army commanders. He extended amnesty to the rebels because he wanted them to 'participate in the reconstruction of the shattered economy', and released those suspected of being rebels to allow them to reintegrate into society (*West Africa*, 6–12 December 1993). Here Strasser was not being doltish as it appears; he was clearly playing a game by attempting to please Sierra Leoneans with the arrests of rebels, and at the same time, pleasing the RUF by releasing the rebels, and then justifying it to the people. Awakened to the love of money, the proverbial 'root of all evil' somewhere along the line, it dawned on the young army officers that if the end of the war were declared so soon, they would have to yield to democratic elections, and they would be out of power without an opportunity to further enrich themselves. The new strategy then was to allow the RUF a hiatus to regroup if they were hard-pressed, and thereafter re-launch. This explains why the people were not allowed to return to their homes, because an RUF re-launch was expected. Additionally, the *sobels* were encouraged to unleash vicious rampages after the fashion of the RUF. In this way, the war would keep going; the NPRC would continue to stay in power; and the military would continue to enrich themselves. Popular memory in the east of the country recalls the period up to the end of 1993 as the period of 'the original rebel war', and thereafter, it was that of 'the sobel war'.

Diamonds and the war equation

The turning point could be traced to quite early in the regime's life. It has been reported that Strasser's troops, engaged in mining diamonds in Kono in mid-1992, were oblivious of the RUF, which surprised them and captured Kono (Reno, 1995: 175). Perhaps more dramatic was the resurfacing of

Antwerp-based diamond dealer, Serge Muller, who, through his partner Mahmud Khadi, had been awarded the contract to market the country's diamonds by President Momoh, and who fled after Momoh's overthrow. Muller is reported to have admitted undervaluing the country's diamonds at the instance of Khadi, who was later ordered by the Marcus-Jones Commission of Enquiry to pay back to government about 1.5 million British pounds. It was believed that this action would have sealed the fate of Muller's involvement in the country, especially as the NPRC was trumpeting an official moral imperative of 'transparency, accountability, and probity'.

But Muller was to make a bold comeback to the astonishment of those who knew what was happening. In 1992, a consignment of diamonds was exported to London which included a big light blue gem. Muller, invoking the Momoh contract that he was the only channel for marketing Sierra Leone diamonds abroad, took out a Court injunction against the public sale by the Government Gold and Diamond Office (GGDO) in London. The consignment was brought back, but there was no official statement about what happened next. Muller however appeared in Freetown later and was entertained by Strasser. On his return, he went with Charles Mbayo and Karefa Kargbo, two top-ranking NPRC officials, in his private jet. A civilian Cabinet Minister at the time protested to Strasser that the government should have nothing to do with the likes of Muller in view of the disclosures in the Commission of Enquiry, and in view of the government's pledge to end corruption. It was to no effect. By this time, it was an established fact that most people in the NPRC 'were more interested in amassing wealth…[and] proved to be more corrupt than the APC government….' (Musa, 1995). By the end of 1993, there was 'growing suspicion that the corruption the boys pledged to clean up may be beginning to defeat them…' (Dowden, 1993).

Not surprisingly, Strasser began his mysterious disappearing acts, performing three of them before the end of 1993 (*West Africa*, 27 December 1993–9 January 1994). On one occasion, out for over a week without even the knowledge of his deputy, Strasser was traced to Antwerp. There was constant allegation that he was out to sell illegally mined diamonds. *Expressen* of Stockholm, Sweden, the largest-selling daily paper in Scandinavia, published a story on 26 September that Strasser had gone to sell 435 carats of diamonds valued at $43 million and was buying houses in UK and elsewhere. The story was carried in a local paper, *The New Breed*, on 13 October. In its editorial, 'Redeemers or Villains', the paper lamented that official corruption had shattered the hope of the people for a better life under Strasser. The editor and several others were arrested and charged for sedition and libel. Bail was refused, copies of the paper were confiscated, vendors were harassed, and the detainees were allowed no visitors (*West Africa*, 25–31 October 1993).

German Ambassador Karl Prinz took up the cause of the journalists, and the NPRC expelled him, giving him ten days to leave. But when it was discovered that it was a serious diplomatic mistake, the NPRC government withdrew the order and denied it had expelled the Ambassador (*West Africa*, 15–21 November 1993). The government was extremely sensitive to such charges, especially when there was a grain of truth, mainly because of the painful realization that it already failed the people, doing the opposite of what it was preaching, and was no better than the corrupt system it came to clean. As a result, it resorted to repressive measures. NPRC official spokesman, Karefa Kargbo, was outraged: The New Breed article not only spoilt our characters but did a great deal of damage to the integrity of the NPRC...The article damaged my character and that of the government...We believe that if you serve your people conscientiously, the truth will come out one day...I always thought that there was no smoke without fire until I entered the political scene...(*West Africa*, 15-21 November, 1993).

In November, Strasser filed a suit in a London High Court against *The New Patriot* magazine, for carrying the story from the *Expressen* in its November issue. The writ was for libel. 'By reason of the publication complained of', the writ stated, 'the plaintiff has been gravely injured in his reputation, and brought into public scandal, odium and contempt'. The writ asked for an undertaking within seven days from the respondents that the article will not be repeated, otherwise an injunction would be applied for and damages sought. No action was taken against the Swedish paper or the originator of the story, Tommy Schonstedt, who welcomed a court action in a Swedish court, for which he was ready. In seizing upon the weaker paper, Strasser' was only attempting to defend the indefensible, and to stop the spread of the scandal. The truth is, even by this time, neither Strasser nor the NPRC had any character or reputation worthy of protection. The NPRC was clearly worse than the APC it replaced in its intrepid corruption.

By the end of 1993, the NPRC came out again with yet another of its corrupt antiques to fool the people. It ordered that anyone who disclosed information leading to the arrest of smugglers would be entitled to 40 percent of the value of the goods seized. This was given excessively wide media publicity, with a skit appearing on TV at least twice an hour every night. Then in early 1994, a 172 carat diamond was seized in a purported anti-smuggling operation. The public was told of the seizure of the stone, but not the person who gave the information. Auctioned for $2.8 million, the NPRC Principal Liaison Officer (super minister) responsible for Mines, instructed the GGDO to pay 40 percent of the amount to Komba Mondeh, another NPRC Principal Liaison Officer. There must have been several other instances. The NPRC had discovered that the quickest way to get rich was through diamonds. By this time, it had lost every iota of the revolutionary intention (or rather pretension) of being a corrective regime to lift the country out of its rabid mess by cleaning the Augean stables the APC had left behind.

A few imponderables: Snippets for the collaboration jig-saw

There are several reported incidents or events that can definitely be seen as pieces of the jigsaw puzzle of NPRC collaboration with the RUF, whether they are direct actions taken, or failure to take actions that were needed in light of the information or intelligence available. A few will be examined. First, is the failure of the NPRC to attack the RUF headquarters. When Pendembu was captured from the RUF, Sankoh made his capital at Giema, some ten miles south east of Kailahun. This was common knowledge. But there was continued official silence about this fact, and throughout the conduct of the war, there was never a single attempt made to attack Giema. When questioned about aerial bombardments against RUF bases, the government explained that the RUF held several civilians and that such an action would lead to unnecessary civilian casualties.

At the end of 1995, some RUF agents were captured in Conakry while on an arms procurement trip. They were handed over to the government, which invited the press to interview them. Mrs Iye Kallon, RUF Public Relations Officer, in a lengthy press interrogation on TV, named Buedu, pretty close to Giema, as Foday Sankoh's seat, and gave valuable information relating to the RUF bases and manoeuvres along the borders of Sierra Leone, Guinea, Liberia and Côte d'Ivoire. Another, Mr Barrie, a diamond valuer for the RUF, was briefly interviewed. Then the interviews were abruptly stopped without official explanation. Speculations were rife at the time that the interviews might have been giving out too much information that could likely establish a connection between the NPRC and the RUF.

Secondly, as the RUF came to extend its area of operations and began taking hostages from 1994, it moved with the hostages right into Kailahun District. The question that comes to mind is whether the RUF did not care so much for security of the hostages and got them to move in small unobtrusive groups across such vast expanses of the country. It is impossible to imagine that such long trips over many days, even weeks, could be undertaken without even a single official detection, when the government troops were indeed receiving and supposedly making use of military intelligence. Was the military covering the RUF?

A third point relates to the NPRC's eastern region secretary, Lt. Tom Nyumah, who was also reputedly engaging the RUF in fierce battles with great valour. He was ubiquitously at all RUF battle-fronts, and hardly a week went by without Nyumah falling into an 'RUF ambush', but came out every time totally unscathed. At first, this was attributed to supernatural powers that Nyumah was believed to possess, and gave him great popularity as the only hero who was successfully battling the RUF. But as these 'ambushes' were repeated with the same pattern time and time again, the local people began questioning the basis of Nyumah's supernatural powers. He came to be openly branded as a 'rebel'. The suspicion was that the ambushes were orchestrated to avoid any hint of collaboration with the RUF, when in fact Nyumah was 'selling game' (switching sides). At the Abidjan meeting between Sankoh and J. M. Bio who took over from Strasser in a palace coup on January 16, 1996, the public noted Nyumah trying to avoid Sankoh, who kept calling to him 'come here my son'. The intimacy displayed by Sankoh gave further support to the popular rumour that Nyumah could have been one of the main links between the NPRC and the RUF.

A final imponderable relates to the death of Dr. Alpha Lavalie. Lavalie was an activist for the Sierra Leone People's Party (SLPP), who gained prominence in organising local hunters in the east to form a civil defence force called the Eastern Region Defence Committee (EREDECOM), which proved very effective against the rebels. In 1995, his vehicle ran into a land mine at an army checkpoint. There was no doubt in the minds of the locals that the soldiers murdered him. If indeed this is true, the question is, why should the army want to eliminate a man who was actually doing some of their official dirty work?

With the rise of the *sobel* phenomenon, the parties to the conflict tended for the most part to avoid each other in direct confrontation, and turned against the defenceless civilian population they were supposed to protect, the army, as its constitutional duty, and the RUF, as its self-professed revolutionary objective. Both took turns at attacking settlements, the RUF first, which usually took away money and valuables of small bulk, then the army would complete the devastation by carting away in lorries, everything the rebels could not take, such as furniture, corrugated iron sheets and windows removed from houses, and then set fire to the town to destroy the evidence. *Sobels* also operated independent of the army, to loot the property of the civilian population, committing atrocities similar to, or worse than the RUF, in order to shift the blame to the RUF. The majority of towns completely razed since 1994 was done in this way.

The mood was correctly captured by *West Africa* magazine when it noted that 'the real tragedy is that both the NPRC and the RUF appear to be out of touch with the majority of the public. None…puts human suffering high on its priorities….[F]or some reason [they] do not seem greatly bothered….' (30 October–5 November 1995). A *New York Times* journalist found Sankoh to be 'a man so blinded by the "rightness" of his vague calls for social justice and his eclectic assortment of ideological influences, that he has become oblivious to the pain his struggle has brought his country' (June, 1996). With characteristic unrepentant arrogance, Sankoh's response to the human suffering is 'when two lions or elephants are fighting, who is going to suffer? The grass of course, I cannot deny it'. If this is countered by the fact that Sankoh has publicly apologised to the nation several times for the pain and suffering his movement has caused, the only response is that he is not genuine because savage atrocities permanently seem to be the most legendary characteristic of RUF operations. It is in response to this situation that Civil Defence Forces (CDF), emerged, the most famous being the *Kamajoisia*,[1] to do for the people what the warring parties could not do: defend them.

Muddied Waters: Disinformation and subterfuge

Once saturated in corruption, the NPRC had to keep the war going as an excuse to stay on in power and continue plundering the state. But it was in their interest to conceal their activities and intentions by confusing the issues as much as possible and thus cause a division among the people. The RUF, for propaganda and political purposes, would take credit for *sobel* activities, thereby giving the NPRC the excuse that they were fighting a formidable enemy. It would then pretend to be bowing to pressure for democratisation, but for the nuisance of the RUF which refuses to go away. The NPRC succeeded to an extraordinary degree by disinformation, subterfuge and legerdemain, to confuse and deceive everybody, but in the end, the forces they unleashed went out of control, putting an end to their diabolical designs.

Institutionally, the NPRC confused the NPRC as a government and NPRC as the army, by creating interference and overlap between the two so as to cloud the role of the Army beyond recognition. With little or no professionalism in the army, 'many of the young military men with their new-found powers have proven unable to perform on (sic) government roles for which they are so unsuited and untrained'. This was a 'serious handicap' which threatened to 'render the entire nation ungovernable' (Conteh,1995). Brig. Kellie Conteh, a professional soldier with excellent training and a fine mind, saw a danger in the marriage between army and government, and wanted a divorce because 'there is a direct link between the political overlap and lack of professional military leadership to the suffering of our people, in terms of looting, displacement from their homes, killing and other atrocities'(ibid). His worst fear for democratisation was 'the constraint of the civil war which can be used as an excuse for extension of military government'. Conteh wanted to restore order and institutional values, and get the army back to barracks as soon as elections were held, but the NPRC wanted the chaos to avoid the elections and continue to stay in power. Operating on completely different wavelengths, Conteh and the NPRC could not coexist for long.

When in April 1993, Pendembu was recaptured from Sankoh, the story was deliberately put out by the NPRC that he had been shot in the leg but managed to escape. To the enquiring mind, this was unimaginable, because a person shot in the leg would obviously lose his speed and therefore be overtaken in no time. So what prevented the government troops from out-running Sankoh and physically capturing him? This tale, fuelled by Sankoh's own silence, gained great currency for two years, until it came to be believed from 1994 that Sankoh no longer existed, having died from gangrene of his leg. So both the NPRC and the RUF deceived the people to believe that the end of the war was in sight, while they continued their plunder of the country's diamonds, the former selling them in Belgium, the latter in Cote d'Ivoire, with each pointing an accusing finger at the other (*West Africa*, 15–21 May 1995).

By the end of 1994, the NPRC which had previously refused to negotiate peace with the RUF, offered to do so for the first time and declared a unilateral unconditional ceasefire (*West Africa*, 15-11, 19–25 December1994). The RUF ignored the invitation, but took advantage of the hiatus to regroup, and in the next few months, 'rebel attacks' spread like wild fire, hitting nearly every part of the country. At the end of the year, Koinadugu and Tonkilioli Districts were hit; in early 1995, Njala University College, Sierra Rutile mines, Sieromco mines (all in Moyamba District), as well as Port Loko and Kambia Districts were all hit and by April, the 'rebels' occupied Songo and Waterloo, only 20 miles from Freetown, 'threatening' the capital (*West Africa*, 6–12 February; 17–23 April 1995; NA: June, 1995). The RUF, taking credit for all these activities, said it had 2000 fighters inside Freetown, and said it would launch an all-out attack, starting with kidnapping the wives and children of government officials. Everyone believed the rebel threat was real (NA: June, 1995; *West Africa*, 17–23 April 1995), but indeed it was the government troops who were doing the job for the RUF.

By all accounts, the pattern of occupation of these districts was the same, and the active collaboration of government soldiers was confirmed by the inhabitants of the places attacked. Usually, the soldiers came and gave assurance to the people that they were safe, and a little while later disappeared from the town. The next thing would be a 'rebel attack' on that town towards the evening. It was reported for instance that government 'soldiers present in Kambia that day [of the attack] and who should have protected [the people] were nowhere to be seen at the time of the attack' (NA: June, 1995).

The same collaboration is true of the ambushes that took place on the highways linking Freetown with the hinterland. The most celebrated was the attack in August 1995, on a food convoy of 70 vehicles escorted by armoured personnel carriers and one helicopter gunship, in which thirty people were killed and over twenty vehicles destroyed (*West Africa*, 21–27 August 1995). The convoy left Freetown at dusk, and was made to pass the night at Waterloo, only twenty miles away. The suspicion was that it was to enable the soldiers study the contents of the vehicles. Half-way to Bo, the convoy was halted by the soldiers who said they were going to comb the area for 'rebels'. At this point, 'rebels' emerged from the bush and attacked the convoy.

To present the war to the people as very intractable, the NPRC hired mercenaries, the Gurkhas and later Executive Outcomes (EO), to help them finish the RUF. In February 1995, the Gurkha leader and Major A. A. Tarawalli, who was ADC, and close confidant and trafficker for Strasser, were killed in a 'rebel ambush' at Matoel, 70 miles from Freetown, where the rebels were reportedly camped and kept attacking convoys on the highway. It was widely believed that these deaths were orchestrated to give the impression that the NPRC was doing its very best. Tarawalli's wife, it was rumoured, was not allowed to see her husband's corpse, apparently because he had been shot at point-blank range.

But when the EO took over single handedly and did a reconnaissance of rebel positions, they launched an onslaught that cost the RUF a quarter of its estimated 2000 fighters. 'Time is running out' for the RUF the EO commander was quoted as saying (*West Africa*, 31 July–6 August 1995). Indeed rumours circulated widely that EO could end the war in no time, but that the NPRC was obstructing their plans. These initiatives which indeed could have ended the war, turned out to be only part of the NPRC game of deception. It is possible to see a direct correlation between the pressure for democratisation and the intensification of the war. As pressure increased, so the war seemed to be getting out of hand. The 1994 pressure was responsible for the massive war spillage of early 1995 as well as the announcement by the government in April of various measures for a return to democracy. But the snag was that the intensification of the war would make all measures impracticable. The western press warned Strasser that as he did not know the strength and determination of the RUF fighting force and that he should therefore not take the threats lightly. Thus, they concluded, the NPRC was 'fighting for its own survival in the teeth of vicious rebel attacks to force the regime from power' (*West Africa*, 15–21 May 1995). 'Instead of crushing the rebels, he finds himself in the embarrassing situation of being crushed by them' (NA: June,1995).

Under strong international pressure for democratisation, Strasser reshuffled his cabinet in April 1995, to demonstrate that he was in line with the international community and therefore was reducing the military presence in the government, in order to concentrate on the war, in preparation for proposed elections later in the year. The position of Principal Liaison Officers was abolished, but principal ministries such as Mines and Agriculture, remained under soldiers. Those who were made to return to the army received unjustifiably phenomenal promotions and placed in all the vital positions. Deputy Chairman Bio was promoted from Captain to Brigadier and appointed chief of Defence Staff. Lt. Komba Mondeh was promoted to Lt. Col. and appointed Director of operations. Capt. R. Glover, promoted to Lt. Col. was appointed Director of logistics and Planning. Lt. Charles Mbayo was promoted Lt. Col. and appointed Chief Intelligence Officer, while Lt. Idriss Kamara was promoted Lt. Col. and appointed Director of Internal Security and Special Operations. Lt. Tom Nyumah and Lt. Karefa Kargbo, promoted Lt. Col. were appointed respectively as general Services Officer for Operations and Director of Public relations. Col. Kellie Conteh, a mature officer who had no part in the 1992 coup, was a different kettle of fish. He was promoted Brigadier and Chief of Staff. As we have seen, his entire background, experience and training, made him want to disengage the military from the government of the country, a principle in direct opposition to the NPRC strategy. Not surprisingly, he was replaced in June by Brig. J.O.Y. Toure, earlier retired, but now re-engaged on contract (*West Africa*, 10–16 April, June 12–18, 1995). Far from being a genuine step in the transition to civilian rule, these changes reduced the visible military presence (though not control) in the government, but tightened the grip of the NPRC on the army.

NPRC complicity

When the NPRC seized power, it said that it had come to clean up the mess of the APC and build a brighter future, and promised the people that it would speedily end the rebel war. But as diamonds entered the war equation, corruption overtook the NPRC, which decided that the only way to stay in power and continue to plunder the nation was to keep the war going. Thus an extraordinary identity of interest emerged between the RUF and the NPRC/ military. Defeated at the end of 1993, the RUF was granted a lease of life by Strasser so that the war would continue. Instead of fighting, the troops tended to avoid each other, and targeted instead, the unarmed and defenceless civilians they were supposed to protect. Government troops engaged in rebel activity, becoming 'sobels'. Seeing elections as a threat to their plundering existence, both the RUF and the NPRC were opposed, and made every effort to prevent it. The NPRC is the worst case of an obscene government that wilfully conspired to literally destroy the state, by sponsoring, in various ways, a rebel war it was supposed to end quickly. Utterly corrupt and immoral, the NPRC government is to be held equally accountable for ransacking the resources of the state, and causing death, pain and misery, in one for or another, to millions of Sierra Leoneans.

Lack of direction? President Kabbah's dealings with the RUF

President Kabbah admittedly inherited a bad situation, but his actions/ inactions, arguably, made the situation worse. In his dealings with the RUF, Kabbah appeared to have been naïve to accept and believe everything he was told on the surface, especially from someone like Foday Sankoh whom he thought would honour his word. Sankoh is a great con artist, with a gift of the garb, who fooled successive negotiators for the better part of a decade, that he was not interested in power. To believe that Sankoh would abide by any number of peace agreements that did not give him the presidency was utterly foolish. Sankoh best understands force, and that was why in every negotiation for peace he had engaged in, he always came up with demands that, if accepted, would inevitably minimise the government military capacity so as to give him the greater advantage to seize power by force.

Few things have been greater anathemas to Sankoh in his rebellion than the Kamajoisia and EO. Kabbah favourably inherited these, whose activities not only ended Sankoh's dithering but made Abidjan possible. A major offensive by the Kamajoi militia, backed by Executive Outcomes (EO),[2] resulted in stunning successes against the RUF. Several major training and operations bases of the RUF were razed with serious loss of rebel lives, including Gambia-Mattru and the RUF headquarters camp, *Zogoda* (Muana,1997). Sankoh complained bitterly. In all probability, it was this military pressure more than any other factor, which put the RUF clearly on the defensive, and made Sankoh to sign the Abidjan Peace Accord. The RUF had never been under such stress in the war since their 1993 rout by the NPRC.

The Kabbah government should have realised this advantage, and had it so elected, could have used this opportunity, notwithstanding the on-going peace process, to press the conflict to a final military victory over the RUF. In the event, it did not. Too narrowly preoccupied with the legal niceties of signing a peace agreement and anxious to demonstrate to the world that it was 'the good guy', the Kabbah government goofed badly. Sankoh did not care much about legal niceties or international opinion, as long as he got his way. When he cared about these, he was on the defensive. What mattered most to him was the reality on the ground. Yet Kabbah bowed to pressure from the IMF, and announced the termination of EO's contract, encamping them even before the agreement was signed. This blunder provided the political and military space Sankoh needed to manoeuvre and muster the capacity for another military strike.

Sankoh wanted desperately to entrench his base in Kailahun and wrote to the OAU Secretary-General in February that the only way for the disarmament process to proceed was for him to re-establish at his Kailahun base. The government agreed to let Sankoh visit Kailahun but not to make a permanent base there until the accord had been implemented. In the midst of this imbroglio, EO left at the end of January, but not before telling government in no uncertain terms that they should start a countdown to a coup that was likely within six months.[3] The government position was seriously undermined by the departure of EO, and as truly predicted, only four months later, Kabbah was overthrown by a coup on 25 May 1997. Even then, Kabbah had received intelligence report about the coup several days before but failed to take any action. Of all the contributory factors that led to Kabbah's overthrow, it appears that the most cardinal was the perceived neglect of the army, and the corresponding perception of the increase in the importance of the *Kamajoisia* with whom the government openly sided. Facing two threats, the *Kamajohs* and the RUF, the soldiers came to 'believe that the threat of elimination of the army as an institution was real' (Position Statement of the SLA and AFRC, 18 September, 1999).

It would appear that the major problem with the Kabbah administration is its inability to detect its potential strength and then to galvanise it into support and loyalty. Of course no one in the Kabbah administration now doubts that the departure of EO was a literally disastrous and silly judgement. If the RUF was so stiff-scared of EO which was acting as a great restraint on its activities, why should any pressure from the IMF or any quarter for that matter, have forced Kabbah to yield to a decision that was not in the military interest of a country at war? The money paid to EO was less important than the lives lost or the peace and stability of the nation-state. With regards to the *Kamajoisia*, Kabbah needed to prevent rivalry between them and the army. But as it happened, the *Kamajoisia* were so upstaged as to incur the hostility of the army, which led to serious clashes between them. In point of fact, the *Kamajoisia* received not much support from government (Gberie, 1997). If pro-government forces engaged in fighting each other, how can they be expected to prosecute the war? And how can anyone not expect the street-smart Sankoh not to take advantage of it?

In May 2000, it was the coalition of pro-government forces comprising of the army, the West Side Boys and the *Kamajoisia* that repelled the RUF attempt to seize Freetown and overthrow the government. But the cracks between them appeared almost immediately, with accusations of unfair and unequal treatment, especially in the provision of logistics and supplies. An equitable accommodation within the framework of a comprehensive defence strategy would have salvaged the situation. A cornerstone of such a strategic policy would have been crafted along the lines of a proper defence architecture that would ensure a national spread and deployment of the Civil Defence Force (CDF) to eventually cover the whole country. Installing such a structure would have required careful consideration and study, because, in the long term, it will be the only instrument that will guarantee the safety and integrity of Sierra Leone against invasion by another misguided lumpen movement.

But 'what is sadly lacking in Sierra Leone', *Africa Confidential* laments, 'is a government with the dynamism and legitimacy to implement…an ambitious programme' (12 May 2000).Widely acknowledged to be effete, inept, and indecisive, with an 'apparent lack of direction' (*West Africa*, 21–27 October

1996), the Kabbah administration did fail to muster all the sinews for war available to it in order to contain the RUF. It made some unpardonable errors (like the assurance in December 1998 that the war will soon be over), all of which combined, have contributed to the prolongation of the conflict in Sierra Leone.

Conclusion

For nearly a decade, the RUF waged a relentless war against the people of Sierra Leone that can best be described as the last word in savagery. It was a weird tale of the grossest human rights abuses, as well as physical and social destruction by people who want to rule the wasteland. While several factors aided the RUF to continue this foul villainy, one important one has been the vitiated approaches of successive governments. Thus, the perpetuation of the conflict has been due less to the strength and power of the RUF, and more to the debased responses by which no government has really put all of its efforts into ending the war.

The APC government of President Momoh, took it as a joke in the false belief that the anti-APC inhabitants of Kailahun District connived to start the war against his government. Had he treated the war as a matter of national priority, he would definitely have aborted the movement before it had chance to develop a self-financing capacity. The NPRC government of Strasser actually defeated the RUF, but in its perversity and perfidy to stay on in power indefinitely to plunder the country's resources, collaboration with the RUF presented itself as the only way to achieve their sordid intention. In the process, the NPRC was also accountable for the humanitarian disaster that engulfed the country during the civil war. The SLPP government of President Kabbah failed to muster all the fighting support it could get to work out a coherent defence policy to contain and destroy the RUF. It also failed to keep up pressure on the RUF by fatal mistakes that undermined government military capacity. All of these acts of omission (Momoh and Kabbah) and acts of commission (Strasser), are in varying degrees, responsible for perpetuating the war.

Notes

1   *Kamajoi* (singular) is a Mende term meaning member of the traditional hunters' guild.

2   A South African mercenary group that was hired by the NPRC government in 1995 which proved very effective in neutralising rebel activity.

3   Personal discussion with ex-Ministers Dr. Harry Will and George Banda-Thomas, July, 1997.

Part II

One step forward, two steps backward

The Political Map of Sierra Leone

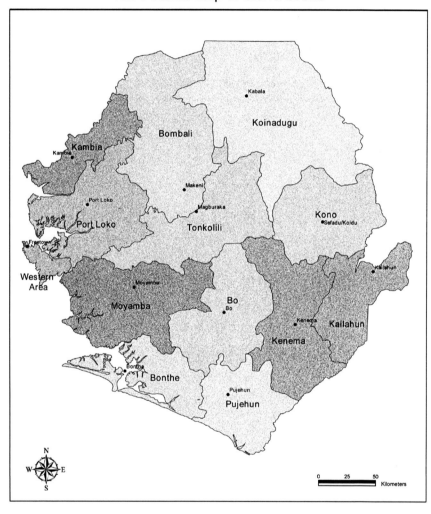

6

In Search of Legitimacy: The 1996 Elections

Jimmy D. Kandeh

After three decades of authoritarian rule and in the midst of a brutal rebel insurgency, Sierra Leoneans went to the polls in 1996 to elect a new president and parliament. Neither the APC, under whose reluctant auspices the process of political liberalization began in 1991, nor the National NPRC, which suspended this process after seizing power in 1992, favoured democratization of the country's political system. Joining the NPRC in opposing the 1996 elections was the RUF, an insurrectionary movement of desocialized marginals. With the NPRC and RUF opposed to the elections, and with both armed factions threatening to derail the exercise by attacking voters, it was quite a remarkable feat that elections were in fact held.

This chapter examines the issues surrounding the decision to proceed with the 1996 elections, the major participants in the process and the election results. As in previous elections, especially in 1962 and 1967, ethnoregional solidarity overdetermined party affiliations and voting behaviour. Elite political realignments after the first round of polling were, however, influenced less by ethnoregionalism than by opportunism and the calculations of party leaders. Whereas the electorate voted largely on the basis of ethnoregional allegiance, party alliances were not always dictated by ethnoregional factors. Political elites are deft at politicizing ethnoregionalism in the mobilization of electoral support but the political alliances they forged have usually been the product of spoils calculations rather than ethnoregional considerations.

Historical background

Prior to 1996, the 1962 and 1967 elections were generally considered the most democratic elections in independent Sierra Leone (Hayward and Kandeh, 1987). Elections during the first decade of independence, 1961 to 1971, were fairly open and competitive. This was, for example, illustrated by the distribution of seats in parliament. The incumbent SLPP lost half of the seats it contested in 1962, winning only 28 of 59. The APC won 16 of the 32 seats it contested while the Sierra Leone Progressive Independence Movement (SLPIM) won all 4 seats in the Kono district. Independent candidates also captured their fair share of parliamentary seats (14) and the small number of unopposed candidacies (four SLPP, two APC and one independent were returned unopposed) showcased the relative openness of the political system during the first few years of independence.

Elections as mechanism for political change faced the ultimate test in 1967 when the opposition APC defeated the incumbent SLPP in the most controversial/hotly contested elections in the history of Sierra Leone. The SLPP nominated candidates for all 66 seats, winning 28, while the APC won 32 of the 52 seats it contested. Not only did the APC win more seats than the incumbent party, it also captured 44.25 percent (286,585 votes) of the popular vote to the SLPP's 35.75 percent (231,567 votes). Independents again did remarkably well, with 20 percent of the popular vote (129,429) and six seats in parliament (Dove-Edwin Report, 1967). APC victory in these elections was, however, thwarted by a military coup led by Albert Margai's ethnoclient and army commander, Brigadier David Lansana. Lansana was replaced within forty-eight hours by a military junta under the leadership of Col. Andrew Juxon-Smith. Juxon-Smith's unpopular National Reformation Council (NRC) was ousted a year later by non-commissioned officers of the armed forces who, rather than form a government, decided to hand over power to the APC party. This was the first time in the history of post-colonial Africa that the military intervened in politics not to exercise power but to facilitate its immediate transfer to a democratically elected government.

The 1968 democratic restoration was, however, short-lived. The APC moved quickly to consolidate power by declaring a state of emergency, harassing and imprisoning political opponents, politicizing the army, police and civil service, adopting a republican constitution and imposing a one-party system of government. Elections under the APC were fraudulent, turbulent affairs involving escalating levels of violence and thuggery. Starting with the 1968 by-elections, violence and organized thuggery emerged as prominent features of the electoral process. This continued into the 1973 elections which the SLPP boycotted out of fear for the lives of its candidates and in protest over the unprecedented level of violence unleashed by the APC government. From 1973 to 1977, Sierra Leone was a de facto one-party state, with the APC as the only party represented in parliament. Anti-government student protests in early 1977 forced the government to dissolve parliament and call for early elections (See Rashid, this volume). As in 1973, violence and thuggery prevented the opposition from contesting most seats; the SLPP, nonetheless, managed to win a total of 15 seats under very difficult circumstances. Immediately after these elections, the APC began preparations for a referendum on a one-party constitution whose adoption in 1978 formally ended the facade of democratic competition that had existed in one form or the other from 1968-1978.

There were three elections (including Momoh's coronation election of 1985) and one referendum during the one-party period. The first one-party election in 1982 turned out to be the most violent. In both Koinadugu North constituency and Pujehun district, the violence was so intolerable that many people fled the area to neighbouring Guinea and Liberia. Port Loko West II also witnessed some of the most extreme forms of violence which shocked even an otherwise inured Siaka Stevens. The 1986 elections, the only election under Momoh, was considerably more open and less violent. Candidates were required to sign a 'code of conduct' the violation of which was punishable by disqualification from the electoral process. Violence in the 1982 and 1986 elections had less to do with ethnicity than the competing ambitions and predatory interests of political elites. Elites from the same ethnic group competing for the same seat in parliament were as likely to mobilize violence against each other as were elites from different ethnic backgrounds.

While the imposition of a one-party system of government was designed to eliminate organized political opposition to the incumbent APC, it failed to silence the voices of popular sectors. The criminalization of opposition to the APC shifted the main locus of opposition activity from patronage parties like the SLPP to popular organizations of students, workers, teachers and women (See Abdullah this volume). Despite past failures (especially in 1977) to forge a student–worker alliance, students were joined in the 1980s by workers and teachers and, in the 1990s, by women's organizations, in constituting the vanguard of popular opposition to APC and NPRC authoritarianism.

Democratic forces opposed to the APC and demanding political change became more assertive after Momoh succeeded Stevens as president. Momoh was locally lampooned as a profligate buffoon who was over his head as president. Many saw his presidency as an opportunity to test the APC's capacity to contain the growing societal opposition to its dictatorship. The end of the Cold War further exposed society and the political system to global currents that could no longer be held at bay by the stratagems of anti-democratic incumbents. Unable to justify its continued political monopoly on the basis of its performance, and facing a groundswell of internal (students, teachers, labour unions, professional organizations and the print media) and external (donor countries, global financial institutions) opposition to its dictatorship, the APC government in 1991 agreed to dismantle the one-party system and conduct multi-party elections.

Momoh, however, did not have the luxury of presiding over democratic elections. At about the same time he was bowing to popular pressures to liberalize the political system, an armed rebellion against his government was launched by the RUF. The insurrection further exposed the degeneracy of the Momoh government as resources allotted to fighting rebels were routinely siphoned-off by members of the APC and military hierarchies. Momoh's grossly inept handling of the RUF insurrection, and the fact that many Sierra Leoneans doubted his party's death-bed conversion to democracy, precipitated the demise of the APC government.

The military coup that ousted Momoh and the APC from power forced the democratic transition into a holding pattern. The NPRC vowed to establish a 'true multi-party system of government' but not before ending the RUF insurrection and restoring state capacities. As it turned out, it was precisely the NPRC's inability to end the war (the war actually escalated during its tenure) and restore probity to state institutions that rekindled public demands for multi-party elections. Taking these demands as well as pressures from donor countries into consideration, the NPRC announced a transition programme for returning the country to constitutional democratic rule. A National Advisory Council (NAC), established to advise the government on the transition to democracy, produced a draft constitution that was supposed to replace the 1991 constitution but was in the end abandoned. The NPRC also appointed an Interim National Electoral Commission (INEC) under whose supervision the elections were organized.

Interim National Electoral Commission

James Jonah, a retired United Nation's Under-Secretary for Political Affairs, chaired the Interim National Electoral Commission (INEC). Jonah accepted the challenge of piloting the democratic transition because he felt he 'should give some service to my country' after 'having worked for 30 years in the UN' (*West Africa*, February 28–March 6, 1994, 346). Before taking the job, Jonah insisted on assurances from the NPRC that the commission would be allowed to operate autonomously of the government. Independence of the commission, as it turned out, was critical to ensuring that the elections did in fact take place.

Ground rules for the elections were specified in three related NPRC decrees (14, 15, 16). Decree 14 required political parties to file financial statements with the electoral commission no later than twenty-one days before the elections. Decree 15 repealed the 1961 *Franchise and Voter Registration Act* and empowered INEC to prepare new electoral lists. Decree 16 replaced the simple plurality system with proportional representation and required each party to pay Le3 million (roughly 6,000 US dollars) to register for the elections. Decree 16 also replaced constituencies with electoral regions and established an *Election Offences Court* to try cases of electoral malpractices. INEC's adoption of proportional representation, instead of simple plurality, helped depersonalize the parliamentary contest, reduce the level of inter-party violence and eliminate unopposed candidatures – all distinctive features of past elections. Depopulation of the countryside rendered the first-past-the-post or simple plurality system impractical and the absence of an incumbent party in the elections, plus the fact that the constitution no longer requires presidents to appoint ministers from parliament, may have also contributed to the low levels of inter-party violence.

INEC encountered serious problems compiling a new voters list. Lack of funds delayed the start of voter registration and many citizens remained unregistered at the end of the first round of voter registration. This forced the commission to compile a second, expanded voters list which was used in the first but not the second round of presidential balloting in the western area. Sierra Leonean refugees in Guinea, estimated at over 200,000, were never registered. INEC's attempt to register these refugees after the first round of elections was overruled by the NPRC, which insisted that the same voter rolls should be maintained for both electoral rounds. There were also reports of discrimination against members of the Fulah ethnic group, many of whom were not registered for the 1996 polling. These reports forced INEC to issue a statement denouncing any attempt to disenfranchise members of the Fula community. Of the 1.6 million Sierra Leoneans on INEC's list of voters, less than 50 percent voted in the first round and approximately 60 percent voted in the presidential run-off election.

Vital to its role in organizing consultative conferences and supervising the elections was the relative autonomy of INEC. The autonomy of INEC was both political and fiscal. INEC's activities were mostly funded by external donors rather than by the government and this eliminated the NPRC's capacity to manipulate the process by withholding funds from the commission. Although the NPRC government contributed the sum of Le27 million (270,000 US dollars) to get INEC started, the $17 million budget of INEC was funded exclusively by donor countries. Backing from the international community emboldened the commission in resisting NPRC efforts to delay the elections. Thus, even after his residence and office were bombed by army regulars, Jonah stood his ground and refused to be intimidated. Without a relatively autonomous electoral commission, it is doubtful whether the 1996 elections would have been held. The final decision to go ahead with the elections was, however, made not by INEC but by the delegates at the Bintumani consultative conferences.

Bintumani conferences

The two consultative conferences held at the Bintumani conference center in Aberdeen provided a forum for political and societal organizations to make their views known concerning the elections. The issue that dominated both conferences was whether to proceed with elections as planned or postpone the exercise until peace was restored. Given the rebel insurrection and the displacement of over a quarter of the country's population, there were many who genuinely felt it was preposterous to hold elections under conditions of insecurity and war. But as it became increasingly obvious that the NPRC (like its predecessor) was using the war as a pretext to remain in power, many citizens who had earlier favored postponement of the elections became vocal advocates of *Elections Now*. Supporters of immediate elections were opposed by advocates of peace before elections.

The first national consultative conference was held from August 15–17, 1995. Among the 154 delegates were leaders of seventeen political parties and the representatives of trade unions, students and women's organizations, non-governmental organizations, petty-traders association, religious groups, the university, the armed forces, displaced citizens, refugees in Guinea and Liberia and representatives of Sierra Leonean groups based in Britain and the United States. One influential organization not represented at the conference was the Bar Association, which declined INEC's invitation to participate because of its objections to NPRC decrees 7 and 8. The main purpose of the conference was to decide whether to proceed with presidential and parliamentary elections or postpone them until the country is at peace. The delegates unanimously opted to proceed with the elections without delay but had to settle for a compromise with the electoral commission on the specific date of the polling. According to the NPRC timetable, elections were supposed to take place in December 1995 but Jonah informed delegates that it would be impossible to meet this deadline, and suggested March 1996 as the earliest date elections could be held. Both sides eventually agreed to move the election date to February 1996.

In addition to settling the issue – at least so it seemed at the time – of whether to go ahead with the elections, the Bintumani I conference also fixed a date certain (February 26) for the elections, ratified INEC's adoption of proportional representation and agreed to hold presidential and parliamentary elections on the same day. The conference adopted a code of conduct for political parties who were called upon to ensure that their functionaries, members and supporters act in accordance with electoral rules and regulations; violation of the code of conduct was punishable by a fine of Le500,000 (equivalent of $950 at the time). At the end of the conference, none of the delegates suspected that another conference to address issues they had resolved would be convened at the insistence of the NPRC. But this was what subsequently happened after a palace coup replaced Strasser with Julius Bio as chairman of the NPRC and head of state.

Upon succeeding Strasser as head of state in late January 1996, Bio announced that elections will be held on schedule. He also, at the same time, started negotiations with Foday Sankoh, the RUF leader, in the hope of ending the civil conflict. Due to these negotiations, and despite the Bintumani I verdict and his own earlier statement that the elections will not be delayed, Bio felt that the elections should be postponed. While dismissing NPRC–RUF talks as a ploy to postpone the elections, Jonah nonetheless went along with Bio's request for a second conference to revisit an issue that had already been resolved at the first Bintumani conference.

The prevailing sentiment among delegates attending the Bintumani II conference was that the NPRC was desperately reluctant to give up power and was using negotiations with the RUF as an excuse to prolong its incumbency. Bio himself actively campaigned among traditional rulers to support postponement of the elections. On the day of the conference, banners calling for *Elections Now* were torn down by military personnel while those calling for *Peace Before Elections* festooned the entrance to the conference hall. Politicians on their way to the conference were roughed-up by men in uniform but this did not deter delegates and their supporters from trekking to the conference site at Aberdeen. Of the seventy delegates who attended the February 12, 1996 consultative conference, fifty-six voted for elections to be held on schedule. Fourteen delegates, including representatives of the NPRC and the RUF (which sent a letter to be read at the conference) voted to postpone the elections until peace is restored. Those favoring elections included representatives of the Petty Traders' Association, the Bar Association (in attendance for the first time), student unions, political parties and women's organizations. Brigadier Joy Turay, representing the armed forces, warned that the army could not guarantee security for the elections but this was dismissed as sour grapes by most of the delegates.

The issue of whether to proceed with the elections despite NPRC and RUF opposition helped to galvanize pro-democracy forces. Both consultative conferences provided an effective forum for public consultation on crucial issues regarding the timing and conduct of multiparty elections. By opting for a consultative conference – the composition of which it had no control over – as the final arbiter on key issues affecting the elections, the NPRC inadvertently ceded control over the transition process to INEC. INEC's position and autonomy were in turn bolstered by consultative conferences whose deliberations and outcome the NPRC could not skew to its liking.

Political parties

Thirteen parties in all took part in the 1996 elections. All but two (SLPP, APC) were products of the transition to multiparty politics which started in 1991 with the promulgation of a new constitution and the partial dismantling of the one-party system. The former northern base of the APC was up for grabs, with both the United National Progressive Party (UNPP) and the People's Democratic Party (PDP) laying claim to what was once exclusive APC turf. There were many prominent APC defectors fielding their own personalist vehicles, all of whom, with the exception of Thaimu Bangura, performed disastrously. But if the fortunes of the APC and its splinter formations were on the decline going into the elections, the same could not be said of the SLPP, a party that had languished in the political wilderness for almost thirty years. As the only other political party to have ruled Sierra Leone, the SLPP's track record (compared to the APC) and the cohesion of its support base in the southern and eastern provinces of the country, ensured that the party would at least trump its historical nemesis, the APC. A fissionalized APC was no match for the SLPP; the challenge to the SLPP had to come from the new parties, namely the UNPP and PDP.

The SLPP describes itself as the 'grand old party of Sierra Leone'. The party's motto – 'One Country, One People' – emblematizes the integrationist ideal of its founding in 1951. Three civic and political organizations – the Sierra Leone Organization Society (SOS) of John Karefa-Smart, the Progressive Educational People's Union (PEPU) led by Chief Julius Gulama, Ahmad Wurie and others and the People's Party (PP) of Rev. Jones (aka Lamina Sankoh) – amalgamated into the SLPP to contest Creole political hegemony and promote national integration (Kilson, 1966; Cartwright, 1970). The party's main adversary in the politics of decolonization was the National Council of the Colony of Sierra Leone (NCCSL) which was opposed to sharing power with members of the SLPP. The separatist orientation and rhetoric of Bankole-Bright, the NCCSL leader, rallied provincial support behind the SLPP. Much of this support, however, was mediated through an elaborate patronage system that sought to absorb the traditional authorities of the three provinces into the SLPP hierarchy.

Conflicts within the SLPP over ministerial appointments and whether to hold elections before independence resulted in defections from the party by aspiring politicians who later came together to form the APC. The APC was handily defeated in the 1962 election by the incumbent SLPP but the death of Milton Margai, the prime minister and party leader, in 1964 left the SLPP in disarray while improving the APC's electoral prospects. Disagreements over leadership succession triggered more defections (mostly by northern politicians) from the SLPP to the APC. The ethnic chauvinism of Albert Margai (Sir Milton's successor) led to the SLPP's stigmatization as a Mende party, and the prime minister's failed attempt to introduce a one-party constitution contributed to his party's defeat in the 1967 elections. More significantly, Albert Margai's reluctance to concede electoral defeat plunged the country into crisis, with three coup d'états in a single year (1967–68).

The SLPP in opposition was hamstrung by the leadership rivalry between Salia Jusu-Sheriff and Mohammed Sanusi Mustapha. The party was split between the supporters of these two men and this sapped its ability to mount a united front against the APC government. In the one-party state, prominent SLPP leaders (including Jusu-Sheriff and Sama Banya) served in various capacities as ministers. SLPP collaboration in the one-party dictatorship did not, however, erode public support for the party in the southern and eastern provinces. The party had the best name recognition going into the 1996 elections and it did not carry the horrendous performance baggage of the APC. In an effort to shed its image as a Mende party, the SLPP actively recruited northerners (including Karefa-Smart and Abass Bundu) for the party's leadership and its final choice of Tejan Kabbah, a non-Mende, as its presidential candidate reflected the party's determination to counter the perception that it is Mende-dominated. While rivalry for the party's presidential nomination evoked images of earlier tussles, the defection of Charles Margai to the NUP after losing the SLPP's leadership contest, may have actually helped rather than hurt the SLPP cause. By choosing Kabbah, a Mandingo and former United Nations bureaucrat, instead of Charles Margai, the SLPP enhanced its appeal among voters in the western area and northern province.

Unlike the SLPP, the United Progressive People's Party (UNPP) of Karefa-Smart was a new comer on the political scene. The party's octogenarian leader had better name recognition than the party he founded. Though a new party, the UNPP can be linked through its leader to the United Democratic Party (UDP) of 1970 and the National Democratic Party (NDP) of 1991–92. In both instances, defectors from the APC dominated the UDP leadership. According to APC propaganda, the UDP of 1970 was 'poisoned by the Temne tribalism of some of the leaders and the grasping personal ambition of others' (*Rising Sun*, 1982, 107). Sensing a threat to its northern base, the APC government banned the UDP and arrested most of its leaders. Two of these leaders, Mohammed Forna and Ibrahim Bash-Taqi, were later executed on unrelated treason charges. The UDP was revived during the brief democratic opening of 1991–92 but it was later banned, along with all other political parties, by the NPRC junta. The party resurfaced under its current name, UNPP, after the NPRC lifted the ban on political parties in preparation for the 1996 elections. The UNPP motto is Unity, Truth and Progress and its symbol is a lamp.

Like most of the other parties, the UNPP is a personalist instrument that is unlikely to outlast its founding leader. Where there was some speculation as to who would be the SLPP standard-bearer, there was no such uncertainty in the UNPP camp. The party attracted many APC retreads, especially those banned from contesting the elections, and was seen by a plurality of northern politicians and voters as an alternative to the SLPP and the APC. The UNPP leader also had better name recognition than any of the other presidential candidates.

The People's Democratic Party (PDP), is also a personalist vehicle formed by a former APC politician and minister, Thaimu Bangura. As minister of information in the government of Siaka Stevens, Bangura gained notoriety for leading efforts to muzzle the print media and for razing two villages to the ground during the violent 1982 elections – the first elections under the one-party system. Bangura left the APC in 1990 for personal reasons and began reinventing himself as an advocate of multiparty democracy. The PDP was a serious contender for the northern vote and the votes of petty traders in urban areas, especially Freetown. The PDP, more so than the UNPP, is identified as a Temne party largely on account of Bangura's credentials as a cultural politician and because most of the party's leaders were Temne. The party's motto, *Sorbeh*, is a Temne word that means dedication, hard work and commitment. With the exception of Karefa-Smart whose defection from the APC predated the one-party state, Thaimu Bangura was the only former APC minister/member to do reasonably well in the 1996 elections.

The All People's Congress (APC) grew out of the People's National Party (PNP) and the Elections Before Independence Movement (EBIM). According to Party lore, the name APC came from a local brand of aspirin (APC) which, for party leaders like Mucktarr Kallay, captured the essence of the party's mission, which was to 'cure' the country of its SLPP headache (*Rising Sun*, 1982, 55). The party was founded and led by Siaka Stevens, a trade union organizer who resigned from the SLPP in 1957 to form the People's National Party (PNP) with Albert Margai and others. As the main opposition party in parliament from 1962–67, the APC led the fight against Albert Margai's unsuccessful attempts to introduce republican and one-party constitutions.

In government (1968–92), the APC was an unmitigated disaster. It drastically shrunk the political arena by adopting the same constitutional provisions (republicanism, one-party system) it had fought against as an opposition party. To add to the layers of irony that characterized APC rule, the party that was the beneficiary of the 1968 democratic restoration did not allow a single free and fair election to be held during the duration of its tenure in power. The imposition of a one-party system of government at a time when the public was clamoring for democratic change retarded institutional development and widened the gulf between state and society. Some prominent leaders began defecting from the party in the early 1990s to start their own political parties; others were banned by the NPRC from contesting the 1996 elections. What remained of the APC in 1996 was led by Edward Turay, a 53-year-old lawyer and former member of parliament from 1986–92. Turay's efforts to reinvent the APC were undercut by the party's disastrous track record.

The National Unity Party (NUP) was founded and supported by the NPRC junta and its civilian supplicants. Divisions in the party between those who wanted the NPRC leadership to contest the elections and those opposed to such an idea, precipitated a palace coup less than a month before the scheduled elections. Although the main reason given for the coup was Valentine Strasser's desire to contest the elections as presidential candidate of the NUP, it was clear that the balance of forces within the NPRC junta had a direct bearing on what transpired inside the NUP. The 'Segbwema Mafia', led by John Benjamin, orchestrated both the ouster of Strasser as head of state and the choice of John Karimu (NPRC minister of finance) as the NUP presidential candidate. By and large, the NUP became indistinguishable from the NPRC in the eyes of the public as most of its civilian leaders were drawn mainly from the ranks of NPRC clients.

In addition to these five parties, eight other minor parties took part in the elections. These were the Democratic Center Party (DCP) which was founded and led by Abu Koroma, a former Attorney General; the People's Progressive Party (PPP), founded and led by Abass Bundu, a former minister in both APC and NPRC governments; the People's National Convention (PNC), whose founding leader Edward Kargbo was another prominent former APC politician and minister; the National Democratic Alliance (NDA) of Ahmadou Jalloh, the first Fula to contest the presidency in Sierra Leone; the Social Democratic Party (SDP) of Andrew Lungay, a United Kingdom resident who returned home briefly to contest the election; the National Unity Movement (NUM) of Desmond Luke, the only former minister to have resigned from the APC government; the National Alliance Party (NAP) of Mohammed Sillah and Geredine Williams-Sarho, and; the National People's Party (NPP) of Andrew Turay.

None of the above parties were mass-based organizations. They were essentially elitist parties that promised to do the same things if elected. Their bases of support were regional, ethnoclientelist and personalist; none could claim a truly national following. The correlation between ethnoregionalism, on the one hand, and party formation and support, on the other, represent an element of party electoral competition in Sierra Leone that has remained unchanged since the 1960s. The participation of thirteen political parties in the 1996 elections, compared to four parties in the 1967 elections, can be attributed to intense factionalism and opportunism among northern politicians. Eight of the thirteen parties in the 1996 elections were led by northern politicians, a fact that made voting more competitive in the north than in the south and east where the SLPP faced only token opposition from the NUP and DCP. Proliferation of parties and fragmentation of the party system mirrored the increased personalization of politics and a general weakening of party loyalty and ethnoregional solidarity among elites.

Party platforms and campaigns

The official campaign period leading to the elections lasted for less than three months. Hardly any campaigning took place in the rural areas due to inadequate security. Campaign efforts focused mainly on urban communities, with political parties utilizing a wide array of resources and strategies to get their messages across to the voting public. Ideology and party manifestos did not differentiate the parties as they all promised to essentially pursue the same policies if elected. The main issues in the campaign were peace, law and order, corruption, rehabilitation and reconstruction. All the parties promised to pursue a negotiated settlement of the rebel war and none seemed to question whether a negotiated settlement was in fact possible or address the issue of what to do if negotiations with the RUF fail. The SLPP, for example, promised to negotiate an end to the war, resettle and rehabilitate the displaced, reconstitute the army, rehabilitate health facilities, reform the educational system, provide decent and affordable housing, invest in infrastructure and usher a 'new dispensation ... free from corruption, extra-constitutional governments, incompetence, nepotism, favouritism, tribalism, regionalism and gender discrimination' (*SLPP Manifesto*, 1996, 2).

The UNPP manifesto outlined several goals of the party. These included the promotion of national unity; the restoration of honesty, integrity and transparency to government; finding remedies for economic mismanagement; use of local resources to improve standards of living of the average Sierra Leonean; proper management of natural resources; assistance to victims of the war, and; reduction in unemployment and stabilization of the economy. On the issue of peace, the UNPP pledged to pursue 'every avenue ... with the help of external mediators, to replace the military option with a conciliatory approach to reach a peaceful settlement between all combatant groups' (UNPP, 1996a: 5). The party's reconciliatory approach was to be based on the offer of 'amnesty to all as the only way to achieve lasting peace' (UNPP, 1996a: 12). The UNPP also committed itself to the decentralization of local government, free primary education, the provision of safe drinking water and primary health care for all, food sufficiency and investment in agriculture.

The *smearfest* between supporters of the SLPP's Kabbah and the UNPP's Karefa-Smart injected a heavy dose of negative campaigning, based on *ad hominem* attacks, into the elections. In an effort to make age an issue, SLPP partisans maintained that the state will be forced to pay huge medical bills if Karefa-Smart was elected president. Some even went so far as to suggest that Karefa-Smart's pursuit of the presidency was fueled by his desire to have a state funeral. In an attempt to channel anti-RUF sentiments into votes against the UNPP, SLPP partisans tried to link the UNPP leader to the RUF. A false report that the UNPP leader had renounced his Sierra Leonean citizenship appeared in the SLPP newspaper (*Unity Now*, 27 November 1995, 5) and unflattering portrayals of Mrs. Karefa-Smart (an African-American) as an outsider unsympathetic to the concerns of the average Sierra Leonean counted as low blows in an SLPP campaign designed to elicit xenophobic reactions from voters.

UNPP supporters pulled no punches going after Kabbah as they sought to highlight the past misdeeds or alleged improprieties of the SLPP presidential candidate. A main focus of UNPP attacks on Kabbah was the report of the Beoku-Betts commission of Inquiry. This commission issued an opinion in 1967 that Kabbah 'lacks integrity ...which ... disqualifies him from holding any high office for which good character and integrity are prerequisites' (Beoku-Betts Report, 1967: 22). Based on this opinion, the APC government under Siaka Stevens confiscated some of Kabbah's assets but these were later returned after the legality of the government's action was questioned in court. By directing public attention to this aspect of Kabbah's record in the civil service, the UNPP sought to portray the SLPP presidential candidate as a corrupt former civil servant who lacked the 'character' and 'integrity' of his opponent, Karefa-Smart.

The politicization of religion by supporters of the SLPP's Kabbah and the PDP's Bangura introduced a potentially dangerous element into the campaign and electoral process. Supporters of Kabbah and Bangura openly called on voters to cast their ballots for their candidate because he shared their Islamic faith. This raw appeal to religion was most conspicuous during the run-off campaign for the presidency between Kabbah, a Muslim, and Karefa-Smart, a Christian. Although he was not known to use the Alhaji title before the elections, supporters of Kabbah suddenly began referring to their candidate as Alhaji Tejan Kabbah; he was also described by local and international media as a 'Muslim lawyer'. In a country where religion has never constituted a significant basis of social cleavage, SLPP efforts to politicize the faith of their presidential candidate obscured and distorted the choices of voters.

A few intimidating incidents prior to election day renewed doubts as to whether the election would in fact be held. On February 10, 1996, there were three grenade attacks in which the offices and residence of the INEC chairman were targeted as well as the residence of Tejan Kabbah. Although there were no casualties and physical damage was slight, the attacks were clearly aimed at derailing the elections by intimidating some of the key players in the process. But if the intention of the army and the RUF was to intimidate and scare voters away from polling stations, the grenade attacks, shootings and other acts of intimidation and violence backfired. People came out of their homes in droves as much to retire a loathed military dictatorship as to elect a new government.

Election results

The first round of voting for president and parliament took place on February 26 and 27. Originally scheduled for February 26, balloting had to be extended for another day due to numerous logistical problems. These problems included the transportation of ballot boxes to the provinces, the late delivery of voter registers to polling stations and the inability of the army to provide security in some areas. Queried about his government's failure to provide adequate security for the elections, the NPRC chairman responded by asking:

> What were we expected to do? Remove soldiers from the war front and send them to guard polling stations ...? Do we have the manpower, and in fact what do you think the reaction would have been had we sent soldiers to guard polling booths? (*West Africa*, March 11–17, 1996, 383)

Security problems prevented several chiefdoms from voting. In the north, no one voted at Mile 91 and the entire Tonkolili district. Eight chiefdoms in Kenema district did not vote and the only voting that took place in the entire district was in the district/provincial headquarter town of Kenema. Pujehun district and several areas of the south also recorded no voting activity. Despite isolated attempts to scare away voters, voting took place everywhere in the western area.

The SLPP's victory in both parliamentary and presidential election did not come as a surprise to many observers. In the parliamentary contest (see table 1), the SLPP captured 36.1 percent of the popular vote, compared to 21.6 percent for the UNPP and 15.3 percent for the PDP. By placing a strong third in both parliamentary and presidential elections, the PDP found itself in a position where it could influence the outcome of the presidential election by supporting one of the two candidates in the run-off. That the PDP chose to form an electoral alliance with the SLPP during the run-off campaign was one of the few surprises of these elections.

The results of the parliamentary elections showed a clear ethnoregional voting pattern (see table 2). The SLPP garnered the bulk of its popular vote from the south (44.3 percent) and east (31.4 percent), where it also captured 84.2 and 49.2 percent of the respective regional vote totals. In the west, the SLPP received 24.9 percent of the region's vote and the party's western vote as a percentage of its overall popular vote was 20.5 percent. As expected, the party did not do well in the north where it attracted only 4.6 percent of the regional vote and 3.7 percent of its overall popular vote.

Table 1: Results of Parliamentary Election

Party	Total Votes	% of Popular Vote	No. of Seats
SLPP	269,489	36.1	29
UNPP	161,618	21.6	18
PDP	114,409	15.3	12
APC	42,443	5.7	5
NUP	39,280	5.3	4
DCP	35,624	4.8	0
PPP	21,354	2.9	0
NDA	20,105	2.7	0
PNC	19,019	2.5	0
NUM	8,884	1.2	0
SDP	5,900	0.8	0
NADP	4,653	0.6	0
NPP	3,989	0.5	0
Totals	750,764	100.0	68

Like the SLPP, electoral support for the UNPP was regionally skewed. The UNPP received over half of its support from the north but fared poorly in the south and east. The party won 44.6 percent of the northern, 21.4 percent of the western, 9.4 percent of the eastern and 2.4 percent of the southern, vote. The regional distribution of the UNPP's popular vote were as follows: north (58.4 percent), west (29.4 percent), east (10 percent) and south (2.1 percent). This correlation between region and party support was also evident in the returns for the PDP. The PDP won 23 percent of the northern, 21.6 percent of the western, 6.1 percent of the eastern and 4.9 percent of the southern, vote. 42.5 percent of the PDP's overall popular vote came form the north, 42 percent from the west, 9.2 percent from the east and 6.1 percent from the south. Although the PDP and UNPP trailed the SLPP in terms of their respective share of the western vote, the western vote as a percentage of party vote totals was greater for the PDP (42.5 percent) and UNPP (29.4 percent) than for the SLPP (20.5 percent).

The APC, PPP and PNC also did relatively well in the north, compared to other regions. Although the APC lost two-thirds of the northern vote to the UNPP and PDP, it still managed to place third in the north, ahead of two of its breakaway reincarnations, the PPP and PNC. The APC received 8.6 percent

Table 2: Results of the parliamentary election by region

Party	Western Area	Eastern Province	Northern Province	Southern Province
SLPP	55,327	84,712	9,929	119,518
UNPP	47,516	16,223	94,453	3,426
PDP	48,076	10,575	48,677	7,081
APC	19,272	2,996	18,414	1,761
NUP	14,554	17,450	3,984	3,292
DCP	2,465	30,426	2,229	504
PPP	7,519	1,092	11,601	1,142
NDA	7,125	3,613	7,961	1,406
PNC	7,605	742	10,246	425
NUM	7,366	345	713	460
SDP	1,377	1,833	1,489	1,201
NADP	2,086	750	989	828
NPP	1,358	1,109	895	827
Totals	221,646	171,866	211,580	141,871

of the western, 8.7 percent of the northern, 1.7 percent of the eastern and 1.2 percent of the southern, vote. The regional breakdown of the APC's overall vote showed 45.4 percent came from the western area, 43.3 percent from the northern province, 7 percent from the east and 4.1 percent from the south. In a rather interesting development, more people voted for the APC in the western area than in the northern province and the party's overall total vote of 42,443 was less than the PDP's northern vote total of 48,677.

Votes for the PPP and PNC also came mainly from the north. The PPP's share of the northern regional vote was only 5.4 percent but the party's northern vote as a percentage of its overall vote total was 54.3 percent. The same pattern held for the PNC, another also-ran, 61 percent of whose votes came from the north. Desmond Luke's NUM received only 1.2 percent of the popular vote but 83 percent of this total comprised votes from the western area. The NUP attracted more votes in the east than the north and south combined; while the party's share of the eastern vote total was a respectable 10.1 percent, its eastern vote as a percentage of its overall vote total was 44.4 percent. Of the DCP's 4.8 percent share of the popular vote, 85.4 percent came from the east, where the party placed second to the SLPP in parliamentary balloting with 17.7 percent of the regional vote.

As a general rule, the parties that performed well in the south and east fared poorly in the north and vice-versa. Three parties (SLPP, UNPP, PDP) were competitive in two regions but only one party (SLPP) was competitive in three regions (western area, southern and eastern provinces). The SLPP received 75.7 percent of its share of the national vote total from the south and east while the UNPP and PDP respectively attracted 87.8 and 84.5 percent of theirs from the north and west. Comparatively, voting was more competitive in the western area than in the other three provinces; the south was the least competitive region, with 84.2 percent of its vote going to the SLPP. By contrast, no single party received more than 25 percent of the western area vote. Of the three major parties, the PDP was the most dependent on the western vote, with 42 percent of its popular vote coming from there.

The three major contenders in the presidential contest were Kabbah of the SLPP, Karefa-Smart of the UNPP and Bangura of the PDP. Kabbah emerged as the top vote-getter in the first round, followed by Karefa-Smart and Bangura (see table 3). Bundu of the PPP, Karimu of the NUP and Luke of the NUM cried foul and questioned the validity of the results. Bangura blamed what he described as his 'dismal performance in the north which is the bastion of my support' on 'rigging of the elections for the UNPP of ... Karefa-Smart by the northern province elections commissioner' (*Sierra Leone Progress*, August 1996, 4). International observers of the elections, however, uniformly concluded that the exercise was relatively free and fair.

Table 3: Results of the presidential election

Candidate	Party	Total Votes	Total Vote (%)
Kabbah	SLPP	267,279	35.8
Karefa-Smart	UNPP	171,603	22.19
Bangura	PDP	119,782	16.1
Karimu	NUP	39,617	5.3
Turay	APC	38,316	5.1
Koroma	DCP	36,779	4.9
Bundu	PPP	21,557	2.9
Jalloh	NDA	17,335	2.3
Kargbo	PNC	15,798	2.1
Luke	NUM	7,918	1.1
Lungay	SDP	5,202	0.7
Turay	NPP	3,925	0.5
Sillah	NADP	3,723	0.5
Totals		745,409	100.0

The regional breakdown of votes in the first round of the presidential election was almost identical to the parliamentary contest (see table 4). Kabbah received 83.7 percent of the southern, 51.1 percent of the eastern, 24.9 percent of the western and 4.1 percent of the northern, vote. With only 35.8 percent of the popular vote, the SLPP candidate placed first in three of the four regions of the country. Karefa-Smart was the top vote-getter in the northern province where he won 46.7 percent of the regional vote. He was second in the west with 22.1 percent, third in the east with 9.9 percent and fourth in the south with 2.3 percent, of the respective regional votes. If performance in the first round provided any clue as to the outcome of the run-off election, then Karefa-Smart's only hope of triumph was to clobber Kabbah in the north and win handily in the western area. Victory in the north and west could not, however, guarantee a Karefa-Smart presidency. For Karefa-Smart to win, he needed a decent showing in the south and east. Kabbah, by contrast, could win the presidency without significant northern support.

Table 4: Results of the presidential election by region

Party	Western Area	Eastern Province	Northern Province	Southern Province
Kabbah	55,615	82,858	8,706	119,714
Karefa-Smart	52,054	16,149	97,112	3,351
Bangura	50,385	1,095	50,930	7,372
Karimu	14,593	17,774	3,970	3,280
Turay	18,240	2,778	15,616	1,682
Koroma	2,035	32,089	2,099	547
Bundu	7,395	1,165	11,784	1,213
Jalloh	5,987	3,615	6,389	1,344
Kargbo	6,357	744	8,225	472
Luke	6,783	744	8,225	472
Lungay	827	1,987	799	1,589
Turay	1.512	610	878	723
Sillah	984	1,111	588	1,242

The result of the face-off between Kabbah and Karefa-Smart had the SLPP candidate once again trouncing his rival in three of the four regions of the country (see table 5). Kabbah's share of the popular vote exceeded the 55 percent required by the constitution to declare a winner in presidential elections. Kabbah won the presidency with 92 percent of the southern, 90 percent of the eastern, 54 percent of the western and 22 percent of the northern, vote. By contrast, Karefa-Smart polled 78 percent of the northern, 46 percent of the western, 10 percent of the eastern and 8 percent of the southern, vote. Where Kabbah was competitive in the north – he had more votes in the north (83,344) than his opponent's eastern and southern votes combined (45,815) – Karefa-Smart's presidential bid failed to gain traction in the south and east.

Table 5: Results of the presidential run-off by region

Candidate	Western Area	Eastern Province	Northern Province	Southern Province
Kabbah	84,635	232,084	83,344	209,462
Karefa-Smart	72,397	26,984	301,114	18,831

Voting data from the provinces suggested grave irregularities in the presidential run-off election. Official results showed a 38 percent increase in overall voter turnout, from 745,409 in the first round to 1,028,851 in the second round of the presidential election. In the northern province, voter turnout increased by 85.4 percent, from 207,507 in the first round to 384,458 in the second round. The east recorded a 59.7 percent increase in turnout (from 162,138 to 259,068) followed by the south with a 59.6 percent increase (from 142,988 to 228,293). Only the western area reported a sharp drop (29.5 percent) in voter turnout, from 222,767 to 157,032. Voter turn-out, based on initial computer printouts of results, was 345 percent in the Pujehun district, 155 percent in Bonthe district, 139 percent in Kailahun district, 117 percent in Kenema district and 90 percent in Bo district. Karefa-Smart's UNPP reacted to these irregularities by issuing a press statement in which it accused the SLPP of massive electoral fraud and chided INEC for accomplishing '...an impossible electoral feat that has eluded other countries like Australia where voting is compulsory by law'. The release went on to state that '...inspite of these glaring irregularities and flagrant violations of the electoral law by both INEC and the SLPP', the UNPP would 'overlook these violations and allow the transition process to move forward' (UNPP, 1996b).

Explaining the results

The SLPP won the 1996 presidential and parliamentary elections in Sierra Leone largely on the strength of its impregnable support base in two of the four regions of the country: the south and the east. Long considered the party's stronghold, there was hardly any doubt that the SLPP would sweep the south and east in these elections. The UNPP was also expected to carry the north but not by as large a margin as the SLPP's victory spread in the south and east. What remained uncertain going into the run-off was who would win the hotly contested western area and by how large a margin. The SLPP's Kabbah could defeat his opponent without carrying the west but the same could not be said for Karefa-Smart. By edging Karefa-Smart in the west, Kabbah more than assured himself of an easy victory.

SLPP victory in the presidential run-off was also aided by its alliance with the PDP, NUP, APC and DCP – four of the top six vote-getters in the first round balloting. The UNPP's electoral alliance, by contrast, featured parties (PPP, PNC, NUM, NADP) that failed to win a single seat in parliament. Thaimu Bangura of the PDP declared his support for the SLPP's Tejan Kabbah after reaching a deal with the SLPP leader that gave his party four cabinet positions, including the finance ministry. In explaining his decision to join forces with Kabbah, Bangura noted that

> Karefa did approach me but I told him I would not support him because he had made an about-face turn on an agreement we reached in London in 1994. When we met in London that year we agreed to work as a team for political power under the PDP *Sorbeh* which was already in existence. But when we parted company and he returned to the US, he formed the UNPP, thus aborting our plan. So how could I have supported him when he was responsible for my own downfall? (*Sierra Leone Progress*, August 1996, 4).

Bangura must have also realized that Kabbah stood a better chance of winning the presidency than Karefa-Smart, hence he chose to side with the odds-on-favourite to win the elections.

Ethnicity or, more broadly, ethnoregionalism was the single most important factor that determined the outcome of these elections. Kabbah could not have won as the presidential candidate of another party. His victory was due primarily to the fact that he was the standard bearer of the SLPP, the party most southerners and easterners identify as their own. People voted for the SLPP rather than for Kabbah; many SLPP die-hards in the south and east knew nothing about the man they were electing president – they simply voted for the *torkpoi* or palm tree (symbol of the SLPP). UNPP supporters, on the other hand, voted for Karefa-Smart the man rather than his party. If Kabbah won the presidency because of party support, the UNPP performed as well as it did on account of support for its founding leader. Voting for an individual

(Karefa-Smart), as opposed to voting for a party (SLPP), did not diminish the salience of ethnoregionalism. In the wake of the APC's demise, many northern politicians saw the UNPP as the only credible alternative to the SLPP. But the northern vote was too fragmented and political horse-trading involving northern elites enabled the SLPP to claim 22 percent of the northern vote in the presidential run-off.

If ethnoregional solidarities help explain voting behaviour in the 1996 elections, the same cannot be said for party alignments which were mainly driven by elite competition for access to public offices and resources. The predatory interests of political elites are at variance with the interests of their ethnoregional constituents even as voting by the latter helps reproduce the domination of these elites. Thus while ethnoregionalism is central to understanding voting patterns in the 1996 elections, they are less relevant to explaining electoral alliances among elites and political parties.

Compared to the last (1967) competitive multiparty elections in which six independent candidates were elected and four SLPP candidates returned un-opposed, there were no independent or unopposed candidacies in the 1996 elections. In both 1967 and 1996, party alignments were dictated less by ethnoregionalism than by intra-elite competition for power and material wealth. The 1996 elections benefited from the fact that there was no incumbent party to contend with, but the absence of an incumbent party did not diminish the sense in which the elections represented a referendum on the NPRC and APC. With the exception of the PDP and its leader, parties associated with these two governments attracted intense hostility and scorn from an enraged public.

Conclusion

What emerges from this discussion of Sierra Leone's 1996 elections is a recognition of the remarkable role played by civil society and the electoral commission in ensuring that the elections were not hijacked or postponed by a government reluctant to give up power. Set in motion by domestic popular forces, the elections replaced a military dictatorship with a popularly elected government. This also happened to be the first time in the country's history that a president was directly elected in competitive elections. Compared to the 1960s when pro-democratic forces were mostly led by professional organizations, the pro-democracy movement of the 1990s has been dominated by popular sectors – reflected, for example, in the leading role of petty traders, students, labourers, women and teachers in the transition to constitutional democratic rule. This popularization of societal democratic forces notwithstanding, maturation of the country's fragile democracy may depend less on the regularity of elections than on the alternation of power between parties and the capacity of elections to bring about genuine political change.

7

The 25 May Coup d'état in Sierra Leone: A Lumpen Revolt?

Lansana Gberie

Introduction

There had not been any apparent signs of trouble in Sierra Leone's capital, Freetown, before renegade soldiers struck on 25 May 1997. The civilian government of President Ahmed Tejan Kabbah, an ex-UN bureaucrat who came to power after four years of military rule in March 1996, had turned the economy around from a negative growth rate of minus 6.4 percent to a positive rate of 6 percent in just one year. Soon after taking office, Kabbah signed a peace agreement with the RUF, whose five-year campaign had devastated much of the country, killed at least 10,000 people (probably over 30,000 – mostly peasants), displaced about a third of the country's population of 4.5 million and wrecked the mineral-dependent economy. Investors and indigenous businessmen who had fled the country amidst the guerilla campaigns were returning, and many in the country concluded that the good times were not far away. International donors generally expressed satisfaction, and the IMF, the World Bank and bilateral donors allocated over half a billion US dollars for reconstruction and rehabilitation.

The first indication that there was renewed trouble was a breathless announcement on the state radio, the Sierra Leone Broadcasting Service, by an unknown soldier, Corporal Tamba Gborie, in the early morning of Sunday, 25 May stating that Kabbah had been overthrown and a 'dawn to dusk curfew' (his words) imposed. Much of what preceded this announcement became clearer only later. That morning about two dozen heavily armed soldiers in civilian clothing had driven up to the main penal centre, Pademba Road Prisons, in three pick-up trucks and blasted it open with grenades. They quickly released about 600 convicts, some of them the country's most notorious criminals, out of the prison and armed many of them with guns stolen from a military depot. These were then led to attack State House, the country's seat of power, where they battled a small detachment of Nigerian troops stationed there under a defence pact signed with the elected government, and overwhelmed them. The next target was the state radio station, and by the afternoon, President Kabbah was ferried out of the country to the neigbouring Guinea. The coupist declared him overthrown, and named Major Johnny Paul Koroma, freed in the prison break (he had been detained there following an earlier failed coup plot) leader of what they were pleased to call the Armed Forces Revolutionary Council (AFRC).

However, the real news of events of 25 May 1997 lay not in the overthrow of Tejan Kabbah. Accusing Kabbah of failing to consolidate the peace with the RUF, the AFRC immediately invited the rural-based rebels to the capital and announced that they were part of the new junta. Without apparent hesitation, the ragtag rebels poured into the seaside capital and took strategic positions in the city. The two forces, now described as the 'People's Army', declared the rebel war over and Koroma exorted Sierra Leoneans to rally to his junta as they had brought peace at last. He declared the RUF leader, Foday Sankoh, who was in detention in Nigeria at the time, as the Vice Chairman of the AFRC – in short the deputy leader of the country.

In fact, the coup was believed to have been planned and executed with the active collaboration of the rebel army (*For Di People*, May 1997), and appears to be the culmination of a long period of collusion between a significant portion of the Republic of Sierra Leone's Military Forces (RSLMF) and the RUF rebels. This bewildering collaboration had given rise to the phenomenon known as *sobels* (soldiers by day and rebels by night). After over six years of unsuccessfully fighting a brutal war to capture state power, the RUF rebels simply 'marched proudly and jubilantly', into the capital, as Major Koroma himself put it, and took what amounted to full control of everything, including the lives of residents. Their appearance triggered a mass refugee movement from the capital to neighbouring states: Guinea, Liberia and the Gambia. More people, about 400,000, left Sierra Leone as a result of the 25 May coup than during any other period in the war.

How can these momentous events, which have aborted a hopeful one year experiment in democratic rule, be explained? Why did the military coup d'etat occur and why was it so violent and difficult to stabilise? Why did the army, which had fought the RUF during the past six years, invite the rebel group to join them in their struggle against the lawfully constituted government? What is the social character of the individuals who made the coup? Is the coup a conventional uprising of disgruntled low ranking military officers, or does it represent a much wider phenomenon of the assault on the state by armed groups who share common values and aspirations with underclass or lumpen element in society? What has been the reaction of Sierra

Leoneans, the regional community of West African states, and the world, to the military coup?

Like the RUF like the Army?

If the coup itself shocked a world which for sometime marvelled at the recovery of a country long dismissed as a hopeless basket case ('beyond salvage', was how Robert Kaplan described Sierra Leone in 1994), the AFRC's public pronouncements have been no less devastating. In its 17 July 1997 'Position Paper' on negotiations spearheaded by ECOWAS with the aim of cajoling them out of power, Major Koroma declared that the RUF and the RSLMF share 'a combination of experience, talent and patriotism that cannot be questioned' (AFRC 1997a). That such a statement could be so openly made after six years of seemingly vicious war between the two forces reflected, perhaps, the naiveté of the AFRC leadership in assuming that they were also stating what many Sierra Leoneans had known all along: that a significant component of the RSLMF was colluding in the acts of banditry and terror perpetuated against civilians by the rebels (See Abraham, this volume).

Sierra Leone's rebel war began in March 1991 after armed incursions by a group of Sierra Leoneans backed by the Liberian warlord, Charles Taylor and Burkinabe mercenaries. In six years, the war engulfed the country with a destructive force, leading to the almost total destruction of the country. By March 1996, an estimated 75 percent of school-aged children were out of school, and 70 percent of the country's educational facilities, already troubled by the time the war began, destroyed. Only 16 percent of Sierra Leone's 500 health centers were functioning by March 1996, almost all of these in the capital and its suburbs (Smillie 1996).

The war, however, was deemed to have been over in late 1993 after the NPRC junta, expending over 18 million US dollars on arming and retraining the RSLMF and other allied forces (the irregulars, mostly local hunters), captured all strategic positions held by the RUF, including their 'headquarters', Pendumbu, and devastated the rebel force itself. Eye witnesses spoke of seeing a convoy of rebel vehicles heading towards Liberia (Richards, 1996) and rumors, published as news by the nation's lively tabloids, freely circulated that the RUF leader himself had been shot. But to the surprise of many, the war escalated in early 1994. By February, the rebels were threatening the capital. Many explanations have been offered for this sudden turn of events, but the real problem seems to have been that a significant portion of the NPRC's rather bloated army, fearing demobilization after the war, simply decamped and drifted to the countryside to engage in freelance banditry, with some actually joining the RUF. Those who did not join actively cooperated with the rebels to create a state of chaos in which they thrived, while still maintaining their membership of the RSLMF. In a shocking admission in late 1994, the NPRC declared that at least 20 percent of its 14,000 strong army was disloyal. Captain Valentine Strasser, the NPRC leader, characterised the sudden escalation of the war as 'nothing short of banditry, looting, maiming and raping'. He warned the public against 'harbouring a soldier who does not possess his authentic document...stringent action will be taken against all civilians found in possession of military uniforms and equipment' (*Vision*, October 1994). A local newspaper, echoing the same sentiments, described the conflict as 'naked banditry, the principal characters being undisciplined soldiers and unpatriotic Sierra Leoneans' (*Unity Now*, November 1994).

Koroma himself appears to have been at the centre of the *sobel* phenomenon. Reputed to have been a delinquent even in high school, Koroma joined the army in the early 1990s and quickly rose through the ranks due to his connections with first the APC, and then, the NPRC leadership, which ruled the country from 1992 to 1996. As head of a detachment of troops stationed at the Sierra Rutile mining company, Sierra Leone's last economic stronghold at the time (1995), he was widely believed to have connived with the rebel leadership to take over the mines and loot the company's property. The mines were thoroughly looted and vandalized. Eyewitnesses reported seeing soldiers in the looting, and some of the company's equipments were later found with soldiers in Freetown. Koroma was subsequently withdrawn from the war-front.

The aftermath of the AFRC coup followed a pattern of 'conquest' long established by the RUF. Looting and apparently aimless destruction of property, raping of women and general vandalism, were the order of the day during the first week of the coup. Over 100 people were reported killed, and the National Treasury, parts of the Bank of Sierra Leone and other important public buildings were burned down. Freetown's cynical residents speculated that the burning of the National Treasury, which held accounts and documents relating to the running of the state's finances, might have been instigated by elements within the military related to civil servants who were then being probed for embezzlement by the Kabbah administration. But the arson sent home a more significant message: formal bureaucratic state structures, particularly those representing accountabililty, were no longer to be part of the scheme of things in the country. The troubled formal state in Sierra Leone had reached the stage which Ali Mazrui would describe as 'normative collapse' (Mazrui, 1996).

It wasn't just that there was a rebellion or a violent and bloody usurpation of power (the bloodiest in the country's history). The formal state structures, authority, not to mention law and political order, had collapsed. After the burning of the Treasury and Central Bank, Major Koroma told the BBC

African Service that his men had not done it intentionally and that they would be rebuilt – a statement which sounded hollow in view of the violent orgy of looting of homes, offices and shops which continued almost unabated during the first six weeks. The junta announced the setting up of anti-looting squads which carried out summary executions of would-be looters, mostly civilian vagrants who had joined the soldiers in the carnage. The move seemed to have had some success insofar as there was hardly anywhere else to loot in the affluent parts of the capital. Even vehicles belonging to foreign embassies, aid agencies and the United Nations had been looted and wrecked. All the main supermarkets and shops had been vandalized. Despite the creation of the anti-looting squads – some of whose members were suspected of complicity in the looting itself – general lawlessness at night, including armed robbery and rape, continued. Some of the looting operations have been dubbed by those who commit them as 'Operation Pay Yourself' – obviously reflecting the financial problems which both the AFRC and the RUF faced in honouring a writ at all, except that they controlled the radio stations, which broadcast daily proclamations from Koroma and his spokespersons (about four in the first month of the coup), and the key military barracks.

There hardly was any control even among the coup leaders. The unlikely coalition of RUF rebels and the RSLMF forces which constituted the AFRC and the so-called People's Army appeared to be particularly prone to instability. In the first weeks of the coup, several clashes were reported between the two forces at the military headquarters (seat of the junta), including at least one gunfight (*Washington Post*, 1997).

Militariat or lumpens?

Steve Riley has attributed the general mayhem which accompanied the takeover to the fact that the coup was the product of the 'militariat' – a social group of relatively junior officers and 'other ranks' in the army, who lack the clientilist ties of more senior officers and are therefore 'prone to institutional instability and some orchestrated political violence' (Riley, 1977). Certainly the take-over was led by junior officers (it was announced by Corporal Gborie), who then initially proceeded to arrest the senior officers. But the ruling council was dominated by brigadiers, colonels and other officers, although the real power brokers seemed to have been army rank and file individuals like Gborie and Zagalo. A large number of junior rank soldiers and rebels were given posts in the Supreme Military Council. If the unnamed position for civilian participation in this council are excluded, the lower rank sergeants, staff sergeants, privates, corporals and lance corporals accounted for 17 of the 22 positions occupied by the military – an unprecedented development in the history of military rule in the country and probably in Africa and the world

(AFRC 1997b). But the chairman himself was a major, hardly a junior rank soldier.

Why is it that the AFRC, in contrast to all the 'militariat' types of junta cited by Riley, has so far failed to establish any sense of order among its men? Six months after the military coup of May 25, the leadership was still complaining about general acts of lawnessness and anarchy perpetrated by its own members and supporters, which, it said, 'was inconsistent with state stability' (Sierra Leone Web page, News section, 19 November 1997). It is certainly not just that opposition to the coup, particularly the armed opposition by the Nigerian-led ECOMOG force, did not allow the AFRC to consolidate. Indeed, much of the opposition was sustained because of the wanton destruction and terroristic behaviour of the junta. The fact is that the convention of military life, never mind discipline, had collapsed because the people who dominate the so-called People's Army – and therefore control the AFRC – are from a social category which, irrespective of their colours, remain criminally disposed and undisciplined. The are the 'lumpenproletariat' of Sierra Leone society.

The case for a class-based or 'lumpen' perspective on the origin and character of the crisis in Sierra Leone has been most persuasively argued by Ibrahim Abdullah (this volume). Abdullah believes that the violence in the country has been peculiarly brutal and directionless because the people who constitute the insurgent forces and the army are mostly socially uprooted and criminally disposed youths who, because of their very nature, lack a progressive and transformative agenda. They are the lumpenproletariat who Marx and Engels described as 'the dangerous class', 'the social scum...that passively rotten mass thrown off by the old layers, may here and there be swept into the movement by a proletarian revolution, its condition of life, however, prepares it far more for the part of a bribed tool of reactionary intrigue' (Marx and Engels 1848). In short, they are incapable of any revolutionary action, much less revolutionary discipline.

The pre-war RSLMF was about 1,500 strong, and was largely made up of nominees of APC party's fat cats who were recruited into the force by a patronage system designed by ex-President Siaka Stevens to ensure that the army remained loyal to the regime. This force, however, proved woefully inadequate to meet the challenge posed by the rebel incursions in 1991, and President Momoh, Steven's successor, was forced to expand the force to about 6,000. Recruits were never properly screened, and Momoh's expanded army happened to consist, as his Foreign Minister, Abdul Karim Koroma, himself admitted, of 'mostly drifters, rural and urban unemployed, a fair number of hooligans, drug addicts and thieves' (Koroma, 1996) – in short, lumpens to the core. They turned out to be little more than a uniformed rabble which easily found more profit colluding with the RUF – an even more criminally-disposed group of lumpens, mostly recruited in Liberia, and in the illicit diamond-mining areas of eastern and southern Sierra Leone.

The army ballooned under the NPRC, which was also dominated by young men, some of whom were products of the rebellious youth culture in the city of Freetown, into a force of about 14,000. The result was that the element of command and cohesion, the hallmarks of military life, became increasingly alien to the RSLMF. Marx's analysis of lumpen capabilities is inadequate in the sense that in at least the Sierra Leone case, the Lumpens had taken action all on their own, without apparently being the 'bribed tool of reactionary intrigue'. Now free from the control of civil society and the state, these armed lumpens have conveniently jettisoned the conventions and restraints of military life, and even its symbols. It was perhaps the first example in Africa of street power taking over the state. At the junta's headquarters, AFRC members move around without their uniforms. Indeed, unlike all military coups in history, this one was made by soldiers who were clad in civvies – and was crucially aided by common criminals who were serving jail sentences. That certainly goes above what could reasonably be seen as a tactical alliance. Major Koroma himself appeared in public, and gave interviews to the international media, sporting denim jeans and trade mark T-shirts. He even drove through the capital once in a stolen UN vehicle, clad in a University of Maryland T-shirt and jeans. RUF members in the AFRC reportedly tore off ranks from the uniforms of RSLMF members who attended a meeting of the council in May. Actions like these go above evidence of institutional instability: there were no institutions to speak of. Things had simply fallen apart.

Evidence of an anti-state take-over could also be seen in the targeting of judges and magistrates, and even the Supreme Court building itself, which was reported to have been torched in the wake of the coup. Many judges and magistrates had to flee the country, as criminals they had convicted took the advantage of their new found freedom to loot their homes and physically assault them. The country's judicial system grounded to halt. It was to remain so for the next nine months of unlimited terror.

AFRC's justification for the coup

In his fist public statement after the coup, Koroma declared that the military had to overthrow the Kabbah Government because his brand of ethnic-based politics had polarized the country into regional and ethnic factions, and that his democracy was flawed. Quite how this was so was not made clear, but the AFRC leader's insistence that Kabbah had given greater privileges to the southeastern-based militia, the *Kamajor*, than that accorded the army, and that this had caused ethnic tensions, reflected a strong sense of resentment not just among the ranks of the RSLMF but increasingly among the country's opposition politicians, most of them hailing from the Northern province.

The *Kamajor*, who then numbered roughly about 37,000, was composed of Mende youths from the Southern and Eastern provinces, areas that were hardest hit by the rebel war, who organized to battle the RUF and the army as a result of the latter's failure to contain the rebel menace or protect them (Muana, 1997). Knowledge of the terrain and high motivation, which compensated for the lack of adequate training and equipment, helped the militia to dislodge the RUF from key areas in the Southern and Eastern provinces and forced them to sign the Abidjan Peace Accord in November 1996. But engaging the RUF had also meant that the *Kamajor* would confront RSLMF members who were colluding with the RUF; the so-called sobels. Prior to the coup, there were many serious clashes between the *Kamajor* and the soldiers, in some cases leading to loss of lives on both sides. The government of Tejan Kabbah even established a commission of enquiry made up of very prominent personalities from a cross section of society, headed by Bishop Keili, to examine the causes of these clashes, which threatened the stability of his government and the security of the country. Koroma charged that his take-over of government removed Sierra Leone 'from the brink of a calamity that (was) too horrendous to contemplate'. The coup, therefore, was 'not actuated by lust for power, nor motivated by malice or a desire to bring untold suffering on the people and Sierra Leone' (Radio Broadcast, 27 May 1997).

One of the junta's earliest radio announcements proclaimed: 'No more *Kamajor* no more civil defence groups. We are the national army. We have to fight for this country'. The junta claimed that Kabbah gave 35 billion leones per month to the *Kamajor* and praised their efforts while the army received only 2 to 3 billion leones per month. This charge is of course false: the *Kamajor* were a volunteer force without pay, and although they were praised for their efforts at combating the rebel menace, they received little logistical support from the government. The soldiers appeared to have been spurred into action mainly by Kabbah's attempt to halve the bloated but evidently incompetent army (reputedly 14,000 strong) partly to accommodate some of the RUF's fighting force (about 5,000 strong) to meet the demands of the Abidjan Peace accord and to transform the army into a professional institution with help from Britian. Koroma and his men understood this move to mean that the army was being 'deliberately and calculatedly marginalized and disadvantaged', citing as evidence the 'drastic reduction in their rations, lack of adequate housing, arbitrary discharge of soldiers and retirement of officers from the army, without availing them of earned entitlements'. They were also very critical of the then Deputy Minister of defence, Samuel Hinga Norma, who allegedly played a leading role in the formation and military activities of the *kamajor* before the Kabbah government came to power in March 1996. He was accused of being partisan in his treatment of the recurring conflicts between the army and the *kamajor*.

The charges are, of course, largely inaccurate, and even if true, might have acted merely as an added incentive for the coup. Most of the soldiers who led the coup were linked to the defunct NPRC, which reluctantly handed over power to Kabbah in March 1996. Koroma himself belonged to the 'NPRC Camp' and owes his rise in the army almost entirely to his connections with senior NPRC officers. Captain Paul Thomas, a spokesperson for the junta, who Riley erroneously claimed is a Krio from Freetown (he is Mende from Njala Komborya), was an aid to Colonel Tom Nyuma, the NPRC's Defence Minister. Gborie was a bodyguard to one other NPRC officer. The first coup broadcast called for the return to the country of two ex-senior NPRC officers, Brigadier Maada Bio, who handed over to Kabbah, and Solomon Musa, a flamboyant former deputy chairman of the NPRC who was dismissed and then sent to study in the UK by Captain Valentine Strasser, the NPRC's first chairman. Musa returned to join the AFRC, and was immediately appointed Chief Secretary of State (in effect Prime Minister). Bio declined the offer to join, but credible speculations place his elder brother, Steven Bio, a wealthy businessman who made his money almost exclusively as an arms contractor for the NPRC, as the main mastermind of the coup. He is believed to have forged the alliance between the soldiers and the RUF leadership while in exile in Abidjan after the first Koroma coup plot that was foiled, which finally gave birth to the AFRC takeover. The AFRC was seen by many to be only a cruder replay of NPRC rule.

There are reasons to believe that the army rank and file were extremely concerned about the imminent demobilization exercise. Ruth First has argued that the military always intervene to seize power when their corporate interest(s) are/is threatened (First, 1965). A survey conducted on the eve of the coup provides a fascinating and highly illuminating glimpse about the army's collective reaction to the impending retirement exercise (Kandeh and Pemagbi, 1997). The report found that the overwhelmingly male (98.1 percent) and young (nearly 60 percent was less than 30 years old) army was predominantly composed of secondary school drop-outs and about 30 percent illiterate, that is, never went to school. Less than 2 percent were university graduates or were medical doctors, lawyers or engineers. Over 60 percent had served for less than six years, which meant that they joined the army in 1991 when the war started. Only 2.9 percent, mainly the old and disabled, indicated that they would want to be demobilised. The rest were hostile to the idea of demobilization mainly because they will be cut off from the free facilities –

free electricity, medical services, accommodation, water, and subsidised rice – they enjoyed as service members. The real problem was that with limited skills and education, the soldiers felt that they would not be able to adjust to normal, wage-earning civilian life.

Bob Kandeh, co-author of the report, disclosed how difficult it was to even carry out the research. Every step had to be approved by Defence Headquarter which had insisted that only soldiers should be part of the entire survey team:

> In co-ordinating the survey, I always found it quite delicate...as the (army) was really an unwilling partner in the exercise...The survey team reported that selected interviewees openly wept as they interpreted their selection into the sample as the first step to their demobilization. Some even professed for insubordination...both officers and private voiced out their bitterness about the demobilization exercise and even hinted that armed robberies etc. would be on the increase if such a large number of personnel suddenly lost the benefits they were used to, however meagre (Ibid).

There can be little doubt that fear of demobilization was a very strong factor leading to the coup, a fear that came close to reality, when President Kabbah, in an incredibly impolitic move, announced that his government would be cutting down on the subsidised rice for the army in a wave of general economic adjustment. Indeed, Kandeh reports that there was an increase in overt insubordination after the demobilization process was announced. There was the case of a group of soldiers leaving for the war-front to engage the RUF, only to disembark at some point with the comment that President Kabbah should select those he was going to retain in his restructured army and deploy them to go fight the RUF. Such insubordination, which was very common and involved attacks against loyal units and the Civil Defence Force (CDF), was only possible because the basic element of command and cohesion had long ceased to exist. The imagined consequences of the demobilization exercise and the collective belief that the CDF were being favoured by the regime touched on the corporate interest of the army. It is not inconceivable that a section of the army, if not the whole army, acted to defend those interests.

Political party reactions to the coup

The coup was condemned universally both at home and abroad, and a massive nationwide effort was almost spontaneously launched to overturn it. The *Kamajor* was the first to vow armed resistance to the AFRC, but the vast majority of ordinary Sierra Leoneans showed opposition to the coup by simply staying at home and refusing to go to work even after repeated threats of dismissal by the junta. Out of this nationwide passive resistance soon sprang the Movement for the Restoration of Democracy (MRD), incorporating almost all the pressure groups and civil organizations plus the local militia – the *Kamajor* and the northern-based *Kapra*, another anti-RUF militia group –

in the country. The local militia constituted the MRD's armed wing, known as the CDF.

Resistance to the AFRC at first seemed to be undermined by the fragmentation of the country along political party/regional lines. The SLPP to which Kabbah belonged, and which drew its support from the Southern and Eastern Provinces, almost immediately condemned the coup. Condemnation of the coup was unanimous in the eastern and southern provinces, with a spontaneous mass demonstration against it in the southern city of Bo, in which soldiers were physically attacked. Parties allied to the SLPP, like the PDP, whose leader, Thaimu Bangura, was Kabbah's Finance Minister, although northern-based, also condemned the coup. Following Kabbah, most of the leaders of these two parties fled into exile in Guinea.

But many members of the UNPP, a largely northern-based party whose leader, John Karefa-Smart, lost the run-off presidential elections to Kabbah, increasingly aligned with the coup makers. The UNPP itself had split into two factions a few months before the coup: 14 out of 17 members of the parliamentary wing had been expelled from the party by Karefa-Smart; these members refused, however, to vacate their parliamentary seats, and colluded with other parties in parliament to frustrate the actions of Karefa-Smart, who was later suspended from parliament for one year. Some members of the parliamentary wing did not, at least initially, follow Karefa-Smart's seemingly pro-junta actions. They joined other parliamentarians in passing a resolution which called for the reinstatement of the country's legitimate government and parliament. In contrast, Karefa-Smart became an envoy of the junta in its diplomatic efforts to frustrate the intervention of the Nigerian-led force in Sierra Leone. He was also one of the junta's delegates in the early rounds of the regional West African meetings to resolve the crisis. After his relations with the junta became strained, he put forward a position paper, which called for a national conference of representatives from all the political actors, ethnic groups and civic organizations, the release of the RUF leader, Foday Sankoh, and the creation of a public service that would reflect the ethnic character of the country (Karefa-Smart, 1997). He also continued to campaign against the ECOMOG intervention in the country. Members of Karefa-Smart's wing of the party allied themselves with, and enjoyed the protection of, the junta. The same is true of the Peoples Progressive Party (PPP) leader, Abass Bundu, who was also a delegate of the junta in the regional peace meetings. Bundu wrote a number of articles questioning the intervention of ECOMOG in Sierra Leone and calling for a national conference of all 'stakeholders' to resolve the crisis. Most members of the APC also supported the junta, with some, like Osho Williams, accepting to serve as ministers.

The alacrity with which these parties rallied to the AFRC helped reinforce the perception that this was a 'northern affair'. But this impression was more apparent than real for with the exception of Karefa-Smart, who was clearly actuated by sheer opportunism, none of these politicians could be said to have significant support from any part of the country. Bundu got less than 3 percent of the popular votes in the elections that brought Kabbah to power, but his animus against the elected president seemed to have derived from the fact that he was disgraced by the Kabbah administration for fraudulently selling Sierra Leone's passports to dubious foreign businessmen. A court case against him was withdrawn by the Attorney General, Solomon Berewa, after he had paid half of the US$200,000 he was reported to have received from East Asian businessmen for the sale of the passports (Government of Sierra Leone, 1997). And the APC could only manage about 5 percent of the votes in both the presidential and parliamentary elections(See Kandeh this volume).

The AFRC attracted mostly frustrated politicians, civil servants, and business individuals from all parts of the country who felt marginalized under the civilian administration. Joe Amara Bangalie, the junta's 'Finance Minister' is a Mende from the south who was one of the APC politicians disgraced by the NPRC and who had since been politically marginalized. Solomon Musa, the 'Chief Secretary of State' and 'Minister of Mines', is also a Mende from the south who was also disgraced by his collegues in the NPRC. Pallo Bangura, a Temne/Limba from the north, who is the junta's 'Foreign Minister', was dismissed as Sierra Leone's permanent representative at the United Nations (a job he got from the NPRC), and replaced by James Jonah when the Kabbah government came to power. Bangura's attitude to the elected government had been, therefore, understandably hostile.

If such conflicting and opportunistic interests tended to initially polarize the country in the wake of the coup and undermine resistance to it, it was the prominent role which was perceived to be played by another frustrated (northern) politician, ex-president Joseph Saidu Momoh, whose APC government was overthrown by the NPRC in 1992, that helped unify the nation. Momoh, whose government was unpopular across the country, is an uncle of the AFRC leader. Strategic meetings of the junta were reportedly held at Momoh's residence, and the ex-president was provided a huge security force and staff. The AFRC's Chief of Staff, Colonel Samuel Sesay, elder brother of the chairman, was drafted into the army by Momoh. The prominence of this so-called 'Binkolo Cabal' (they are Limbas from Binkolo, a small northern town) helped crystallize the nationwide opposition to the AFRC. This was exemplified by a letter to the Nigerian Head of State, General Sani Abacha, signed by all the traditional heads from different ethnic groups in Freetown and other civic organizations calling for an armed intervention to overturn the coup in August and prevent the APC from coming back to power (Community Leaders, 1997). The Limba Chief was the only chief in Freetown who did not sign the document. A highly effective radio station, FM 98, installed by the ousted government in ECOMOG-controlled Lungi, also helped to solidify opposition throughout the country against 'the common enemy', the so-called People's Army or the AFRC/RUF and their collaborators.

Dynamics of popular resistance and regime terror

On 25 June, the AFRC announced that it had foiled a coup plot and proceeded to arrest and detain a number of senior officers, including Colonel Tom Carew, a northerner, and other prominent officers who originated from all regions of the country. Prominent politicians linked to the SLPP, including Sama Banya, Elizabeth Lavalie (the country most prominent female parliamentarian) and Abu Aiah Koroma, Kabbah's Minister of Presidential Affairs, were also arrested and detained. They were all released without charge about a month later. But the junta launched a vicious offensive against towns and villages they believe to be habouring *Kamajors*. Moyamba town in the south of the country was attacked in June and sacked. About a hundred people were reported killed by the AFRC forces. On 28 June, AFRC forces struck parts of Bo district, killing 25 people and razing to the ground Telu, headquarters town of Jaiama Bongor chiefdom. This was the chiefdom in which Samuel Hinga Norman, Kabbah's Deputy Minister for Defence and leader of the *Kamajor* movement, was regent chief. They also cold-bloodedly murdered octogenarian Paramount Chief, Sami Demby, uncle of Kabbah's Vice-President, Albert Joe Demby.

The attack on press freedom and the political rights of vocal Sierra Leoneans was unprecedented. Incidentally, although the AFRC claimed in its first post-coup broadcast that the Kabbah government's assault on press freedom, particularly the passing of the widely condemned Newspaper act (which was bound to restrict press freedom if signed into law), was one of the reasons for the take-over of the government, the junta clamped down on journalists in a way that was inconceivable under previous regimes. Soldiers beat up, detained, tortured and intimidated journalists opposed to the coup, and in some cases, their offices were ransacked and their cars confiscated. In the event, only six of the 52 newspapers in circulation before the coup remained on the streets. Two leading independent papers, *Vision* and *The Standard Times*, in announcing their suspension of publication in August, cited the AFRC's hostile attitude towards the press in general and their editors in particular, for their decision to close down.

The AFRC remained a pariah junta, shunned by every government in the world. Sierra Leoneans in the diaspora also condemned the coup. About a week after the take-over, 1,500 Sierra Leoneans demonstrated in Washington DC against the AFRC and called for United States' military intervention to overturn it. Through the Sierra Leone discussion group, Leonenet, some formed the Citizens for the Restoration of Democracy and quickly dispatched a letter to the UN Secretary General supporting the efforts of ECOWAS to overturn the take-over. Many of these agitations were launched in North America, largely as a result of the inspiration provided by John Leigh, Kabbah's ambassador to the US, and James Jonah, the country's permanent representative at the UN.

Internal opposition to the coup took a dramatic turn in August after members of the National Union of Sierra Leone Students (NUSS) announced a massive demonstration against the AFRC in Freetown and other parts of the country. The plan received the support of the Labour Congress, the Sierra Leone Association of Journalists (SLAJ), the Women's Movement and other civic organizations. But it was ruthlessly crushed in Freetown on Monday, 18 August by the rebel soldiers who attacked just about everyone on the streets with machetes, sticks and even live bullets. At least two students were killed at the Nursing Home, in the city centre, and another murdered in his room in one of the students' hostels when the rebels invaded the Fourah Bay College Campus. About 80 people were arrested and detained. In Bo, the country's second largest city, about 100 people who turned up for the demonstration were dispersed by units of the rebel army who attacked them with tear gas. Live bullets were also fired in the air to scare others away from the streets. At Lungi, however, where the AFRC has no presence, the demonstration went on without incident, with hundreds turning up to cry down the junta and demand the restitution of the elected government.

Naked savagery won the day in the capital but the point was clearly made: 'the brutal action of the Council in killing, wounding and maiming pro-democrats is an affront not to the people of this country but to the whole world' (*Standard Times*, 22 August 1997). The paper went on to note that '…the nation, particularly the students, had nonetheless succeeded in letting their voice heard, that they have not and will not tolerate the leadership of the junta no matter what resistance they would face' (Ibid).

In spite of this overwhelming national opposition to the coup, the international media continued to portray the crisis in Sierra Leone mainly as a stand-off between the junta and the Nigerian-led ECOMOG. The caption of one article on the coup in the *US News and World Report* (16 June 1997) simply read 'Non-democrats to the Rescue', and concentrated exclusively on Nigeria's role in trying to reverse the take-over and raising the tiresome moral issue of a military dictatorship fighting to restore democracy in another country while continuing to keep their own elected president in detention. Not surprisingly, supporters of the junta are harping on the same theme. In a letter to the UN secretary General calling for a halt on Nigeria's 'aggression' against the AFRC regime, Abbas Bundu, a former Secretary General of ECOWAS who lost to Kabbah in the electoral race for the presidency, raised the same point about the Nigerians and declared Nigeria's military actions as 'totally unwarranted and unjustified' (*Christian Science Monitor*, 1997). The ECOMOG factor has been significant in the anti-junta movement, but this has to be placed within the context of the wide-ranging forms of resistance that Sierra Leoneans have shown at various levels to undo the military coup.

ECOMOG's intervention and international pressures

Armed resistance to the coup from the Nigerian-led ECOMOG force in Freetown was sustained, albeit limited, and carried out within the context of an international and regional sanctions regime, which did not explicitly endorse the use of force to enforce the embargo and weaken the resolve of the junta. Immediately after the coup was announced, the Nigerians, who were overwhelmed by the rebellious soldiers on the day of the take-over, quickly reinforced their positions in the capital. By 31 May, there were 3,000 Nigerian troops in Freetown and about 1,500 Guinean soldiers. Ghana also sent a small detachment of troops but insisted on a negotiated settlement. By early July, after the failure of talks brokered by prominent Sierra Leoneans, Nigerian military officials and Western governments, aimed at providing a safe passage for the coupists and reinstalling the elected government, the Nigerians were prepared to strike. But the operation, code named Wild Chase, was botched after John Karefa-Smart, who was privy to the plans as a result of his earlier role in attempting to get the junta to step down, announced to the public the Nigerians' intentions. In the event, the junta and its rebel allies struck first, overwhelming the Nigerian forces that were thinly spread across the capital. The Nigerians responded by using their gunboats to attack the junta's military headquarters from the sea and in the ensuing confusion, the junta carried out air-strikes against civilian targets and claimed that the Nigerians were responsible. Over 60 people were reported killed as a result of this exchange.

The UN and OAU condemned the coup and gave support to the regional organization, ECOWAS, to reverse it. The Commonwealth, describing the coup as 'a setback for the continent of Africa as a whole', suspended Sierra Leone pending a re-establishment of constitutional rule. The European Union suspended development aid, and all foreign missions hastily vacated the chaotic capital. The US, Britain and France quickly airlifted their nationals and other foreigners from the country. ECOWAS foreign ministers met in Conakry on 27 June and agreed to pursue a three-pronged strategy, which was highlighted in a 14-point communiqué: 'dialogue, economic sanctions and an embargo, as well as a recourse to force' as a last resort. It added that 'in order to increase the effectiveness of the above measures, the minister... recommended prior consultations among member states at the highest level' (The Ministers of Foreign Affairs, 1997). The communiqué stressed that no country should recognize the junta, and called on the international community to support the ECOWAS initiatives and to provide humanitarian assistance to Guinea and other countries affected by the flood of Sierra Leonean refugees.

A four-nation committee comprising of the foreign ministers of Nigeria, Ghana, Côte d'Ivoire and Guinea, as well as the Secretary General of the Organisation for African Unity, Salim Salim, was appointed to dialogue with the junta and to report back to the chairman of ECOWAS, General Sani Abacha, after two weeks. Of the two West African countries involved in the crisis, Ghana and Côte d'Ivoire took a more cautious approach – they pleaded for dialogue as opposed to the outright use of force to overturn the coup. Nigeria took a much tougher stand, arguing the case for urgent and rapid intervention to prevent the situation from further deteriorating and endangering other countries in the region. The OAU's Secretary General was in favour of 'any method that would restore the legitimate government in Sierra Leone'. The junta rejected the ECOWAS communiqué and, in a concerted effort to frustrate the plans of ECOWAS, sent emissaries to countries that were felt to be less belligerent to plead their case and ask for support.

Upon the advice of Ghana's President Jerry Rawlings and Côte d'Ivoire's Konan Bedie, ECOWAS, initiated negotiations with the AFRC in July to effect a peaceful resolution of the crisis in which Kabbah would be restored to power and some of the grievance of the soldiers addressed. Ghana's Deputy Minister of Foreign Affairs, Victor Gbeho, visited Freetown as part of the efforts to engage the junta. His reported statement that the situation in Freetown was peaceful and that the international community was being fed with misinformation about acts of lawlessness and mass killings, provoked strong rebuttal from the ousted government and Sierra Leoneans at large. Further diplomatic discussions and pressures led to a meeting in Abidjan on 17 and 18 July between the ECOWAS Committee of Four and the Freetown junta. A joint communiqué called for the implementation of an immediate cease-fire and 'the early restoration of constitutional order, consistent with the objectives of ECOWAS as spelled out in paragraph 4 (1)' of the communiqué. This paragraph called for 'the early restoration of the legitimate government of President Tejan Kabbah'. The junta's delegation was given time to 'return home and hold further consultations with the regime in Freetown in order to facilitate a consideration of the detailed modalities for the return of constitutional order to their country' (Economic Community of West African States 1997a). Although the provisions of the communiqué were very clear about what was meant by 'constitutional order', the junta's chief delegate, Alimamy Pallo Bangura – and, subsequently, Johnny Paul Koroma – insisted that the statement meant that the government of Kabbah could be reinstated, but did not guarantee that this would happen. The two sides agreed to reconvene in Abidjan on 25 July.

The meeting reconvened on 28 July but broke down on 30 July after Koroma announced that his junta 'would not be stampeded into hurrying matters beyond their appointed course' and proceeded to announce a transition programme which would see him in office until 2001. He defiantly asserted that his junta will fight 'aggression internally and externally... to the last drop of our blood' should ECOWAS decide to intervene militarily. The ECOWAS member states especially those who had argued the case for dialogue, felt embarrassed by Koroma's posture. It became clear to all especially the Committee of Four that the junta was not negotiating in good faith. Indeed, the communiqué of the meeting 'expressed dismay at the announcement by the illegal regime of Freetown, while the meeting was still in session, of its decision to suspend the constitution of Sierra Leone and remain in office illegally until the year 2001', and 'found the new position of the Sierra Leonean delegation on the issue of the reinstatement of President Kabbah totally unacceptable'. Nigeria's Foreign Minister, Tom Ikimi, later told reporters that he believed the AFRC's envoys did not have any real mandate to negotiate. He concluded that the Committee of Four had no choice but to recommend to the Heads of state that the economic embargo against Sierra Leone should be tightened. The chief delegate and foreign spokesperson of the junta, Alimamy Pallo Bangura, may also have felt let down by the behaviour of his master. He defected, sought asylum from the authorities of Côte d'Ivoire, and tried to secure an international job as a reward for his defection. The junta's leader, Johnny Paul Koroma, later wrote a letter to him to reconsider his decision (AFRC, 1997c). Bangura went back to resume his duties with the junta.

At an ECOWAS summit meeting in Abuja on 28 and 29 August, the Kabbah government, which was officially invited to participate, lobbied hard for tough action. On the recommendation of the Commitee of Four, member states endorsed stronger sanctions against the junta, and agreed to extend ECOMOG's mandate to include Sierra Leone. This was dubbed ECOMOG 11 but under a central command based in Liberia. The Committee of Four was subsequently expanded to Five, with Liberia as the new member. ECOWAS reaffirmed its position 'to restore constitutional order to Sierra Leone as soon as possible'. It decided to place 'immediately a general and total embargo on all supplies of petroleum products, arms and military equipment to Sierra

Leone and abstain from transacting any business with that country'. Member states further agreed to 'prevent from entering their territories, all members of the illegal regime, as well as military officers, members of their families, and other entities' directly connected to the regime. The funds held by members of the junta and civilians directly or indirectly connected them were to be frozen. The export and import of commodities between Sierra Leone and member states were to be prohibited. The delivery of humanitarian goods could only be done with the 'prior approval of the Authority of Heads of States and Governments of ECOWAS'. ECOMOG, was also entrusted with the responsibility to 'employ all necessary means to impose the implementation of the embargo'. This was to include the close monitoring on 'the coastal areas, land borders and airspace of Sierra Leone'. ECOMOG's was mandated to 'inspect, guard and seize any ship, vehicle or aircraft violating the embargo' (Economic Community of West African States, 1997b).

The ECOWAS Committee of Five, Sierra Leone's permanent representative to the UN, James Jonah, and other African representatives at the Security Council, got the British government to sponsor a resolution to back the ECOWAS sanctions regime in Sierra Leone. The United Nations Security Council voted unanimously on the resolution on 8 October 1997. Acting under Chapter VII (enforcement) and Chapter V111 (regional arrangement) of the United Nations Charter, the Council empowered ECOWAS to enforce an embargo against Sierra Leone. The resolution authorized ECOWAS to halt ships in order to inspect and verify their cargoes and destinations. As in the ECOWAS sanctions regime, the Security Council's measures included a ban on the sale or supply of petroleum and petroleum products and weapons and military equipment to the junta. The resolution also called for an international travel ban on all members of the junta and adult members of their families unless permission was granted by a special committee on Sierra Leone to be created by the Security Council. The Council was to periodically consider reports on violations of the measures adopted, and decide on requests for exceptions to the ban on importation of petroleum products and travel by members of the junta or their families. The resolution provided for the termination of the sanctions if the military junta relinquished power and allowed the restoration of Sierra Leone's democratically elected government. The sanctions were to be reviewed by the Security Council 180 days after adoption of the resolution if they were still in force (UN Security Council, 1997).

The Conakry Peace Plan

Although the junta declared its intention to remain in power until 2001, sustained military and civic pressure, both national and international, forced it to sign a 'Peace Plan' on 23 October 1997, which committed it to hand over power in May 1998. In the two weeks leading to the peace meeting in Conakry, the ECOMOG force sustained its military pressure on the Junta with a number of target bombings, some of which led to the complete destruction of the junta's military headquarters at Cockerill. With the intensification of the bombings, local residents, including opinion leaders, intensified their pressure on the junta to accede to the demands of the international community. Kabbah also made a very good impression at the UN General Assembly meeting in October, where he briefed member states about the nature of the crisis and the need to restore his government and constitutional order. He was to follow this up with a one-day workshop on his government's plans for its post-coup first ninety days in office, organised by the British Ministry of International Development in London. Kabbah also had the opportunity to push his case at the Commonwealth Heads of State Summit in Edinburgh, to which he was specially invited by the host government and the Commonwealth Secretariat. It was during this same period that the Security Council passed its unanimous resolution on the immediate restoration of the Kabbah government and support for the ECOWAS-initiated sanctions, including the banning of the junta and members of their immediate families from foreign travel (United Nations Security Council, 1997). It was a combination of these pressures – internal and external – that caused the Junta to crack and to agree to cede power to the Kabbah government at the meeting.

Brokered by the ECOWAS Committee of Five, the Conakry Peace Plan (Economic Community of West African States 1997c) called for the immediate cessation of hostility, the restoration of the government of Ahmed Tejan Kabbah on 22 May 1998, the demobilisation of all combatants by ECOMOG (to start on 1 December 1997), the commencement of humanitarian assistance (to start on November 15), the return of the refugees from neighbouring countries, the granting of immunity to members of the AFRC, and the release of the RUF leader, Fonday Sankoh, who had been detained in Nigeria before the coup on allegations of gun-running. The latter 'could continue to play an active role and participate in the peace process'. The accord also called for the formation of a broad-based government after Kabbah's restoration to power and ethnic balance in top level appointments to public service.

Both the ousted government and the AFRC accepted the Plan in principle but its implementation was undermined by the legendary unpredictability of the junta. A few preliminary meetings were held between ECOMOG and the junta to establish the groundwork for the deployment of ECOMOG troops in the country. Progress was made in a number of areas, though the junta continued to raise objections in a few vital ones. The junta first called for the removal, and then reduction, of Nigerian troops in the ECOMOG force, as well as the immediate release of Foday Sankoh as conditions for the implementations of the Peace Plan. It was also opposed to plans to disarm the army on the grounds that it is a national institution protected by the constitution. The AFRC continued its propaganda war against the Kabbah regime even as it 'agreed' to relinquish power. These conflicting signals coincided with the new Liberian government's growing opposition to ECOMOG and the sanctions regime against Sierra Leone. It should be recalled that Charles Taylor, the president of Liberia, had worked closely with the RUF. According to the ECOMOG Commander, General Victor Malu, the illegal junta had no authority to decide the makeup of the ECOMOG force. He has also insisted that the peace agreement did not include the immediate release of Foday Sankoh.

But the junta was also riddled with serious internal problems. On November 1997, the AFRC announced that it had foiled a coup plot organised by some of its own members and staunch supporters. This coup was said to have been led by Steven Bio, a wealthy businessman who allegedly sponsored the foiled August 1996 coup plot against Kabbah. Bio, elder brother of the former NPRC leader Brigadier Julius Maada Bio, a powerful figure in the AFRC was reportedly opposed to the Conakry plan to restore Kabba to office. A large number of soldiers and RUF rebels were reportedly arrested. The leader of the junta, Koroma, was also reported to have sacked a top level official of the AFRC and suspended eight other soldiers because of their involvement in 'some dubious activities' aimed at undermining 'the revenue-generating capacity' of the Ministry of Mines and Mineral Resources. These are said to have been under 'mess arrest'. It is reported that the eight had 'set in place a reign of anarchy inconsistent with state stability' (Sierra Leone Web Page: Sierra Leone News, 19, November). Corporal Tamba Gborie, the man who announced the coup on 25 May, was said to be among those arrested.

By January 1998, the Nigerians had amassed about 10,000 fresh troops from Nigeria. But the assault against the Junta forces was not a totally Nigeria affair. Operation Sandstorm was co-ordinated between the Nigerians and the CDF, and Hinga Norman allegedly played a significant role in the whole operation. The CDF began the operation by carrying out strikes against the juntas forces in strategic parts of the country, including the diamond regions of Kono and Tongofield. This strategy was intended to keep the bulk of the Peoples Army away from the capital, and it worked. In the event, when the Nigerians struck in February, most of the juntas best commanders, like Sam Bockarie, were away in the hinterland battling the CDF. By mid-February the capital had been secured. President Kabbah triumphantly returned to Freetown on 10 March, and by April, 90 percent of Sierra Leonean territory, including the diamond-mining areas, were secured by Nigerians and the CDF.

8

Unmaking the Second Republic:
Democracy On Trial

Jimmy D. Kandeh

The birth of Sierra Leone's second republic in 1996 marked the culmination of a long and bitter struggle for democratic change that dates back to the nationwide student demonstrations of 1977. Attempts to forge a student-worker democratic alliance during this period were thwarted by the government's clientelization of labour leaders and repression of students. Rather than leverage a democratic opening, student political activism in the late 1970s hastened the contraction of an already shrinking political arena. A one-party state was declared in 1978 and all opposition to the incumbent APC government was criminalized. After twenty-four years in power, the APC was finally thrown out of office in a coup d'état led by disgruntled junior officers of the Sierra Leone Army (SLA). Students were the first social group to welcome the change of government and to identify with the new power structure. But the popularity and promise of the 1992 coup soon dissipated, and the inability of the new leaders to distinguish themselves from their discredited predecessors rekindled popular demands for democratic change through the ballot box. Pressured by a resurgent civil society and Western donors, and in the midst of a brutal criminal insurgency, the National Provisional Ruling Council (NPRC) reluctantly ceded power to a democratically elected government on March 29, 1996 (See Kandeh this volume).

Fourteen months into the second republic, *sobel* elements (rogue soldiers) of the Sierra Leone Army (SLA), joined forces with the RUF rebels to overthrow the government of Ahmad Tejan Kabbah. The agenda of this *sobel*-rebel alliance did not rise above the criminal expropriation of public resources and private property. As the country became convulsed by criminal terror, the international community reacted by imposing sanctions on the new regime and encouraging efforts by regional leaders to return President Kabbah to power. Kabbah was eventually reinstated in March 1998 by a Nigerian-led West African intervention force but he was almost toppled again in January 1999 by the same forces that ousted him in 1997. The Nigerians were once more called upon to repel the January 1999 invasion of Freetown, in which over 5,000 civilians were killed and many more mutilated by desocialized marginals. In the wake of this brutal invasion, a severely weakened President Kabbah signed a peace agreement that, among other things, granted a blanket amnesty to rebels and rewarded some of their leaders with ministerial positions. This power-sharing agreement left many Sierra Leoneans confused, demoralized and angry.

This chapter reviews three identifiable phases of Sierra Leone's turbulent second republic: pre-coup (1996–1997), post-restoration (1998–1999) and post-invasion (1999-). It probes the functioning and role of the executive, parliament, political parties, judiciary, armed factions and civil society before and after the new republic was twice (1997, 1999) upended. Of particular interest are the miscues of the Kabbah government and the institutional weaknesses of the second republic. How the elected government went about the task of governing, why the democratic experiment unravelled so quickly and the prospects for long term peace and security are among the broad issues examined.

The executive: Composition and policies

The logic behind the selection of the first cabinet of the second republic, as well as the personalities chosen, were early pointers of the type of governance to expect under President Ahmad Tejan Kabbah. In the past, cabinet appointments were patronage-driven and for the most part unrelated to the qualification and integrity of appointees. This skewed appointments in favor of cultural politicians, sycophants and opportunists. First republic cabinets were drawn mostly from parliament, a branch of government not particularly known for its expertise and probity. Constitutionally empowered to choose his cabinet from outside parliament, Kabbah had a rare opportunity to put together a formidable team that would signal a break from the interminable spoils politics of the first republic.

Kabbah's first cabinet, however, turned out to be a yawning disappointment. Despite the President's declaration that his choice of ministers would be based on competence and integrity, most of his appointments failed to meet this test. Not only was the cabinet bloated (44 ministers and deputy ministers), the inclusion of politicians discredited by their complicity in past dictatorships did not inspire confidence in the new government. The choice, for example, of Maigore Kallon as Minister of Foreign Affairs and Thaimu Bangura (an old APC hand) as Finance Minister were not remotely connected to the qualification and honour of these men. It was no secret that Bangura's ministerial appointment was part of a pre-election deal and that Kallon's inclusion in the cabinet was dictated by parochial loyalties and ties. Thus, rather than assemble a competent and honourable cabinet, Kabbah settled for a bunch of recycled politicians and spent cronies.

The post-restoration cabinet was, save for a few exceptions, hardly any better. The number of ministers and deputy ministers was trimmed from forty-four (23 ministers and 21 deputy ministers) to twenty-seven (18 ministers, 9 deputy ministers). The appointments of James Jonah (Finance, Development and Economic Planning), Julius Spencer (Information, Tourism, Culture) and Alie Bangura (Trade, Industry and Transport) were positively received by the general public. All three men had played important roles in mobilizing resistance to the AFRC and paving the way for the restoration of the Kabbah government in 1998. Spencer and Bangura, for example, operated Radio Democracy (FM 98.1), which was the voice of the elected government during the AFRC interregnum. But the selection of Sama Banya, who was earlier rejected for a parastatal position by the pre-coup parliament, as Foreign Minister baffled many who saw his appointment as yet another glaring reminder of the president's inability to free himself from discredited cronies and practices.

Kabbah's cabinet was again reshuffled after the 1999 invasion and the signing of the Lome peace accord. Included in the cabinet for the first time were rebel and *sobel* leaders, eight of whom became ministers and deputy ministers. This power-sharing arrangement ended after the RUF made yet another attempt to shoot its way to power in May 2000. Some RUF leaders are still in detention awaiting trial for human rights abuses and war crimes. Under pressure from domestic popular sectors and donor countries, Kabbah has called on the United Nations to put Sankoh on trial because his government allegedly lacks the capacity to do so.

In terms of policy, Kabbah identified 'the pursuit of lasting peace' as his top priority and expressed his willingness '...to meet the leader of the RUF ... at the earliest opportunity' (Sierra Leone Government, 1996, 6). Given his commitment to dialogue with the RUF, the President moved quickly to arrange a meeting with Foday Sankoh, the RUF leader. Negotiations between the two sides, which was started by the previous military government, resulted in the signing of a peace accord that was supposed to end all armed hostilities. This accord, *inter alia*, assumed that appeasement of the RUF would yield a durable peace. But Sankoh's obduracy, intransigence and delusional flights of grandeur doomed the Abidjan peace accord (Bangura, 1997; Abraham this volume). The RUF warlord refused to nominate members to the Demobilization Committee, which was established to supervise the encampment and disarmament of RUF combatants. He opposed the deployment of a 720-

member United Nations peacekeeping force and declined to meet with the Peace Commission even after the latter temporarily moved its sessions from Freetown to Abidjan. While RUF members on the Peace Commission (Philip Palmer, Fayia Musa, Mohammed Deen-Jalloh) supported implementation of the Abidjan accord, Sankoh and his bush commanders were clearly opposed to any such move. An attempt in 1996 by RUF Peace Commissioners to oust Sankoh as their leader resulted in their abduction and incarceration by Sankoh loyalists.

A major shortfall of the Abidjan accord was its indemnity and appeasement provisions. Amnesty International raised strong objections to Article 14 of the agreement which stated that 'no official or judicial action will be taken against members of the RUF/SL in respect of anything done in pursuit of their objectives' (*Abidjan Accord*, 1996). A peace without justice formula also formed the basis of the 1999 Lome agreement, which incorporated the amnesty provisions of the Abidjan accord and sanctioned the inclusion of rebels and *sobels* in the government. Kabbah's capitulation, especially his decision to share power with an unrepentant horde of mass murderers, rapists and arsonists, was inconsistent with the president's earlier position on power sharing and at odds with public sentiments on the issue. As was true of the Abidjan accord, the disarmament provisions of the Lome accord only became a reality after the arrest and detention of Sankoh in May 2000.

The beneficiaries of Kabbah's policy of reconciliation were not limited to rebels and *sobels*. Charles Taylor, the external grand-patron of the RUF, also profited from Kabbah's naïve pursuit of peace through appeasement. Even in the face of mounting evidence that Taylor was still running guns and diamonds for the RUF, Kabbah stubbornly continued to see Taylor as part of the solution rather than the problem in Sierra Leone. Instead of breaking-off diplomatic ties with Liberia to protest Taylor's backing of the RUF, Kabbah chose to appoint a new ambassador to Liberia and has paid several visits to the Liberian warlord.

Rogue politicians associated with the first republic also profited from Kabbah's policy of forgiveness, amnesty and reconciliation. Based on the recommendations of P.L.V Cross, a judge from Trinidad and Tobago, Kabbah ordered the return of most of the assets of APC politicians that were confiscated by the NPRC dictatorship. The President also lobbied parliament to enact NPRC Decree No. 6, which granted NPRC leaders immunity from prosecution for their actions while in office. But the presidential action that triggered the most intense public outrage was Kabbah's decision to grant ex-president Momoh a lucrative pension package. The political fallout from this controversy was so damaging to the president that he later sought to refine his offer by insisting that Momoh could only collect his pension after retirement from active politics. This qualifier provoked the following response from the APC secretariat:

...the All Peoples Congress (APC) is of the view that denying ex-president Momoh partial benefits already accorded him by government simply because he remains leader of the All Peoples Congress (APC) party would be discriminatory and a violation of his human rights (*The Pool*, March 20, 1997: 6).

In the end, Momoh chose to forgo the pension rather than retire from active politics (*New Sierra Leonean*, March 20, 1997, 1).

Reconciliation, first with APC politicians and later with rebels and *sobels*, squandered the government's credibility and failed to end the criminal insurgency. Having inherited a rogue army whose interests were at odds with society, Kabbah could not rely exclusively on that same army to provide security. Widespread renegade activity among government troops had forced the NPRC junta to hire mercenaries (Gurkhas, Executive Outcomes) in 1995 – a policy continued by Kabbah in his first few months in office. After the first unsuccessful coup against his government, Kabbah turned over responsibility for his personal security to a unit of Nigerian soldiers. The Nigerians were also asked to help retrain and restructure the armed forces. This Nigerian involvement, coupled with the presence of Executive Outcomes (a South African mercenary/security outfit with interests in diamond mining), provided a modest but robust counter-weight to a disloyal and unpopular army. The deterrent value of this alternative security arrangement was, however, lost when the government, in accordance with the Abidjan accord and in deference to the International Monetary Fund (IMF), decided to prematurely terminate the services of Executive Outcomes.

Security provided by the Nigerian soldiers and Executive Outcomes was mainly confined to Freetown and a few prized diamond-mining areas of interest to the corporate affiliates of Executive Outcomes. To protect and safeguard the rest of the country, the government had to rely on army regulars and civil defence militias. But clashes between these militias, especially the *Kamajors*, and the army inflamed an already volatile environment and helped precipitate the 1997 coup.

The *Kamajors* were first mobilized under the NPRC government to help protect the countryside from marauding gangs of rebel and *sobel* bandits. The effectiveness of the *Kamajors* as a counter-insurgency force contrasted sharply with the unholy alliance between army regulars and the RUF. It was the *Kamajors*, bolstered and supported by Executive Outcomes, that flushed the RUF from its main bases in the East of the country during 1996 – a reversal for the RUF that many believe forced Sankoh to negotiate the Abidjan accord so as to buy time and regroup.

Ties between the SLPP and the *Kamajor* militia remain controversial and potentially destabilizing. These ties have created the perception, especially among Northerners, that the SLPP is assembling a parallel military force or, more specifically, a Mende militia. What happens to the *Kamajors* and other civil defence militias in the second republic is anybody's guess but unless the links between militias and political parties are severed, electoral competition in the future is likely to escalate into full-blown militarized contests.

Failure to restore the protective capacity of the state limited the ability of the Kabbah government to forge ahead with its plans for rehabilitation and reconstruction. A new ministry of Rehabilitation, Resettlement and Recovery (the triple R ministry) was created to address the pressing needs of those dislocated and traumatized by the rebel-*sobel* insurgency. This ministry worked closely with the United Nations High Commissioner for Refugees (UNHCR) in formulating and implementing a plan to resettle refugees and displaced persons. With an estimated 450,000 Sierra Leonean refugees in Guinea, and another 50,000 spread across the border with Liberia, government activities were largely funded by international humanitarian groups and donor agencies.

A Round Table Donor's Conference, convened in Geneva in September 1996, netted $231.2 million in pledges toward Sierra Leone's recovery efforts. These efforts, as outlined by the Sierra Leone delegation at the conference, included a Quick Action Programme (QUAP) tailored to address post-war emergency needs and a medium-term programme geared toward poverty alleviation. The areas targeted by the government's medium-term poverty alleviation plan were agriculture, education, health and infrastructure. Food sufficiency, reduction of mass illiteracy by 40%, establishment of a health clinic in every chiefdom, and improvement in the quality of life of the rural population, ranked high among the government's list of priorities (*West Africa*, January 13–19, 1997: 62).

The economic goals of the Kabbah government emphasized growth, price stability, job creation, private sector development and improvement in the country's investment climate. Increasing productivity, improving income and employment opportunities, reducing rice imports by 50% in five years and increasing exports of cash crops by 40% over four years, were among the government's performance goals. The economy (GDP) grew by 5.6 percent in 1996 (compared to -10 percent in 1995), inflation was down from 38.8 percent in February 1996 to 5.6percent in November 1996 and external reserves rose from $31 million in 1995 to $55 million in 1996. In September 1996, the country's national debt stood at $1bn (108% of GDP) and debt service as a percentage of merchandise exports in 1996 was a hefty 83.4 percent (*West Africa*, April 14–20, 1997, 594–596).

Economic recovery was threatened not only by the rebel war but also by entrenched corruption. Corruption in the Kabbah government was rampant and although the president himself was not directly implicated in specific acts of malfeasance, his policy on corruption was conceived in the spirit of amnesty and shaped by his pursuit of reconciliation. This prevented the prosecution of high profile cases like that involving Abass Bundu, a former presidential candidate and one-time minister in both APC and NPRC governments. Bundu was arraigned in court during the first few months of the second republic on charges of operating a passport scam while he was foreign minister in the NPRC government. This case, which involved the sale of Sierra Leone passports to Hong Kong Chinese for large sums of money, was mysteriously settled out of court, with Bundu agreeing to pay back to the state the sum of $200,000 (US dollars). Rather than prosecute those involved in official corruption, Kabbah's policy simply required officials to reimburse the state in amounts roughly equivalent to what was misappropriated or embezzled. Reminiscent of the Momoh years, this 'reimbursement' approach to the problem of corruption served neither to punish nor deter corrupt officials.

Overall, Kabbah inherited a bad situation that got worse under his watch. Whereas the problems facing the country cannot be simply blamed on personalities, the lack of a firm and decisive leadership in a period of crisis contributed to a heightened state of insecurity. An otherwise astute leader could have prevented the 1997 coup and the 1999 invasion, the two events that exposed the complacency and ineptitude of the Kabbah government. Kabbah's apparent naivety, especially his belief that appeasement could end the war, has exposed Sierra Leoneans to increasing levels of danger. Whether the issue is rogue politicians, rebels and *sobels* or Charles Taylor in Liberia, Kabbah's approach has been to pursue peace and reconciliation through appeasement. A critical failure of political leadership in the second republic has been the government's inability and/or unwillingness to develop an independent military force to replace the army after the 1998 restoration. Part of the reason for this failure was Kabbah's preference for foreign over local solutions. The President would rather have Nigerians fight and die for a country that is not theirs than arm his own people to take the fight to the rebels. Fears that local militias would become too powerful and pose a threat to the government explain the government's fitful and tepid support for the only fighting force that has remained loyal to the government throughout the second republic. By relying on foreign troops to rescue Sierra Leone, Kabbah failed to seize the opening created by the war to mobilize the citizenry and construct a new regime from the ravages of war. It is this lack of leadership that has prompted observers to demand a UN take-over of Sierra Leone as a trust territory. According to one such proposal, 'the only effective long-term solution is to declare a UN trusteeship or protectorate over Sierra Leone, just as a bankrupt company is placed in receivership. Like Somalia, Sierra Leone is a failed state, its government long ago hijacked by gangsters (Ayittey, 2000: A26).

Kabbah, for his part, wants the British to 'stay forever' in Sierra Leone. What the President does not realize, however, is that none of the western countries, including Britain, who can get the job done in Sierra Leone are interested in undertaking such a mission. And it is because no serious thought was given to what should be done in the event that appeasement and reconciliation failed that Sierra Leone now finds itself at the mercy of the international community for both its security and sustenance.

Parliament and political parties

A listless appendage of the APC in the first republic, parliament in the second republic continued to be weakened by disarray within the opposition and opportunism among politicians. The decision to adopt proportional representation, rather than the single-member district system, in the 1996 parliamentary elections affected the quality of parliamentary representation. Since parliamentary membership was no longer a requirement for appointment to the cabinet, party leaders were generally unenthusiastic about serving in parliament.

Parliamentary approval of cabinet and other top-level appointments was a novel feature of the 1991 constitution. Chaired by S.B Marah, SLPP parliamentary leader, the Committee on Appointments and the Public Service included the parliamentary leaders of all six parties. Although some of Kabbah's appointees (Maigore Kallon, Thaimu Bangura, Amy Smythe) ran into initial problems, only one ministerial appointment (Sheki Bangura) was rejected. A few parastatal and judicial appointees also failed to make it through parliament but on the whole most of the president's appointees for various top-level positions were confirmed. In the words of one MP, 'confirmation hearings to clear the president's nominees provided parliament an important mechanism for holding state officials accountable' (Dumbuya, 1999: 12).

Among the important bills enacted by the pre-coup parliament were the National Reconciliation Commission Act (1996); the Constitution Reinstatement Act (1996); the National Provisional Ruling Council Decrees Act (1996); the Road Transport Authority Act (1996); the Minimum Wage Act (1997); the Ombudsman Act (1997); the Newspapers Act (1997); the Media Practitioners Act (1997), and; the Appropriations Act (1997). The Indemnity Act (1996), which sought to absolve NPRC leaders of responsibility for acts committed while in office, was tabled but rejected by parliament. In the wistful summation of one MP, the rejection of the Indemnity Act meant 'for all intents and purposes, the NPRC government remained fully liable for all acts done by that government during its tenure of office' (Dumbuya, 1999: 12).

Arguably, the most contentious bill passed by the new parliament was the Press bill which, among other things, sought to establish guidelines and an ethics code for journalists. Among its provisions were the requirement that editors must be university degree holders with ten years experience in journalism, or; must possess an advance certificate or diploma in journalism from a recognized institution, plus ten years experience in journalism, or;

should have at least fifteen years experience in journalism (*Sierra Leone Gazette*, 1997). The Sierra Leone Association of Journalists (SLAJ) and the New York-based Committee for the Protection of Journalists (CPJ) raised strong objections to this bill, which the government argued was necessary to upgrade the quality of journalism and curtail journalistic abuses.

A vexing issue that dogged the pre-coup parliament was dissension within the UNPP. Karefa-Smart, the UNPP leader, attempted to unseat fourteen of the seventeen UNPP members in parliament by expelling them from his party. This created an uproar within his party and an awkward situation for all concerned as parliament was called upon to resolve what was essentially an internal party dispute. A Special Committee established to look into the matter recommended that the fourteen MP's should not be expelled. The Committee on Privileges, on the other hand, advised the Speaker to suspend Karefa-Smart from parliament because of statements he had made that were deemed contemptible of the speaker and parliament (*Expo Times*, 1997, 1; *Concord Times*, 1997, 1). Justice S.M.F Kutubu, the speaker in question, accepted the recommendation of both committees and announced the suspension of Karefa-Smart after a motion was approved by parliament with 46 yes votes and 6 abstentions. The parliamentary Committee on Privileges based its recommendation to suspend Karefa-Smart on Section 99(3) of the 1991 constitution, which states that

> Where a member refuses to render an apology pursuant to the provisions of sub-section (3), the speaker shall suspend that member for the duration of the session of parliament in which the defamatory statement was made and a member so suspended shall lose his parliamentary privileges, immunities and remuneration.

Suspension from parliament embittered Karefa-Smart who was not only at odds with his own party but with the entire parliament. His frantic efforts to get the president to intercede on his behalf were rebuffed by Kabbah who maintained that it would be improper for the executive to interfere with the work of the legislative branch of government. Kabbah's refusal to come to Karefa-Smart's political rescue may, according to the president, help explain why the UNPP leader became such an outspoken apologist of the AFRC junta.

Reviews of the pre-coup parliament have been generally negative. In the opinion of James Jonah, the former Interim National Electoral Commissioner and post-restoration Finance minister, the pre-coup parliament did not perform

> ... to the ... degree that most of us would have accepted, and why? Again refusal to change our attitudes. And one of the things which has surprised me ... is I do not sense that all parliamentarians are proud to be parliamentarians. They should be proud. Being in parliament should not be seen as a parking lot to become ministers (*For Di People*, April 8, 1997: 7).

This downgrading of parliament into a weigh station for politicians is likely to continue to compromise its effectiveness in the second republic. Paradoxically, it is precisely at a time when parliament finds itself in a stronger constitutional position to exert influence and establish its autonomy from the executive that many politicians are choosing not to be members. During the AFRC interregnum (1997-98), most MPs fled the country or went into hiding. Parliament, however, was far from united in its response to the AFRC/RUF usurpation. There were those, notably Karefa-Smart and some APC politicians, who saw the coup as an opportunity to pursue their selfish agenda. The vast majority of parliamentarians, however, opposed the coup although there was not much they could do to reverse it. A press release denouncing the junta and calling for the reinstatement of the Kabbah government was issued but nothing was heard again from parliament until after the March 1998 restoration.

The legislative arm of government suffered the same contortions as the executive during the post-1999 period. With many parliamentarians, including prominent SLPP members, blaming the president's lack of leadership for the invasion, Parliament was more inclined to endorse sharing power with the AFRC/RUF after than before the invasion. UNPP parliamentarians were the first to declare support for the inclusion of *sobel* and rebel leaders in a government of national unity. Many SLPP partisans interpreted northern parliamentary support for power sharing as an attempt to gain power by means other than the ballot box. In the end, however, even SLPP diehards in parliament voted to ratify the Lome agreement. The only dissenting voice within the SLPP's leadership circle came from Peter Tucker, author of the 1991 Constitution, who denounced the Lome agreement as an unconstitutional act of unfathomable appeasement. Tucker was relieved of his position as Chairman of the National Advisory Committee and denounced as unpatriotic by the President.

The six political parties represented in parliament are, without exception, elitist parties. Two of them, the SLPP and APC, remain unreconstructed patronage parties while three others (UNPP, PDP, DCP) are personalist outfits. The sixth party, the National Unity Party (NUP), had its origin in the NPRC's attempt to perpetuate its rule through participation by some of its leaders in competitive politics. Compared to the SLPP whose political fortunes have been on the rise in the second republic, the bottom seems to have fallen out from under the APC, which is less competitive today than at any other time in its history. The fracturing of the APC in the 1990s has electorally transformed the north into the most competitive region after the western area but the parties that are competitive in this region are mostly splintered reincarnations of the APC.

Intra-party rifts have generally overshadowed inter-party differences in the second republic. Internal party squabbles have centered on personal ambitions rather than ideology or party policy. SLPP stalwarts were angry with Kabbah for appointing many of their political opponents to the cabinet. UNPP parliamentarians were furious at Karefa-Smart for pursuing his presidential ambition at their expense and many never forgave him for opting out of an agreement with Kabbah that would have ensured substantial UNPP presence in the cabinet. Bickering among PDP leaders stemmed from the loss of three ministerial positions in the cabinet after Kabbah's first reshuffle. In none of these three cases of party infighting did the issues rise above the level of what individual politicians stood to gain personally from specific alignments and arrangements.

The proliferation of parties in the second republic suggests not a flowering of democracy but a weakness of the party system. Self-serving considerations continue to dictate party formation/alliances and electoral support for parties still exhibit an ethnoregional bias – all the parties in parliament attracted the bulk of their support from specific regions. This aspect of party competition is a carry-over from the first republic that is likely to continue into the future, especially in the absence of ideological differences among political parties.

Judiciary

The jailbreak that accompanied the May 1997 coup represented a major setback for efforts to restore law and order in Sierra Leone. Not only were hardened criminals unleashed on society, public records of all sorts were destroyed. Another jailbreak in January 1999 re-emptied the Pademba Road prison of all its inmates, including ex-president Momoh. Both the coup (1997) and invasion (1999) jailbreaks exposed judges and government prosecutors to horrendous human rights abuses at the hands of armed fugitives, rebels and *sobels*. Over 250 policemen were reportedly killed and 80 percent of police stations in Freetown were set ablaze during this invasion. Judges, including the Chief Justice whose house was razed to the ground, fled the country *en masse*. Upon their return in April 1999, many judges insisted on adequate protection of their homes and offices as a precondition for resuming work. In essence, the collapse of the security order meant the collapse of the legal order.

The weakness of the judiciary as a democratic institution was on full display in the days following the May 1997 coup. The swearing-in of Johnny Paul Koroma as head of state by the Chief Justice reinforced the public's image of the judiciary as a tool of incumbent governments. Although the Chief Justice claimed to have acted under duress, what saved him from prosecution after Kabbah's restoration is a specific provision (Section 120, sub-section 9) of the constitution which states that 'a judge of the superior court of judicature shall not be liable to any action or suit for any matter or thing done by him in the performance of his judicial functions'.

Kabbah's restoration in 1998 was followed by the arrest of a large number of elites who, according to the government, had collaborated with the AFRC junta. Among those arrested were lawyers, academics, politicians, community leaders, journalists, civil servants and senior army officers. Some of these individuals were later tried for treason, convicted and sentenced to death. Twenty-four soldiers, including those who had orchestrated the May 1997 coup, were court-martialed, sentenced to death and executed. The fact that most of those arrested and arraigned were northerners gave rise to fears of an anti-northern witch-hunt. As Yusuf Bangura (2000: 8) notes,

> It was reckoned that more than 60 percent of elites who were tried were of Northern and Western Area origin. Even though the government was on very firm legal grounds to conduct the trials, and that these elites committed these crimes as individuals rather than as members of ethnic groups, the trials widened the ethnopolitical divide and undermined efforts to create a united front against the rebels.

Foday Sankoh's treason trial created quite a spectacle in the law courts of Freetown. Sankoh, who was extradited to Sierra Leone from Nigeria in 1998, insisted that the government's case against him lacked merit because it violated the terms and spirit of the 1996 Abidjan accord. The government maintained that the treason charges against Sankoh only covered his actions since the signing of the Abidjan accord. Amnesty for future crimes, the government maintained, was not covered by the Abidjan accord; hence this accord could not be invoked as defence for crimes committed after it was signed. In the end, Sankoh was convicted of treason and sentenced to death by hanging. He was on death row awaiting his appeal when rebels and *sobels* stormed the city in a brazen attempt to capture state power in January, 1999. After the invasion, and as called for by the Lome agreement, Sankoh and his armed loyalists were granted a blanket amnesty. The invasion, in short, saved Sankoh from the gallows.

The Lome appeasement represents a mockery of justice and a debasement of the judicial system. It is very difficult to envisage the credible functioning of Sierra Leone's judicial system when the worse offenders of the law are granted immunity. Already, following the May 2000 arrest of Foday Sankoh, the government announced that it lacked the capacity to put the rebel leader on trial. It has since called on the United Nations to explore the possibility of establishing a special court for Sierra Leone that would try RUF leaders. Such a trial, if and when it takes place, can go a long way in restoring a semblance of justice for Sierra Leoneans.

Sobels, rebels and militias

To no one's surprise, *sobel*s and rebels continue to pose the most serious threat to Sierra Leone's political, social and economic recovery. Clashes between *sobels* and the *Kamajor* irregulars are believed to have been among the factors that triggered the May 1997 coup. In the first year of the Kabbah presidency, at least three attempted *sobel* coups were reported. These failed coups resulted in the forced retirement of the few remaining NPRC officers in the army and the arrest of some of those believed to be responsible. Kabbah, however, decided not to court-martial coup plotters, choosing instead to refer their cases to the civil courts. It was while waiting for his day in a civil court that Johnny Paul Koroma was sprung from his prison cell by armed *sobels* and declared head of state.

The fact that Kabbah inherited a rogue army severely constrained his security options. Because of the rebel insurgency, the president could not simply disarm or disband the army. Even though the *Kamajors* were loyal to his government, they were not in a position to prevent or suppress a coup. Absorbing *Kamajors* into the regular army could have been one way of challenging *sobel* hegemony in the army, but this was a move the president was neither willing nor prepared to make. It was only when he was forced into exile in 1997–98 that Kabbah, out of desperation and lacking an army of his own, embraced civil defence. Once reinstated, the president refocused his attention away from bolstering civil defence militias to creating a new army. This failure to prioritize national defence as a civic duty made the government more dependent on external forces, especially the Nigerian army.

The government's failure to see civil defence as a credible alternative to a disloyal army can be partly blamed on Kabbah's estrangement from the masses and fears that civil militias could be hijacked by powerful warlords determined to make a run at state power. As Yusuf Bangura (2000, 6) writes:

> It has been reportedly suggested that one of the reasons why the civil defence force does not feature prominently in the overall strategy of the government is because of the lack of control of the president over this force. Strengthening this force was seen as undermining the president's grip on power and consolidating that of his deputy defence minister.

Furthermore, arming the population requires a certain degree of confidence in the people on the part of rulers. Kabbah not only lacked this confidence, he was out of sync with popular currents. He could not, therefore, be expected to vigorously pursue the civil defence option.

Since signing the Lome agreement, the government has reversed its position on the issue of whether the army had been disbanded. The government's position after it was restored to power in 1998 was that the army had dissolved itself as a result of its mass complicity with rebels. As part of its appeasement strategy, the government later claimed that the army was never disbanded. The Kabbah government has already paid salaries to some renegade soldiers and is prepared to integrate a couple of thousands into the 'new army'. Although the Lome appeasement calls for the inclusion of AFRC/RUF combatants in the army, the rearming of bandits by the government does not augur well for peace and security in Sierra Leone.

The *sobel*-rebel alliance that had ransomed state and society in the second republic came to an end after Lome. Foday Sankoh, the rebel leader, and Johnny Paul Koroma, the *sobel* leader, were hardly on speaking terms before the capture of Foday Sankoh. Forces loyal to both men clashed repeatedly, with each side accusing the other of insincerity in their commitment to the Lome agreeement. The unraveling of this criminal alliance is rooted in minor political differences and deep-seated personal animosities. Politically, most *sobels* harbor vestigial loyalties to the APC, the party against whom the RUF took up arms. Furthermore, Sam 'Maskita' Bockarie, the former RUF field commander, held Johnny Paul Koroma, the *sobel* leader, captive for much of 1998. This incident embittered Koroma who was later appointed as Chairman of the Commission for the Consolidation of Peace. Koroma, now a born-again Christian, has been busy trying to rehabilitate himself in the eyes of the public. He was aided in his reinvention project by the RUF's attempt to seize power in May 2000. Ex-SLA soldiers loyal to Koroma helped beat back rebel forces, winning kudos from a forgiving public.

Civil society

Although professional associations played a critical role in contesting Albert Margai's authoritarian tendencies in the 1960s, most of these groups lost their political voice in the first republic. Political activism by the labour movement was silenced through co-optation of labour leaders during the 1977 student crisis, and then crushed in the wake of the 1981 labour unrest. Since protest activity against the APC was illegal, societal groups were generally forced to either toe the party line or withdraw from overt political activity. One group, however, that successive governments in Sierra Leone have been unable to coerce into submission are university students. Students were not only in the forefront of popular agitation to dismantle the one-party state, they were also in the vanguard of popular efforts to resist AFRC/RUF terror.

Student relations with the Kabbah government soured over the issue of Momoh's pension. Reflecting the sentiment of most Sierra Leoneans, students were incensed by the very idea of pensioning Momoh. To express its disapproval, the National Union of Sierra Leone Students (NUSS) scheduled a March 10, 1997 meeting at the Circular Road Parade Grounds. This meeting erupted into open confrontation between students and security forces attempting to disperse them. Many students were seriously injured in a show of excessive force by the government. By violently suppressing the right of students to demonstrate against government policies and perceived injustices, Kabbah alienated the most reliable pro-democracy constituency in the country. Remarkably, students were able to set aside their misgivings about the Kabbah government in leading societal efforts to reinstate the very government that had tried to silence their voice. Like most Sierra Leoneans, students saw their support for Kabbah's reinstatement not as an endorsement of his performance in office but as an expression of underlying commitment to the principles of democratic governance.

Among the influential groups that emerged during the transition to the second republic were women's organizations. The Women's Forum and Women for a Morally Engaged Nation (WOMEN) championed popular demands for democratic renewal in the 1990s. After the 1996 elections, Zainab Bangura (the leader of WOMEN), together with Joe Opala and Julius Spencer, founded an autonomous non-governmental organization to monitor government activities and enhance government capacities. The Campaign for Good Governance (CGG), as the organization came to be known, attracted generous funding from the US-based Office of Transnational Initiative (OTI), the National Endowment for Democracy (NED) and the Overseas Development Agency (ODA). Most of these funds targeted specific training and capacity enhancing programmes for parliamentarians, the cabinet, judiciary, civil service and mass media. As symbol of Sierra Leone's fledgling democracy, the CGG experienced a momentary setback when one of their leading lights became a full-fledged politician.

WOMEN were by no means the only politically active group in the second republic. Teachers and labour unions also continued to make their voices heard. High unemployment (especially among university graduates), the late-payment of salaries and dilapidated facilities, were among the issues of immediate concern to teachers. Layoffs, high unemployment, hyperinflation and late payment of salaries equally agitated workers. Both the Sierra Leone Teachers Union (SLTU) and the Sierra Leone Labour Congress (SLLC) condemned the AFRC/RUF coup and demanded the reinstatement of the Kabbah government. United in their position that insecurity and violence made it impossible for their members to return to work, the SLTU and the SLLC instructed their membership to disobey the junta by not reporting for work. This act of civil disobedience was critical in consolidating domestic opposition to the AFRC junta.

Recent events have once again pitted popular sectors against the Kabbah government. After the capture of Sankoh in May 2000, the government did not know what to do with the rebel leader. The government's indecision was in sharp contrast with public demands that Sankoh should be made to pay for the crimes he and his followers have committed against the people of Sierra Leone. When Lansana Kouyate, the ECOWAS Secretary-General, announced that the Sierra Leone government had agreed to a plan that would have transferred Sankoh to another country, there were spontaneous demonstrations in Freetown protesting any such move. Had the international community not insisted that Sankoh should be tried, Kabbah was poised to ignore popular demands for Sankoh's trial.

Conclusion

Arguably, perhaps the only redeeming aspect of Sierra Leone's turbulent second republic has been the unflinching support by popular sectors for democratic rule. The role of civil society in ending the NPRC dictatorship and resisting its AFRC sequel is unprecedented in the annals of military rule in independent Africa. In resisting the AFRC/RUF for as long as it did, Sierra Leone added to its long list of firsts among African states – the first country where an incumbent was voted out of office (1967), the first country where a coup restored a democratically elected government (1968) and the first country where a democratically elected government was reinstated by sub-regional military forces (1998). These critical junctures suggest irrepressible public support for democracy but power contenders have seldom found democratic openings and restorations to be in their best interest.

That rebels and *sobels* became Kabbah's partners in running the government was a major setback for democracy and the rule of law in Sierra Leone. Largely as a result of one of the worst leadership failures in Africa, Sierra Leoneans have neither peace nor justice in the second republic. A series of aggravating miscues by the Kabbah government compromised state security and exposed the average citizen to great danger. The premature withdrawal of Executive Outcomes, the failure to take adequate steps to foil the May 1997 coup, the excessive reliance on ECOMOG to provide security and the unwillingness to develop new defence structures capable of mobilizing the population for self-defence – all contributed to a deteriorating security environment. Both the May 1997 coup and the January 1999 invasion could have been averted and thousands of lives saved had the president been up to his job as commander-in-chief.

9

Civil Society Against the State: The Independent Press and the AFRC-RUF Junta

Olu Gordon

We know death to be the inevitable end of any man born of woman ... be it by gunshots or any other means, death will come when it will come... What is important is giving our people the necessary information needed for their survival at a crucial time like this. [It] is a worthy cause and it is better to die for such a cause than to live for nothing.

Standard Times, July 25, 1997

'Press Freedom has to stop where the security of the state begins.'

AFRC Secretary-General, Colonel Abdul K. Sesay, November 24, 1997

Between May 1997 and February 1998 most sections of the independent press in Sierra Leone were locked in a bitter confrontation with the Armed Forces Revolutionary Council (AFRC), one of the most vicious military regimes Africa has ever seen. The AFRC, which most Sierra Leoneans simply called the 'Junta' (with a hard J), was an alliance of unruly subalterns in the army and the lumpen rebels of the RUF.

The AFRC coup d'état of May 25, 1997 toppled Sierra Leone's first democratically elected government in nearly thirty years; barely a year after it had assumed office. The regime unleashed a nine-month nightmare of looting, murder and mutilation, which Jimmy Kandeh calls 'subaltern terror' (Kandeh,1999). AFRC functionaries criminally accumulated enormous resources from public and private coffers through the use of violence.

Like most sections of the Sierra Leone public, the independent press showed great courage in standing firm for the restoration of democracy and the elected government in face of rampant gangsterism by the junta. Editors, journalists and most media practitioners and their staff were called on to run great risks, make huge sacrifices and show extraordinary ingenuity as they struggled to maintain their newspapers as forums for free expression of mass public opinion. As Sierra Leone went through its most serious crisis since independence the oft-derided independent press rose to the occasion.[1]

However this is only one level at which the situation can be analyzed. Rather than marking a sharp break from all that had come before it, the AFRC era represented an intensification of the repression that had been directed against the press since Sierra Leone's independence. Indeed by the time it was finally booted out of power in February 1998, the AFRC was reduced to trying to enforce all draconian press laws that it had inherited from previous regimes – including the very 'democratic' administration that it had displaced. This, despite having a whole array of other extra-legal means of coercion at its disposal.

The struggle of the independent press against the AFRC junta was in essence a struggle of civil society against the state. The struggle neither began with the May 25 coup nor has it ended with the restoration of 'democracy'. Within two years of the overthrow of the AFRC junta, its erstwhile leader, Johnny Paul Koroma, was incorporated into the Kabbah administration as chairman for the Committee to Consolidate Peace (CCP) and the leader of the RUF, Foday Sankoh, was installed as chairman of a commission set up to manage the country's most precious resource – diamonds. Both these appointments were made over the express opposition of the independent press and the great mass of the people of Sierra Leone. As Kandeh notes:

> By paying ransom (four ministerial posts) to war criminals in a last desperate effort to hang on to power, the political class has once more demonstrated that no evil goes beyond its opportunistic embrace (Kandeh 1999).

Yet the fact that this 'political class' as Kandeh describes it, went ahead to appoint its former antagonist to state positions really just demonstrates the fundamental antagonism between the interests of civil society and the interests of those who occupy state positions and seek to use them as a primary instrument of capital accumulation and class formation.

And yet these forces are also playing a more important role in the scheme of things; keeping shop for Western hegemonic interests. The 1999 Lome Peace Accord, which elevated both rebel chieftains, was reportedly drafted by a United States Department team and received full endorsement from Western countries, Western NGOs and other members of the international community.

Chole, in his introduction to a 1995 book on the problems and prospects of Democratization Processes in Africa, enjoins the need to go beyond the 'widespread euphoria' and seek answers to the following questions:

Is what is taking place democratisation in content or merely in form ... how much substance does it involve? ... If it is more form than content, what justifies the celebrations? What are the limitations and contradictions of this process? What are the social forces – internal as well as external – behind it? How compatible ...are the interests of these forces? What is the link between economic reform and democratisation? What guarantees, if any, are there against the reversibility of the process? (Chole, 1995)

A study of the conflict between the press and the AFRC-RUF may help shed some light on these questions; and an understanding of these questions is certainly key to charting the way forward for true democratization in Sierra Leone.

A smallholder's media

Freedom of expression, freedom of the press and all other hallowed liberal bourgeois freedoms do not exist in a vacuum. They always evolve/develop within a particular historical context and are situated within a definite environment. These freedoms are mediated by conflicts and consensus between classes and socio-economic groups competing for influence and power. Freedom of expression within the specific realities of Sierra Leone has always meant the freedom to expose and denounce those who controlled the system of predatory capitalism that gave rise to the colonial and neo-colonial system. Sierra Leone grew out of the small coastal settlement around Freetown, which the 'abolitionists' set up in the late 1700s to provide a home for Africans liberated from slavery. Its earliest newspapers were set up and run mainly by dissatisfied settlers articulating grievances against the colony's administration and agitating for participation in the colony's affairs.

Both Fyle and Abrahams have laid out, in some detail, how the competing commercial interests of European colonial powers led to the annexation of the hinterland as British imperialist interests attempted to ensure that trade routes fell under their suzerainty. By the turn of the century the press was centered in Freetown partly because this was where the whole colonial enterprise was administered from and also because it was the home of the western modernity – the place where one could find those literate in English, the official medium of communication (Abraham, 1978; Fyle, 1979).

Agitation against colonial abuses was the basis for the development of the independent press; this reached its highest level in the *West African Standard*, the organ of the West African Youth League set up in the 1938 by the tireless Pan-Africanist and labour organizer, I.T.A. Wallace-Johnson. The colonial government brought a whole battery of legislation to muzzle the *Standard* and cripple Wallace-Johnson politically. By the time war broke out in 1939, colonial officials had pushed through a series of laws that made it possible for them to 'legally' trap and detain him for the duration of the war (Abdullah, 1995).

By the late 1940s, two trends had been established which still affect the operations of the independent print media in Sierra Leone today. The first was the relatively small (often personally owned) and under-financed natured of its operations. The second was, and is, the use of the state's coercive legal machinery to attempt to license, regulate or otherwise control the content of newspapers. Sierra Leone never developed large media conglomerates and although Mbayo correctly identifies the consistency with which 'privately owned media organizations come... directly at odds with political authority and are primary victims of repressive governments of the day', he fails to locate the source of this constant friction in the specific realities of neo-colonial Sierra Leone (Mbayo, 1999). Under neo-colonialism, the state lacks 'relative autonomy'; it does not stand above competing fractions organizing the political domination of subordinated classes while pretending to serve societal good. In the main, the state is the primary instrument of class formation and, as Kandeh correctly points, 'highly amenable to the interests of the political incumbents' of state power' (Kandeh, 1999). It means little whether these incumbents are one party adherents, young pseudo-radical students, elected politicians or lumpen subalterns: its fundamental behaviour has to be the same because though the names and faces of the state's apparatichik may change, their interests do not. As Frantz Fanon presciently observed, they are there to run the racket for imperialism while prosaically filling their pockets (Fanon, 1961).

If indeed as Mbayo argues, the private media is an independent entity actively engaged in the production of a consumer product-media content (Mbayo, 1999) then the smallholders of the print media in Sierra Leone knows very well what sells; the exposure of corruption and the underhand dealings of the denizens on the corridors of power. One only has to glance at the headlines of Freetown's independent press over the years to verify this 'over-concentration': on corruption/rumors of corruption which is what brings the independent press head-to-head with the powers that-be on a consistent basis over the years.

Neo-colonial press freedom

One consistent theme, which the political class has sounded over the years, is that 'negative' press reporting about corruption 'drives away foreign investors'. The state cannot deny the existence of corruption – it just seeks to stop the press writing too much about it. This could jeopardize 'foreign investors' – that is foreign venture capitalists out for a quick killing in Sierra Leone diamond fields – coming in to be bilked by a predatory state apparatus. To end negative press reporting the neocolonial state, like its colonial predecessor, creates a whole armoury of repressive laws designed to limit the independent press reporting on the accountability of and transparency of state officials. In 1980 the Newspaper (Amendment) Act was passed by the APC one-party dictatorship. The act gave the minister wide powers: to grant newspaper licences/to suspend, cancel or refuse to grant them if 'advised' by a press council which he personally handpicked and whose members received allowances directly from the state coffers. This law was first utilized against *For Di People*, *Weekend Spark*, and two other Freetown tabloids in 1986. But President Momoh later reversed the suspensions after he was petitioned (*For Di People*, March 1986))

When the Young Turks of the NPRC overthrew the APC in April 1992, they declared a 'revolution' and a 'war against corruption'. The NPRC set up public probes headed by senior judges, to uncover the corrupt practices of the APC. However when stories of the past abuses became stale news and the press began to peddle new merchandise about corruption in senior NPRC circles, the young 'revolutionaries' soon resorted to old APC tactics. In January 1993, the new regime brought in the restrictive licensing regulations, which excluded over 24 of Freetown's 33 independent newspapers. NPRC information Secretary, Hindolo Trye explained that this move was necessary to 'make the press more responsible' (*For Di People*, January 1993). He did not explain to whom they were supposed to be responsible but the message became clearer that year when six *Newbreed* journalists were arrested, denied bail and eventually brought to trial for daring to reproduce a foreign newspaper's allegations that NPRC Chairman, Valentine Strasser, had been involved in the illicit diamond trade.

Although the Sierra Leone Association of Journalists (SLAJ), the media's umbrella body supported the pro-democracy movement at the first and second Bintumani conferences that led to the end of the NPRC rule in 1996, it has received little thanks from the government that it helped to install. Within its first eight months in power, the SLPP prosecuted two newspapers, *The Point* and *Expo-Times* under the 1965 Public Order Act, invited several journalists for 'routine police questioning' over several stories critical of corruption in cabinet (*The Point* and *Expo-Times*, February–April 1997) and even 'banned', albeit briefly, a radical newspaper sympathetic to the opposition party before it even issued its maiden edition. The SLPP continued in the tradition of anti-press legislation when it introduced the Media Practitioners Act and the Newspaper Act in 1997. Both bills were taken before parliament and shot-gunned through in a matter of days (*For Di People* April 1997). Under the terms of the new laws the state would, under the guise of improving 'professional practice', give itself the right to license newspaper and ensure that editors were 'sufficiently' qualified to practice as journalists/editors. To qualify meant having at least ten to fifteen years professional experience in addition to academic qualifications arbitrarily set by the government. The Attorney General, Solomon Berewa, claimed that the SLAJ executive had suggested the bill; a point which the Information Minister also echoed.[2] 'The Bills were meant to bring sanity into the profession and save the trade from deadwoods', charged Abdul Thorlu-Bangura the then minister of information.

SLAJ had indeed requested legislation; but it had asked for repeal of existing repressive laws as well as the enactment of a freedom of Information Act. In alliance with other members of civil society, particularly the student union, the journalists vigorously lobbied against president Kabbah signing the two bills into law. The two bills remained on the president's table and awaiting his signature when the rebellious army subalterns stormed the State House early on the morning of May 25, 1997 sending the incumbent members of the political class scampering into exile in neighbouring Guinea.

Revolutionary press freedom

In their analysis of the May 25 coup, Earl Conteh-Morgan and Mac Dixon-Fyle argue that the Kabbah administration while making efforts to create a positive image for the state (Conteh-Morgan and Dixon-Fyle, 1999), undermined the legitimacy and constitutional status of the army by encouraging the development of a parallel structure – the civil defense forces or *Kamajors*. This led to the army disrupting the new democratic arrangements and its corresponding human rights gains. However the Kabbah government did more than just alienate the army, it systematically delegitimized itself by relying on the same patrimonial arrangements and repressive anti-people measures of preceding regimes; making itself almost indistinguishable from those same regimes.

As late as March 1997, the Kabbah government was tear-gassing college students protesting against the SLPP's decision to award a pension to the discredited former president, Joseph Saidu Momoh. It had also, in addition, to the proposed press bills, resurrected a colonial law which had never been previously used to charge three journalists from the *Expo Times* for espionage. The charge was based on the discovery of old military briefing papers in the offices of the newspaper during a 'routine' police search. It is clear, as Conteh-Morgan and Dixon-Fyle observe that the government played into the hands of the army by failing to take decisive action to halt the deterioration of relations between the army and the *Kamajors* (Conteh-Morgan and Dixon-Fyle, 1999). What is less clear is why the regime systematically alienated its own support base in civil society which brought it to power. Days before the coup, columnists in the *Democrat* newspaper were warning that the Kabbah administration was preparing the ground for its own overthrow. In one of its editorials, the *Democrat* maintained, 'When the government harasses the press, you can be sure that some ambitious army captain somewhere is already preparing his takeover speech denouncing repressive and corrupt civilian leaders' (*Democrat*, May 18, 1997).

The ambitious army captain presented himself just a few days later. Captain Paul Thomas had been aide-de-camp to a senior NPRC member and had seen his former patron enrich himself and depart for an all-expenses paid academic scholarship in the United States. He was dismissed from the army several months later on allegations that he was involved in coup plotting. On May 26, 1997, as spokesman for the AFRC he declared the SLPP government overthrown for the usual reasons: corruption, nepotism, tribalism and so on. But, he also added an intriguing point: the army had stepped in to prevent the SLPP repressive press bills from becoming law! (SLBS Radio Broadcast May 25, 1997) On the morning of May 26, 1997, while drunk and unruly soldiers continued their looting which had started the previous day, Captain Paul Thomas presented himself at the central Freetown residence of the SLAJ Secretary-General calling on journalists to make common cause in the 'revolution' against the deposed regime which had introduced the press bills. Given a non-committal but generally negative response, the AFRC strong man departed while the SLAJ Secretary-General moved to a safe house.

The regime continued to maintain that it had come to safeguard the 'freedom of the press'. At its first rowdy press conference held at the Cockerill Military headquarters on Wednesday May 28, the new AFRC chairman, Major Johnny Paul Koroma continued to claim this was 'a fact'. When it was pointed out to him that there was a clear contradiction in his regime's claim to uphold press freedom while at the same time banning public marches and assemblies and taking the nation's only two independent radio stations off the air, he lapsed into incoherence (AFRC Press conference May 28, 1997).

The AFRC desperately tried to make friends with the press allegedly doling out millions of leones in the early days of their 'Revolution' to unscrupulous pressmen who claimed that they needed money to print their newspapers. The only friends the regime was able to garner amongst the ranks of the press, however, were those editors who felt victimized by the actions of the deposed SLPP regime: *Torchlight*, edited by Sheka Tarawally who had served a month in prison for the contempt of parliament, *Expo Times* (edited by Sega Shaw) was still facing legal charges arising from the espionage allegations while *The Pool* (Chernor Ojukwu Sesay) was a long-time confidant of the AFRC strongman and Chief Secretary of State Captain Solomon A.J. Musa. These papers were amongst the very few who broke ranks with their colleagues and gave their support to the junta.[3]

The reaction from the majority of the people, civil society and SLAJ was to call for the rebellious soldiers to hand over power to the elected government immediately. It was not that they loved the Kabbah administration; they deplored military rule more. Barely fifteen months had passed since the consultative conference on the electoral process had voted by a margin of three-to-one for the NPRC to leave power. Sierra Leoneans remembered all too well the arbitrary and brutal nature of military rule – irrespective of whatever the AFRC might say in justification for the coup. The violence and mayhem that accompanied the May 25 upheaval only further convinced them that the soldiers must return to the barracks. Kabbah had alienated his army so much that the loyal sections of the military barely fired a shot in his defence. The major resistance came from Nigerian troops stationed at State House and members of the paramilitary Special Security Division (SSD) who held off the attacks of the mutineers for over eight hours – long after Kabbah had fled by helicopter first to the ECOMOG base at Lungi airport and then by jet to Guinea.

The rebellious soldiers then embarked on an orgy of looting. They also targeted banks, foreign exchange bureaus and private houses in search of easy money. In the process, they ignited the Central Bank after unsuccessful attempts to use rocket propelled grenades to open the vaults (Interview, AFRC soldiers, September 1997). The soldiers also did a little work as arsonists for hire; setting fire to the Treasury Building which held records implicating seven state officials who were due to go on trial the next morning for falsification and theft of state resources (Interview, AFRC soldiers, September 1997). On the morning of Tuesday 27 when it was safe to come out, thousands of Sierra Leoneans gathered at the site of the burned Treasury in mute protest. It was the first but not the last of the AFRC wanton arsons and in the coming months, Freetown was to become accustomed to the smell of burning buildings.

This unprecedented destruction and the decision of the AFRC to 'invite' the RUF to join them in a 'revolutionary' junta and the People's Army basically lost the army whatever popular sympathy they might have hoped to gain. The court of public opinion had already delivered verdict on the junta on the very morrow of the coup, although it would take nine bloody months to execute that verdict.

Civil society resistance

On Tuesday May 27, the Sierra Leone Labour Congress issued a statement denouncing the coup and calling upon the regime to step down. The Labour Congress told workers to stay home until this basic demand was accepted (*For Di People*, June 3, 1999). Denunciations of the coup also came from the National Union of Sierra Leonean Students (NUSS), the Women's Peace Movement, university dons, the petty traders' association and the association of journalists, SLAJ. In its formal position paper issued on May 28, 1997, SLAJ called on all its members to remember that freedom of expression and of the press could only be guaranteed within the framework of a democratic constitution and rule of law (SLAJ Statement May 28, 1997). This was a rather optimistic statement given its recent travails with the Kabbah regime. Due to widespread disruption and social and economic dislocation caused by the coup, it was not until early June that the first independent newspapers were issued. A public hungry for news of political developments eagerly snapped them up. Throughout the period of Junta rule, the papers consistently sold 2-3 times more than normal circulation.[4]

In many ways, the lack of resources and publication facilities turned out to be the major strength of the independent media during the period of AFRC. In an interesting pamphlet produced by an international NGO, journalist Umaru Fofana explains that most press houses lacked computers or phones and had to outsource their basic production of its copy (Fofana, 1999). This resource disadvantage enabled journalists to operate in a clandestine manner; to be on the move and to escape being caught. It often became impossible to pin down exactly where the newspapers were being published since their stated offices were just addresses in their imprints.

Guerilla journalism and subaltern press repression

One of the proponents of guerilla journalism was the *Standard Times* which quite early fell victim to the strong-arm tactics of the military. Three days after the coup, Phillip Neville, the managing editor of the paper was beaten up and robbed by soldiers when he was overheard denouncing the coup during a private conversation near his residence (*Standard Times* June 10, 1997) Standard Offices were raided three times within the first six weeks of the coup for what the AFRC Secretary General, A.K. Sesay called 'publication of disturbing and alarming stories' (Sierra Leone Web Archives). At one point in early July they suspended publication indefinitely due to what they described as unrelenting harassment from Junta forces. Publication was however resumed a week later with a stirring editorial and the quote at the start of this article (*Standard Times* July 5, 1997).

To cope with the 'unrelenting harassment', *Standard Times* devised a unique method of compiling their paper and distributing it. The *Standard Times* offices at Bathurst Street were generally opened up and left empty. A group of secretaries and messengers mingled with the residents of the neighbouring houses keeping a watchful eye on the front doors. If friends stopped by, they would emerge to redirect them to the actual site were the newspaper was being printed, several miles away. If the strangers suspected to be AFRC personnel or plain-clothes policemen entered the office they wait fruitlessly and leave the office in bewilderment (Interview, *Standard Times* staff, 1998). When the AFRC-RUF armed gangs began to target the vendors who sold popular newspapers both producers and distributors came up with an innovative response; copies of *Standard Times* were sold to trusted customers hidden between the covers of pro-junta publications which no one really wanted (Interview, Gbonor Kamara, Chief vendor 1998). The tactics were eventually adopted by most, if not all, of the Freetown's pro-democracy tabloids as the struggle against the Junta intensified.

The AFRC's attempts to woo the press soon came to an end. Isolated internationally and soon subjected to economic sanctions rigidly enforced by the Nigerian ECOMOG military contingents based at Lungi airport and Jui near the neck of the of the Freetown Peninsular, the AFRC dug in its heels. At first the attacks against the press were relatively mild. The state radio carried a press release denouncing *For Di People* for reporting on a secret AFRC-RUF delegation which travelled to Libya to seek support. The AFRC warned the press that 'Sensitive state matters must be cross-checked before publication'. Soon 'negative' press reporting the abuses of power by junta functionaries attracted a more vigorous response from the AFRC (Sierra Leone Web Archives). In July, the *New Tablet* editor, Gibrill Foday-Musa and correspondent, Emmanuel Senessie were beaten up and arrested for reporting on internal frictions between the AFRC and its RUF allies; six people were held at the offices of the *Democrat* newspaper on the suspicion of being reporters for the clandestine pro-democracy radio station FM 98.1 and Frank Kposowa, SLAJ president was declared 'wanted'. The junta swooped on his office, arrested four media workers, and claimed to have discovered documents tying the paper to an underground opposition movement (Sierra Leone Web Archives). This wave of repression did not stop the 'negative' reporting on the junta arbitrary use of power, simply because that abuse of power continued, and as pointed out earlier, this made good copy apart from other more altruistic considerations.

Throughout July, *For Di People*, Freetown's best-selling independent, continued to expose atrocities like the beheading of a paramount chief related to the vice-president Joe Demby, massacres by the army to quell low-intensity resistance from the *Kamajor* militia and the cold-blooded murder of one Miriama Sesay of Kissy. Miriama was shot by an AFRC soldier for listening to FM 98.1 radio (*For Di People*, July 1997). *Awoko* newspaper edited by VOA stringer Kelvin Lewis was the first to cross into ECOMOG territory at Lungi, and report on the tightening noose that Nigerian Commander Maxwell Khobe was drawing around the Junta. These trips continued until the AFRC discontinued ferry service to Lungi in late July (*Awoko* July 1997).

The press did not restrict its war against the AFRC to everyday reporting; almost daily an editorial, special commentary or a 'letter to the editor' (usually made up by the newspaper staff) called on the military to surrender and return power to civilians. The tone of these attacks necessarily had to be muted for tactical reasons but the message was clear: the junta should step down and save Sierra Leoneans 'further suffering'.[5]

As economic and military pressures mounted, the AFRC became more repressive. In September, freelancer and BBC stringer Umaru Fofana was shot in the leg and almost had his eyes gouged out by rebels incensed at ECOMOG bombing of the junta headquarters. (Fofana 1999). Fofana's predecessor, Victor Silva went into hiding and eventually fled to ECOMOG lines when an angry mob accused him of under-counting the victims of the Mabela bombing, a bloodly event allegedly staged by the Junta itself (Interview, Mabela and Mountain Cut residents 1998). Six journalists, including the editor of the *Independent Observer*, Jonathan Leigh, a stringer for the *Democrat*, Jon Foray and a freelancer, Mohamed Koroma were arrested in October and tortured so badly that one was left with permanent disability (Fofana, 1999). But the physical intimidation and brutality proved to be ineffectual methods for controlling the press since the junta could not simply round up all independent journalist to stop them from publishing. And from August they began to sound the need for 'responsible journalists' to register their newspaper under the terms of 'existing laws,' namely the 1980 Press Act and Kabbah's press bills (Sierra Leone Web Archives).

Like its predecessors, the Junta denied that the intent was to muzzle the press. The Information Commissioner for Junta, Sedu Turay claimed that 'we are only drawing attention to a clause in the law which has been frequently ignored'. Coming from the functionary of a regime which received no formal diplomatic recognition from a single country during its period in power, the statement could not have been more ironic. SLAJ took the decision not to follow any of the AFRC proposed guidelines 'because this would imply the recognition of an illegal regime' (SLAJ Statement November 1997). Most papers refused to obey the call for registration and continued publishing until ECOMOG launched Operation Sandstorm in mid-February 1998, which finally flushed out the Junta from power.

Shaping public opinion: Civil society and the press, 1997–1998

In a paper written well before the events of 1997, Amadu Sesay describes civil society in Sierra Leone as 'very weak' with 'few well-organized and autonomous institutions'. He argues that a 'strong' civil society can exert 'relatively high pressures for social consumption' and such pressures can lead to high politicization and debate over resource allocation (Sesay, 1999). This argument appears to be postulated on how civil society operates in the developed capitalist countries where the market is the main mediating force of resource allocation because all classes accept, almost without question, the fundamental legitimacy of capitalism. Matters are very different in a neocolonial formation where violence, especially direct physical violence, is the underlying method by which social classes take power, hold power and allocate resources.

The coercive pressure of the state can either be overthrown by a radical-revolutionary party with an entirely different vision of society and resources allocation or it can be resisted by civil society. As Robert Fatton quoting Babhia explains, 'civil society is the place where especially in periods of institutional crisis, de facto powers are formed that aim at obtaining their own legitimacy, even at the expense of the legitimate power [of the state]' (Fatton, 1992). Fatton also points out that civil society is always potentially a 'highly subversive space' where new structures and norms may take hold to challenge the existing state order. He notes, in particular, that this generally includes 'the phenomenon of public opinion understood as the public expression of agreement or dissent concerning existing institutions' (Fatton, 1992). This provides a more comprehensive explanation than Sesay's analysis of the role of civil society in Sierra Leone, especially of how the press resisted AFRC-RUF junta for nine months. The pen is never mightier than the sword except where the press both reflects and also helps shapes the articulation of powerful social interests that cannot simply be suppressed out of existence. Daring, courageous and ingenious though the independent media was in resistance to the AFRC-RUF, it survived because it was a part of a larger coalition opposed to the regime.

The coalition of interests opposed to the regime included students, teachers, labour leaders and ordinary workers, market women, university lecturers, and even sectors of the state's coercive apparatus like judges and the police. However, only the press was in a position to articulate those interests on a consistent and daily basis. Despite their hunger for power and brutal methods, the junta simply could not eliminate those who articulated those opinions; they knew they were generally unpopular. To return to Fatton once again, 'coercion generates different forms of non-compliance' (Fatton, 1992) and the AFRC could not ignore thousands of people 'voting with their feet' for exile in Guinea and the Gambia, teachers refusing to teach and reopen schools or even the passive muted hostility which their armed personnel encountered on the street on a daily basis.

The press served as a mirror to reflect the opposition to the junta both internally and externally. It covered the press releases of various civil groups, carried out interviews with leaders of organizations like the Labour Congress. Labour leaders used the newspapers as a medium to strengthen the workers solidarity in the anti-junta struggle, while simultaneously de-selecting the news items designed to paint the military in a more favourable light (*For Di People*, May 1997).

But the press was not simply a reflective surface, it also helped shaped and strengthened civil society's democratic resolve through choosing what it highlighted in reports, and by also actively working with more organized and stronger social forces which were challenging the junta. One good example of this collaboration was the role played by the media in organizing and executing the August 18 student march for democracy. Students used the offices of the *For Di People* newspaper to hold meetings to plan the demonstrations and were assisted with press funds to facilitate the action. Members of SLAJ, NUSS and radical youth groups like the Pan-African Union and Women's' movement for peace were all actively involved in the execution of this operation (Interviews, Dr. Fatmata Boie-Kamara, Karim Bah & Egerton Macauley, 1997–1998).

In times of 'institutional crisis' civil society begins to exert its influence to fill the space which the fracturing of state hegemony leaves vacant. The fact that AFRC was not only denied international recognition but also subjected to a punishing academic embargo in itself reduced its confidence and limited its effectiveness – a neocolonial state, even one ruled by drug-crazed subalterns, needs the support of 'foreign investors'. Neocolonial sate functionaries, like the fictional 'Mr. Johnson' cannot exist without a good white Massa to ape, bow to and serve (Cary, 1947).

It may be a slight digression, but a fascinating one nonetheless, to note that when Princess Diana died in a car crash in Paris the head of the AFRC junta, recognized by nobody in the world, found time to send a message of condolence to her Majesty Queen Elizabeth II consoling her on the loss of her (ex) daughter-in-law. He also ordered flags to fly at half-mast. The whole episode was thoroughly ridiculed at the time by the satirical columnist Professor Peep (*For Di People,* September 1997).

While the confidence, solidarity and working relationships between segments of civil society got stronger, the cohesion of the AFRC-RUF alliance got weaker as the weeks went by. The junta was confronted with the enormous task of containing the various avaricious tendencies it had unleashed in all ranks of the army. It had to resort to shooting its own foot soldiers to put a halt to massive looting and nightly armed robberies (Sierra Leone Web Archives). Even at the higher levels it ended up arresting and detaining operatives like Corporal Tamba Gborie, a key figure in the May 25 Coup, after he was caught looting the Iranian Embassy (Sierra Leone Web Archives). Captain S.A.J. Musa's wife later admitted in a press interview given after his death that her late husband and Colonel S.F.Y. Koroma, the Chief of Army Staff, fell out over the appropriation of a 200-carat diamond (*Vision,* January 1998).

In the test of wills between the subaltern usurpers and civil society it was clear that whoever had the greater staying power would win. Contrary to Abdel-Fateh Musa's assertion that British mercenaries from Sandline played a 'key role' in what he rather mischievously called a 'coup' (the restoration of the elected government), journalist who accompanied ECOMOG into battle do not remember any European mercenaries being present, much less playing a major role (Musa, 2000). Musa's assertion uncritically reproduces Sandline's own propaganda and minimizes the 'key role' that non-compliance civil society in Sierra Leone played in creating the conditions for ECOMOG military intervention and assurance of its success. These and similar views by sometimes well meaning NGO commentators based abroad have been instrumental in muddying the water and prolonging the agony of the people of Sierra Leone.

'Den die for natin': Victory, betrayal, and defeat

President Kabbah finally decided to return from exile on March 10 – over a month after Freetown had been retaken by ECOMOG from the AFRC-RUF alliance. The public was euphoric. The press too reflected that euphoria with headlines welcoming the president and the restoration of democracy. But the president returned to a battered country. Before the junta pulled out of Freetown, they had turned their guns on the people and burnt most of the houses in the main streets of central Freetown chanting the slogan 'No AFRC – No Salone!' Over 70 billion leones (about US$ 35 million at 1998 exchange rates) had been looted from the central and state-owned commercial banks. The AFRC appointed parastatal boards had systematically milked state enterprises like Sierratel, the telecommunications company, and State Lottery Board (*For Di People*, 1999). AFRC forces withdrew to remote areas of the country where they were later to launch operation 'NO LIVING THING' – a calculated campaign of genocide designed to alienate rural people from the government and cripple the infrastructure of the country. The public mood, as reflected in the independent press, demanded that those who imposed immense suffering on the people be brought to justice and swiftly (*For Di People*, February 1999).

President Kabbah responded to this public mood when he declared that his restoration marked a 'new beginning' for Sierra Leone and promised a non-partisan cabinet of technocrats (apparently in comparison to his pre-1997 SLPP based cabinet). Few of these euphoric promises survived for long. Though a few non-SLPP members were co-opted into the cabinet – mainly on the basis of their contributions to restoring Kabbah while abroad, rampant corruption within the state apparatus was not tackled. Indeed, short of a radical overhaul at both structure and function of the neo-colonial bureaucracy, it is difficult to see how this would come about. Both Kabbah as an individual and the SLPP as a patronage party were incapable of carrying out such a far-reaching project.

The 'new beginning' for the press lasted less than two and a half weeks after Kabbah's triumphant return. On March 27, 1998, Sorie Fofana, the editor of the *Vision* was arrested 'for the usual routine police interrogation' over a story alleging that national security adviser 'Sheka Mansaray had arbitrarily detained several policemen whom he claimed were taking bribes at checkpoints' (*For Di People* March 28, 1998). Fofana who had been a leading member of the radical wing of the independent press was released a few days later but the damage had been done. Government–press relations returned to the pre-1997 status. Some members of parliament who returned from exile even accused the press of 'fomenting the coup' through its 'irresponsible reporting' and demanded that the president sign the pre-coup press bills into law. The media was not the only sector of civil society to be repaid with ingratitude for its sacrifice to return the legitimate government to power. Teachers had to threaten strike action, when their salary arrears remained unpaid until October.

Kabbah dithered between 'retraining' and 'dissolving'. As usual he took no decisive steps in either direction. Nigerian General Maxwell Mitikishe Khobe who was seconded to serve as Chief of Defence and restructure the forces found little or no cooperation from senior state functionaries who appeared to hold the view that it was both possible and politically desirable to simply upgrade the pro-SLPP *Kamajor* militia into a modern professional army. The committee to recruit new personnel into the army met only twice between its creation in June 1998 and the cataclysm of January 1999. Both vice-president Demby and deputy defense minister Sam Hinga Norman made themselves unavailable to meet with General Khobe (Interview, Maxwell Khobe, 1998 & 1999).

The Kabbah government was dithering at a time of inauspicious developments and slow deterioration of the security situation. Nigeria was gradually scaling down its troop commitments to ECOMOG following the sudden death of military strongman, Sani Abacha. Junta troops, reinforced and rearmed by Charles Taylor, president of Liberia, made military gains east of the country. The NUSS executive met Kabbah in October and volunteered to recruit 1,000 students to serve in an expanded civil defense force. Kabbah refused. 'It is not always safe to give unknown people guns', he reportedly told the students (Interview, Egerton Macauley, NUSS President 1998–1999). So distant was Kabbah from the realities on the ground that he said in a speech in early December that the remnants of the AFRC-RUF rebels would be 'mopped up' and the 'war would end by the end of 1999' (*For Di People*, 1999). Within two weeks of the speech, Kono, in the diamond-rich district, and Makeni, the headquarters town of the northern province, had fallen to the AFRC-RUF offensive. Within another week the rebels stormed Freetown, after Julius Spencer, the information minister, had denied until the last moment that the 'rebels were coming' (*For Di People*, 1999).

Once again, a turbulent crisis broke upon the heads of the hapless population of Sierra Leone. They were disorganized and unprepared for the ferocity of the revenge attack which left over 5,000 civilians dead in the first three weeks of murder and mayhem. Human Rights Watch has extensively documented the abduction, rape, murder and mutilation carried out by the rebels on the residents of Freetown; a phase they called 'junta two' (Human

Rights Watch, 1999). Kabbah and the SLPP could not defend, organize or mobilize the people against the depredations of the rebels. When the new 'institutional crisis' erupted, many state functionaries simply abandoned their posts and fled into exile.

The people organized Civil Defense units (CDU) in their local areas to cooperate with ECOMOG as they slowly pushed out the rebels from Freetown's central and eastern zones. CDU volunteers set up roadblocks to screen and identify junta collaborators. Meanwhile Kabbah had decided to meet the detained Foday Sankoh in his place of confinement in an ECOMOG warship off the coast and get him to agree to a unilateral cease-fire. The wily Sankoh gave an ambiguous message which he promptly repudiated as he was flown to meet his commanders for talks in Conakry.

The AFRC-RUF attack on Freetown was an act of pure calculated barbarity. The *sobels* (soldier-rebels) targeted all of those who they believed had 'betrayed' them during the AFRC time in power. Journalists were prime targets. The former Secretary-General of SLAJ narrowly escaped death by leaping a back wall when armed rebels surrounded his house. SLAJ treasurer, Dorothy Awoonor-Gordon who had testified against the AFRC ringleaders during the court-martials that led to their execution, had to go underground, when a rebel squad stormed her home and asked for her. They left after unsuccessfully trying to torch the building (Interview, Dorothy Awoonor-Gordon 1999). Not all journalists were fortunate. Paul Mansaray, a senior editor with the *Standard Times* was killed with his entire family when he sought sanctuary in a church at Kissy, in the East End of the city (*Standard Times,* January 1999).

The weeks following the rebel assault on the city were chaotic. The government seemed too ready to strike a deal with the rebels at any price. However civil society and the people, who had borne the brunt of the rebel atrocities, laid down stiff conditions at the April 1999 consultative conference meeting. By consensus, they proposed to the Kabbah government that:

> Notwithstanding any arrangements for a cease-fire, immediate action should be taken to remove the rebels from areas they now occupy, particularly strategic and economic zones before the conclusion of any cease-fire arrangement *(Consultative Conference Report,* 30).

The conference rejected any form of power sharing; the RUF was to be recognized as a political party and would have to campaign for power through the ballot box (*Consultative Conference Report,* 3). The participants proposed that the rebel leader, Foday Sankoh should not be 'unconditionally amnestied' but could be pardoned in the interests of peace and reconciliation provided he 'renounces violence, unconditionally releases all abductees and allow his combatants to go through the (disarmament) DDR programme' (*Consultative Conference Report* 37). The Kabbah government jettisoned all of these recommendations when it signed the Lome Peace Accord on July 7, 1999 after two months of backroom haggling with the rebels.

On the eve of the signing of the Lome Accord. The Civil Society Movement, a coalition of the main activist groups which had engaged the junta, launched a 24-hour general strike and shut down the major cities in the country. But it was a futile and last-ditch effort; the deal had been done! It was left to the independent newspapers once more to articulate the disappointment of the voiceless majority. On the eve of the accord, the *New Tablet* ran this poignant headline which captured the public imagination: *Den Die for Natin* (They died in vain) (*New Tablet*, July 1999). The paper editorialised: 'Yours were the sacrifices made so that some people will have power while others stay in power'. Most of the major tabloids echoed this sense of betrayal. Some tried to find something redeeming or hopeful in the agreement, advocating swallowing the Lome 'bitter pill' for the sake of peace. Yet, many press commentators correctly predicted that the RUF would never be satisfied with half a loaf when it could have it all. They maintained that by rewarding violence and murder, the government had not only delegitimized its democratic credentials but had also entered an open gladiatorial arena for a vicious struggle for power.

The collapse of the Lome Peace Accord lies beyond the scope of this chapter. It is fitting however to note that when the masses marched on May 8, on Sankoh's residence to demand the disarmament of his men and the release of abducted United Nations peacekeepers, Saoman Conteh, a journalist, was one of the 21 people who died when the rebels opened fire on them.[6]

Notes

1   The Sierra Leone press is often condemned for its sensationalist reporting and poor grammar.

2   SLAJ Recommendations on Media Reform presented to Minister of Information June 7, 1997.

3. *Torchlight* even accused the SLAJ executive of taking a US$ 15,000 bribe to support democracy August 1997.

4   *For Di People*, for example, sold 4,000 copies per run before the 1997 coup; it shot up to 15,000 by mid-July 1990.

5   *For Di People*, in its July 5, 1999 edition suggested that Johnny Paul Koroma step-down to save 'poor Sierra Leoneans' from an imminent ECOMOG invasion.

6   Saoman Conteh was one of the first journalists to be detained by the AFRC-RUF junta.

Part III

Other players in the drama

Sierra Leone Diamond Areas

10

The Elusive Quest For Peace: From Abidjan to Lome

Arthur Abraham

Introduction

Contemporary Africa is at crossroads with nearly one-third of the continent convulsed in intra-state wars that are characterised by a kind of violence against civilians unprecedented in the history of conflicts on the continent. Yet, these wars are just one of the commonest manifestations of what has come to be termed 'the African Crisis', exemplified by political instability, economic failure, state collapse, social cleavages, crime, and random violence (Chabal and Daloz, 1999: xvi). The crisis itself is popularly explained by the concept of 'state failure' or 'state collapse', a situation in which the state 'withers' to the extent that it is unable to perform its most basic functions of protecting the lives and properties of its citizens, defending the state from internal and external aggression, or even controlling state agents or resources (Zartman, 1995: 5). Thus while Africa at the end of the twentieth century may appear to some as a reinvented 'dark continent', it must be admitted that these wars have not only been caused by internal factors but also by external factors which have contributed in varying degrees to the origin, progress and sustainability of these wars, most notably in the supply of arms from developed countries in return for local resources. This chapter examines the many peace initiatives and how they were botched by the rebel movement itself, and argues that the major reason for the collapse of successive initiative rests squarely with the intransigence of the RUF.

The leopard comes to town: The Revolutionary United Front

When the RUF leader Corporal Foday Sankoh and his band of mercenaries and RUF combatants took Bomaru in Kailahun in March 1991, he informed the BBC that the movement was not interested in power. His project, he declared, was a 'people's war' to 'liberate' the masses from 'the corruption and oppression of the APC government' which had ruled Sierra Leone for 23 years. Paul Richards argues that the RUF saw itself 'as a people's movement for national recovery' aimed at replacing 'Sierra Leone's patrimonial system with a revolutionary egalitarian system' (Richards, 1996: 59). There was however, no social or political agenda other than a smattering of disarticulated and undigested ideological droppings appropriated mainly from Gaddafi's vague populist formulations about a 'people's revolution'. The conduct and progress of the war was also characteristically unusual: it was not directed against its target, the APC as an organisation or as the government, nor did it specifically target APC party officials. In Kailahun district where the RUF launched the war, the main targets were chiefs, traditional office holders, local traders, prosperous farmers, and even religious leaders, who were subjected to public beheadings, forced labour and other forms of humiliation including the rape of women and girls (Abraham, 1997: 108; Muana, 1997: 79). In one of the greatest mysteries of the time, the government troops sent to battle the RUF, partnered with them, earning the sobriquet *sobels* (soldiers-cum-rebels). Then, in a deftly contrived disinformation campaign, they confused everybody by blaming each other for their actions (Keen 1995; Abraham 1997; Richards, 1996: 6).

The indiscriminate pogrom and mayhem that came to characterize the war, is admitted by everyone including the RUF which has openly confessed this 'nightmarish experience'(RUF/SL, 1995: 8) forcing Sankoh to contemplate apology on several occasions.[1] Yet abductions, rape and mutilations continue to individuate the RUF strategy. Girls as young as ten are made sex slaves, while boys of similar age and above, are drugged and conscripted as child soldiers and made to complete their 'initiation' or 'de-institutionalization' by committing their first atrocities against members of their own families (Richards, 1996: 31; Gberie, 1999: 3; *New York Times*, May 13, 1998; January 26; February 4, 1999; *Time,* January 25, 1999; *Washington Post,* January 12, 1999; *Amnesty International,* reports 1991–1999; US State Department Report in *Reuters*, February 26, 1999). This rather peculiar style of waging war transformed the countryside from small, sparsely populated, and widely dispersed villages into 'pockets of dense urban settlements' as villagers who cannot flee to other countries flocked to the main hinterland centres 'as ultimate bastions of safety' (Bangura, 1997: 218).

How do we explain this kind of violence in a movement supposedly fighting to liberate the 'masses'? First, it would appear that violence against civilians was an atavistic inheritance from the immediate Liberian ancestry of the movement, even though the contexts were not identical.[2] 'Taylor taught Sankoh a way of war', writes Michael Kelly, 'that was the last word in savagery, corrupting innocents to murder innocents' (2000: 1). But once started, violence got out of control and assumed an independent character of its own. Second, the apparent egalitarian ideology from Gaddafi's Green Book misguidedly saw all traditional office-holders and prosperous people as 'enemies of the revolution'. The problem of indiscriminate violence was opposed by the educated and disciplined members of the movement. This gave Sankoh, whose official position was 'head of ideology', an opportunity to orchestrate the execution of his rivals and thus become the sole leader of the RUF (Abdullah, 1997: 72; 1998: 23–24).

Third, the original invasion force was small, numbering 'no more than about 100 or so guerrillas' (Richards, 1996: 5), so that to increase the ranks quickly, it was necessary to capture young people by force. Trying to obtain the confidence and favour of the local population would have been difficult if not impossible. To maintain a hold on the captives, they were then inducted into the culture of violence through mind-altering drugs and forced to commit horrendous crimes in their home communities. Severed of all community linkages, the captive would have no where to run to but to stay with the RUF. As part of this culture, the boys were indoctrinated to believe that they had lost all members of their families, but had a surrogate 'father' in the person of Sankoh who would take care of all their needs. Finally, once the RUF established itself by force, terror became the sole basis of its existence. Clearly the RUF got caught in a vicious circle that has made it impossible to abandon terror and violence. Thus by its lumpen social character and terrorist methods, the RUF is, by implication, innately anti-democratic. Therefore it cannot enter an open electoral contest. It is important to remember this background in the assessment of all the abortive efforts at bringing peace to the country especially as the RUF has successfully hoodwinked many by consistently masquerading under a democratic mantle.[3]

The tortoise's short hands: Early peace initiatives

The initial peace moves to end the war did not come about as a result of external intervention. On the contrary, it originated from the communities that were attacked in 1991 when the RUF invaded Sierra Leone. Unable to wipe out the small number of the rebels before they had time to swell their ranks by terror and capture, the corrupt and decadent APC regime allegedly put out a propaganda claiming that the rebellion was a plot by the anti-APC local inhabitants to overthrow the government. Incensed by this erroneous misrepresentation, the Kailahun District Descendants Association (KDDA) mounted a huge demonstration in Freetown in mid-1991. The Association petitioned the President by emphasising the unity of Sierra Leone pointing out that an attack on any part should be seen as an attack on the whole country. They then urged him to consider the rebellion as a national crisis and to respond appropriately. But the President's reply was anything but encouraging: the army which is a peace-time army, he told the delegation, had been sent to contain the situation. He then advised the Paramount Chiefs to return and help with local defence by organising vigilante groups arming themselves with stones, slings, machetes, and spears to confront rebels using automatic weapons (KDDA minutes, 1991–92; *West Africa* culled in *Daily Observer*, Banjul, 20 August 1997).

Meanwhile, the rebellion gradually gained momentum. In April 1992, disgruntled young soldiers who had been sent to fight the RUF came to Freetown to protest inadequate salary and deteriorating conditions. This was a cover for a coup that had been planned well in advance. The young officers seized power and formed the National Provisional Ruling Council (NPRC) under their most senior officer, Captain V.E.M. Strasser. The RUF leadership was expecting the coupist to invite them to join the new government but this did not materialise because of the excessive demands of the movement. The NPRC's suggestions for a half-way compromise was rejected by Sankoh after Charles Taylor advised that the plan was a foreign ploy to get rid of the RUF (Abdullah and Muana, 1998: 181). Sankoh thereafter made a surprising volte-face and accused the 'rebel NPRC' of being the 'watchdogs of the APC government', who had been 'introduced to hijack the revolution', by whom, we do not know. He denounced the NPRC as undemocratic because it did not represent the people and was simply illegitimate, corrupt and repressive like the APC. Sankoh claimed he wanted a 'people's government' and he chided international organizations for their recognition of the NPRC (RUF/SL 1995; *New African*, July 1993, 12–14).

Other peace initiatives involving the Commonwealth, the Organisation of African Unity (OAU) and the UN, proved difficult mainly because Sankoh appeared elusive. This was because he was distrustful of them with the exception of one, International Alert (IA), a London-based conflict resolution non-governmental organization, whose agent, Ayaaba Addai-Sebo, a Ghanaian, had once been Charles Taylor's publicist and was known to Sankoh and the RUF (Richards 1996: 15–16; IA 1995: 1). From early 1995, Addai-Sebo became a close adviser to Sankoh and a frequent visitor to the RUF bases. He actually warned the RUF against dealing with 'imperialist' organizations like the UN and the Commonwealth which would just ruin their cause, and attempted to monopolise access to the RUF.[4] Far from facilitating the process of bringing peace, International Alert actually made the task more tortuous. Much of the hard-line posturing and evasive tactics of the RUF in subsequent negotiations may be attributed, in part at least, to the influence and advice of Addai-Sebo, who was officially International Alert's 'special envoy' to the Sierra Leone peace talks.

'The future is in your hands': Rebels, *sobels* and elections as a peace strategy

A combination of domestic and external pressures pushed the NPRC to announce a democratic transition programme in November 1993. The people were utterly disgusted with the ruthlessness and rampant corruption of the NPRC government as well as by its refusal to end the war, while the international community, drawing from little experience elsewhere, saw elections as the best hope of goading the RUF into a political position that would eventually end the war. This peace strategy in itself would have been problematic even if conditions were different precisely because it was based on the rather misleading assumption that the RUF was interested in peace. It is therefore difficult to understand the thinking behind organising the elections when the RUF had neither surrendered nor been defeated; when the RUF and government soldiers were in control of diamond-mining fields and known to be collaborating; when the RUF controlled its supply lines and access to its political patron, Charles Taylor of Liberia who received diamonds and supplied arms to the RUF. Above all, there was no reliable army for a new democratic government to inherit. However much the people might want a democratically elected government, the means to protect them and assure them of peace simply did not exist.

After the announcement of the electoral timetable, Sankoh was invited by the Interim National Electoral Commission (INEC) to register the RUF as a political party and participate in the elections. Instead he threatened to disrupt the elections: 'democracy and elections will have to wait until we have freed the country,' he declared from his base in the Gola Forest reserves (*West Africa*, 1–7 May, 10–16 July 1995). The Bintumani National Consultative Conference (Bintumani I) held in August voted overwhelmingly for elections to be held on 26 February 1996 (See Kandeh this volume). At this point, the interests of the RUF and the NPRC in forestalling elections and the return to democratic rule became overtly congruent. Thus at the OAU meeting with the RUF held in Abidjan in December, Sankoh made an extraordinary statement that flabbergasted observers, considering that the RUF was at war with the NPRC. Sankoh remarked that he was not targeting Strasser and the NPRC, but rather 'corruption, which is the ideology of the APC'. A foreign journalist observed that 'in fact, the RUF appeared to have been complaining about the APC and its excesses, rather than the NPRC' (*West Africa*, 8–14 January 1996).

Then in January 1996 a palace coup removed Strasser as head of the NPRC government; his deputy, Julius Maada Bio, whose sister was a top ranking RUF official became the new head of state. Bio contacted Sankoh about proposals for ending the war and both agreed to begin peace talks in Abidjan on 28 February. To demonstrate his commitment to the proposed peace talks, Sankoh immediately declared a temporary ceasefire for two months (*West Africa*, 22–28 January 1996). In a bid to scuttle the elections, Bio suddenly informed the nation that it was preferable to postpone the elections until the end of the war, prompting a second Bintumani conference which was duely held on 12 February. The conference voted overwhelmingly for elections to be held as scheduled. A last fling at scuttling the elections came from the army chief who immediately warned that the army might not be in a position to provide adequate security for the elections (*West Africa*, 19–25 February 1996).

Confused over a clear strategy for prolonging its stay in power, the NPRC had toyed with the idea of transforming itself into a political party, but painfully aware of its profound unpopularity, supported instead the fabrication of a surrogate outfit controlled by civilians called the National Unity Party (NUP). This party clearly had no chances, and some other means had to be found to sabotage the elections. Soldiers stole ballot boxes, and on polling day, began heavy firing to intimidate the people. The RUF, for its part, tried to stop the elections by carrying out several attacks in rural areas, killing several people and burning houses and villages (*West Africa*, 4–10 March 1996). According to the RUF:

> RUF fighters in the bush went on the rampage and as their own way of stating their objection to the planned elections, they proceeded on a campaign to cut off the hands of innocent villagers as a message that no voting should occur…. These men decided to employ the tactics of APC men…. These learned [sic] thuggery and cruel inhumanity is [sic] one of the most regrettable part [sic] of the entire RUF war... (RUF Political Wing Press Release, January 15,1999).

The indiscriminate amputations extended to babies and children of non-voting age, which raises serious doubts about whether the RUF was really 'making a political statement', or another exhibition of its character as a terrorist organization. The elections went on as scheduled, and a legitimate government was elected under Ahmed Tejan Kabbah of the Sierra Leone People's Party (SLPP) in what was described by international observers as the 'freely expressed choices of the people' (African-American Institute, 1996: 26).

Playing a yo-yo: The road to Abidjan

Bio and Sankoh resumed talks in Abidjan on 28 February, two days after polling, as promised. The RUF demanded an annulment of the election results because, according to Sankoh, the elections were a UN-sponsored plot to take control over Sierra Leone. After much groundwork by the UN and other international agencies, Sankoh and President Kabbah, who took office at the end of March agreed to an 'indefinite' truce. The next four weeks were consumed by a flurry of top-level discussions and negotiations, preliminary to the actual peace conference in May. International Alert openly took sides with the RUF instead of acting as a neutral facilitator, and advised that 'a level playing field cannot be constructed if any of the mediating organizations are [sic] seen by a party to the conflict as an instrument of the national interest of a foreign power and/or 'foreign troops and mercenaries' (International Alert, 1996: 15).

Not surprisingly, the RUF insisted that all foreign troops and mercenaries should leave the country before disarmament, to which the government responded that 'disengagement of friendly forces would commence in tandem with the encampment and disarming of RUF fighters'(*West Africa*, 17–23 June; 1–7 July; 29 July–4 August 1996). By trying to diminish the military capacity of the government and correspondingly increase that of the RUF, it appears that International Alert, or its representative, would not have been opposed to the RUF seizing the government undemocratically. And interestingly, no one in all the peace negotiations ever referred to the RUF's own mercenaries, the Liberians, Burkinabes, and South Africans. According to Ivorian officials, Sankoh was not disposed to sign any peace agreement. He was in touch with former NPRC military personnel who intimated him of a coup plot and Sankoh's real preference was to enter a power-sharing arrangement with them (Jones, 1999: 42). Thus, when government covertly presented the RUF with a list of possible appointments Sankoh again raised the issue of foreign troops and demanded the Vice-Presidency and several ministerial positions for his rebels as a condition for laying down arms, which the government was unable to concede (*West Africa*, 29 July–4 August 1996).

The mediators however continued to encourage Sankoh to accept the government's offer. Meanwhile, for the first time ever, Sankoh, on behalf of RUF, issued a public statement broadcast over national radio on 18 June 1996, apologising to the nation for the atrocities his men continued to commit against fellow Sierra Leoneans. He told Sierra Leonean students in Abidjan that he was prepared for a lasting peace agreement with the new government (*Expo Times*, 14 August 1996), and vowed never to return to the bush (*Freedom Now*, 24 August 1996). Yet frequent cease-fire violations became a public concern in Sierra Leone.

Then at the end of August, Sankoh suddenly announced that he was dropping his objections and was consequently given permission to be flown to his bases to brief his fighters about the new development. A week later, on 8 September, the government announced the discovery of a coup plot and arrested several people, including Major Johnny Paul Koroma, a suspected *sobel* with NPRC connections (Gberie, 1997: 152). Are there any connections between Sankoh's departure and the coup plot? Back at the UN, President Kabbah urged the international community in his maiden address to impose sanctions on the RUF, because despite extensive government concessions,

Sankoh was still being evasive. After that, he told the press that 'there are now no insurmountable differences between the…RUF and the government' even though at that material time a high-powered RUF delegation was in Belgium, reportedly on an arms purchasing mission' (*West Africa*, 21–27 October 1996). It appears that Kabbah did not have any proper appreciation of the kind of leadership he was dealing with. Or if he did, he was incapable of devising a robust alternative.

The robust alternative – the military option – was perhaps what Sankoh was capable of understanding best. A major offensive by the *Kamajoi* militia, backed by Executive Outcomes (EO),[5] resulted in several major training and operations bases of the RUF being razed with serious loss of rebel lives (Muana, 1997: 93–94). The RUF had never been under such stress in the war since their 1993 rout by the NPRC. The government, had it so elected, could have made the fullest use of this advantage. But it goofed badly when it ostensibly bowed to pressure from the IMF, and announced the termination of EO's contract. This blunder provided the political and military space that Sankoh needed to manoeuvre and muster the capacity for another military strike.

On 30 November 1996, the Abidjan Peace Accord was eventually signed, signalling the end of the war 'with immediate effect'. A blanket amnesty was granted to the RUF, and a Commission for the Consolidation of Peace (CCP) was to be set up, which in turn was to create several other bodies including the Demobilization and Resettlement Committee. The RUF was to transform into a political party, while its demobilised combatants were eligible to be considered for recruitment into a restructured national army. A Neutral Monitoring Group from the international community was to be deployed to monitor cease-fire violations, while Executive Outcome were to be withdrawn. Finally, the accord bound the signatories to respect international humanitarian law, implying the targeting of unarmed civilians.

In its generosity, the Abidjan Peace Accord was clearly an RUF victory. It protected the RUF from prosecution, and even though no government positions were given to the RUF, the treaty put both on the same political pedestal, making the RUF a potentially important player in the political future of the country. But the treaty was not without flaws. With respect to the most important organ to be set up, the CCP, there was no time-frame pegged to the implementation of the tall order of its work. The Abidjan peace accord was surprisingly silent on atrocities and a truth commission as part of a healing process. It was also silent on the *Kamajoi* militia, even though it was involved in the conflict and needed to be demobilised like other armed groups. Above all, the treaty lacked a review mechanism which would have been able to detect flaws and recommend appropriate action in time.

Rough ride: From Abidjan to Bloody Sunday

The ink was still fresh on the signed accord when Sankoh started his usual theatrics. This time he not only refused to nominate members to the critical Demobilization and Resettlement Committee which was responsible for disarmament but opposed the decision to send 720 UN peacekeeping observers. He accused Berhanu Dinka, Special Envoy of the UN Secretary-General, of being an 'obstacle to peace' for supporting the elections which he called a 'coup d'état', aimed at placing a former UN official in charge of the country (Dumbuya, 1999: 2). Meanwhile, Executive Outcome left the country at the end of January 1997, but not before warning the government that it should watch out for a coup, which was likely within six months (Personal Interview with two cabinet ministers, July 1997.) Not unexpectedly, accusations and counter-accusations of cease-fire violations increased and the security situation deteriorated. Efforts to pursue and track down rebels who had been attacking civilians and ambushing passenger and food convoys on the highways were described by Sankoh as unprovoked attacks on the RUF aimed at preventing his return to Sierra Leone and thus jeopardising the peace process (*West Africa*, 3–9 March 1997). This was the situation in Sierra Leone when in March 1997 Sankoh turned up in Lagos, Nigeria allegedly to finalise arrangements for the purchase of heavy weapons from Ukraine. He was picked up at the airport for illegally carrying a personal weapon and ammunition (*For Di People*, 4 April 1997).

On 15 March 1997, the external delegation of the RUF met in Abidjan and issued a press statement removing Sankoh from the leadership of the RUF for his unyielding determination to thwart the peace process and prolong the suffering of the people of Sierra Leone'. Captain Philip Palmer signed the release and the new leadership pledged to co-operate with the Kabbah government and the UN. This group comprised the *crème de la crème* of the RUF, educated, professional or semi-professional, as opposed to the lumpen, uneducated mass with their hardened commanders, who saw no future for themselves if they dropped their guns. The battle group commanders did not support the breakaway group. But the government immediately welcomed the change. Captain Philip Palmer, the new leader, then led a delegation through Guinea to the Kailahun District RUF stronghold to discuss with the loyalist. He was promptly arrested and detained by the senior battlefield commander, Sam Bockarie (*Unity Now*, 24 March 1997; *The Point*, 2 April 1997; *For Di People*, 4 April 1997; *West Africa*, 7–13 April 1997).

These events culminated in the bloody Sunday overthrow of the Kabbah government on 25 May 1997, a joint action of a faction of the army and the RUF, putting an end to the one-year-old democratic experiment. A military junta, the Armed Forces Ruling Council (AFRC/RUF), was established. Sierra

Leoneans were assured that the peace they so badly longed for was now theirs as the army and the RUF became the 'People's Army'. The President later admitted that he had been informed about the coup several days before but failed to take the necessary precaution (*West Africa*, 20–26 January 1997). Major Johnny Paul Koroma, already in detention for his part in a previous coup, was sprung from gaol and prevailed upon to head the AFRC. Sankoh became the deputy, even though he was still detained in Nigeria. Koroma accused Kabbah of 'failure to consolidate...peace in our motherland' which threatened to degenerate into 'factional conflicts', an obtuse reference to the *Kamajoisia*, hated by both the soldiers and the RUF, although for different reasons (See Gberie this volume). Other grievances included failure to address welfare problems of soldiers and the 'killer Press Bill' (*The Point*, May 31, 1997; *Expo Times*, June 12, 1997).

The popular perception at the time of the coup was that the RUF was marginal to the take-over, having been invited by the soldiers *ex post facto*. One perceptive observer has argued rather convincingly that it was the other way around, that the RUF was dominant, 'the military...merely used as a conduit for an RUF-led invasion' (Sesay, 1997). It is now known that rebels had infiltrated the city some three weeks before the coup. Many of the soldiers who staged the coup were from Daru barracks in Kailahun District, the RUF stronghold. The pattern of the take-over had RUF written all over: indiscriminate looting and destruction of that which could not be looted; disregard for all diplomatic immunity in the looting process; raping of women (a sore point in Freetown) and harassing of civilians; recruitment through jail breaks; use of civilian clothing as camouflage; communication through gun shots; battle cries mostly in Liberian dialects; graffiti-like death squads and death angels painted on vehicles and walls (Sesay, 1997). This was the most unpopular coup ever staged in the history of Sierra Leone; it was bereft of both internal and external support. The international community was outraged; the OAU and the Commonwealth condemned the bloody take over, the UN later followed with suffocating sanctions and embargo. The OAU for the first time gave a mandate for the restoration of the legitimate government. But the involvement of frustrated politicians who rallied to the junta compounded the problem.

An ECOWAS Committee of Five (Nigeria, Ghana, Côte d'Ivoire, Guinea and the OAU) was set up to dialogue with the Junta. They were under intense pressure to 'discuss the early restoration of constitutional order'. But while a meeting was going on in Abidjan in July, Koroma announced, *à la* RUF, a transitional programme that would see the junta in office until 2001. The meeting was forced to reschedule another round of peace talks in Conakry. The Conakry Peace Plan was signed on 23 October 1997, providing for a six-month transition, and eventual restoration of the Kabbah government in

May 1998. But the junta began to filibuster and Koroma set forth a number of 'concerns and conditions' including the 'formation, composition, duration and role' of the government the junta would hand over to while calling for Nigerian ECOMOG troops to leave the country immediately.[6]

These mixed signals convinced ECOMOG commanders that the junta had changed from its position taken in Guinea. In January, junta ministers made several phone calls to *West Africa* magazine in London informing them that contrary to the Conakry Plan, the junta would not step down, the rebels would not demobilise, and fresh elections would have to be arranged (*West Africa*, 16–22 February 1998). Then on 8 February, an ECOMOG patrol vehicle hit a landmine at Kissy in the east of Freetown whereupon, it came under 'concentrated fire' from the junta forces, killing some Nigerians. This provided the occasion for ECOMOG to start a full-scale offensive that eventually led to the take over of Freetown on 15 February 1998. Several junta ministers and key players were captured but Koroma and the RUF top-notch escaped. Kabbah himself returned on 10 March.

Restoration of democracy or from the frying pan to the fire?

President Kabbah's restoration was most unprecedented. Yet, it was marred by a popular desire for revenge, set out in his Address to the Nation on the Restoration of Democracy in March 1998. Two thousand people were arrested and detained for 'collaborating' with the AFRC/RUF. Amendments were made to the law to make it easier to convict anyone arraigned before the Courts.[7] For several reasons, the massiveness of the incarceration was doltish and counter-productive. In the first place, the country lacked the capacity to handle, process and try such a large number of people without making a mockery of justice. The decayed, antiquated, and slumberous judiciary, pitiful and reputed to have long lost its basic attribute of dispensing justice, coupled with a scanty bench dominated by mediocrity or incompetence, and a self-seeking and corrupt bar, guaranteed that if the President's Herculean task was to be accomplished, justice might well not have been expected. Secondly, the exercise would have been exceedingly time-consuming and financially costly if it was to be conducted in a fair and just manner. Thirdly, if the meaning of the term 'collaborator' were to be stretched to its fullest elasticity, collaborators might well have tried collaborators. The dynamic of the situation was such that many people, although opposed to the junta, but with no capacity for a sustained resistance, could have been goaded to serve the junta under duress or out of fear. Yet no distinctions were made. In all, 59 civilians who served the junta were charged with treason and conspiracy and tried by two tribunals which sentenced 16 to death in August and another 11 again in October, respectively.

A Court Martial trial of 38 military personnel on charges of treason, murder and collaborating with the enemy ended in October, with 34 convicted and sentenced to death by firing squad. As there is no legal appeal from a Court Martial verdict under the laws of Sierra Leone, international appeals for clemency or a stay of execution poured in. Kabbah commuted ten sentences to life imprisonment but approved the execution of twenty-three men and one woman which took place on 19 October 1998. Kabbah came under severe international criticism. At home, the RUF issued a statement that they would avenge the execution of the military officers, while the AFRC said they would attack Freetown in retaliation.

The month of October also saw the dramatic trial of Sankoh, who had been repatriated from Nigeria at the end of July. In September, he was charged with treason, soliciting support for forces hostile to the state of Sierra Leone, and invasion of Sierra Leone. No lawyer was forthcoming to defend Sankoh, and so the Kabbah government, towards the end of September, passed a law under emergency regulations stating that 'a trial shall not be invalidated or adjourned merely because of the absence of a legal practitioner representing' a defendant, who had a right to represent himself. This undignified perversion of the justice system by President Kabbah who is apparently said to be a lawyer himself, is difficult to fathom, much less justify. To have got an ill-educated terrorist like Sankoh to defend himself in technically prone criminal proceedings in the High Court without the government going all out to ensure that he got the best representation, would seem to be nothing short of making a mockery of justice. On 23 October, Sankoh was found guilty of treason and sentenced to death.

To all intents and purposes, there existed a conjuncture of events by the end of October, which was ominous for the state. The trials, which did not give the impression of having been conducted according to the highest standards required by law, and in particular, the executions, vexed and provided renewed courage for all the rebel groups to strike back. This was not apparent to the government, which throughout this period, kept talking tough, even dismissing the AFRC/ RUF request for peace talks to be sponsored by the UN or Commonwealth. The AFRC soldiers therefore began making plans to attack Freetown; the RUF joined the AFRC. Charles Taylor, as usual, provided shelter to the RUF, whose attack squads were trained in Liberia by erstwhile South African Defence Force Colonel Fred Rindle with the support of Libyan military trainers and other mercenaries. These squads hid in the Freetown suburbs days prior to the January assault (*Africa Confidential*, 12 May 2000). The collaboration of an international cartel of criminal gangsters harboured by Taylor, was intended to create a satellite state directed by him, so that they would have free rein over Sierra Leone's diamonds and other resources in order to pillage them (*London Times*, 11 February 1999).

Reportedly led by the AFRC junta whose fleeing soldiers a year previously had hidden lots of arms in tombs in the city cemetries, the assault on the capital of Freetown in January 1999 was the most brutal offensive in the then eight-year war. The invading force included several nationalities (*London Times*, 11 February 1999; *Reuters*, 19 February 1999; *Sierra Leone News – Sierra Leone Web*, [SLN-SLW] January 19, 1999). In fact arrested Israeli reserve colonel, Yair Klein, who recruited the mercenaries,[8] 'admitted to shipping arms from the Ukraine and Libya to the rebels' using Liberia as the base (*Reuters*, 29 January; 19 February 1999). On the first day, the eastern and central districts of the city were taken in a lightening flash with monstrous devastation. The rebels broke open the central prisons and not finding Sankoh there, instead released the prisoners they found including junta soldiers and coup convicts. Top RUF commander thought to be second to Sankoh, Sam Bockari, who glorifies in killing for the purpose of becoming famous and redeeming his marginality and physical stature, told reporters that 'what we want... is Kabbah to leave', and at another time, that the attack would only stop if Sankoh were unconditionally released (*Associated Press*, January 8, 1999; *Reuters*, January 15 and 29, 1999). By the time ECOMOG was able to secure Freetown, over 3,000 children were reported missing and more than 5,000 lay dead. One third of the population of the city was made homeless (Coll 2000, 25; *SLN-SLW*, January 14, 1999).

President Kabbah and Foday Sankoh met secretly the following day and agreed on a seven-day cease-fire, a return to 1996 Abidjan Peace Accord in return for Sankoh's release. Sankoh ordered his combatants to hold on while Kabbah informed the nation of the cease-fire. As pro-government and ECOMOG troops pushed back the invaders to the eastern suburbs the following week, Sankoh was flown to a meeting of ECOWAS foreign ministers in Conakry where he flatly denied having agreed to a cease-fire with Kabbah. He told the BBC, 'I have not declared any cease-fire. No, no, no, that's wrong...We just have to negotiate...A military option will never succeed in Sierra Leone... As long as I'm in prison, [the rebels] will never obey any cease-fire' (*SLN-SLW*, March 8, 10, 12, 1999; *BBC Online News*, January 9, 10, 12, 1999). Shortly after, at a press conference in Monrovia, Charles Taylor announced a one-week unilateral cease-fire on behalf of the RUF while reiterating a call for the immediate and unconditional release of Sankoh. Sankoh was not released; the cease-fire did not hold! (*SLN-SLW*, January 14, 15, 19, 1999; *Associated Press*, January 18, 1999). For the first time, Britain and the United States directly accused Taylor of sponsoring the rebels and warned him to desist.

Crucifixion: Justice carries its cross in Lome

As frantic diplomatic efforts continued, the RUF reiterated its commitment to peace on the understanding that it had never questioned the legitimacy of the Kabbah government, and that the RUF was not fighting against the civilian population, but against ECOMOG and the civil defence militia. The RUF declared it 'constituted a single unified structure' with the renegade army, and agreed to a cease-fire to facilitate 'dialogue' but wanted no preconditions to be set by either party, although it requested the release of Foday Sankoh.

President Bill Clinton sent his Special Envoy for Africa, Rev. Jesse Jackson, to urge Kabbah to 'reach out' to the RUF, and be more flexible in dealing with some of the rebel demands. Jackson brokered a cease-fire agreement, which was signed by Kabbah and Sankoh on May 18 (Lizza, 2000: 22). Substantive talks could not get under way for several days because the RUF again raised the issue of the 'immediate and unconditional' release of Sankoh as a pre-condition and argued that by accepting 'the legitimacy of President Kabbah's government, it was in effect dropping its proposal for a transitional government'. The RUF had clearly perfected its consistent inconsistencies of shifting the political goal post whenever it suits it needs.

In the negotiations, the RUF demanded the vice-presidency, ten ministerial portfolios in a proposed 20-man cabinet in a transitional government, and a tall order of senior positions. The list of RUF demands for a power-sharing arrangement, almost looks like a total surrender of the government to the RUF[9] (*SLN-SLW*, June 9, 10, 1999; *Associated Press*, June 10,1999). The government's offer of four was rejected as 'not enough'. However, at the instigation of Charles Taylor, the RUF dropped its latest demands and accepted to sign the peace agreement (*Agence France Presse*, July 5, 1999; *BBC Online News*, July 7, 1999). The Lome Peace Agreement was signed on 7 July 1999, between the government of Sierra Leone represented by President Kabbah and the RUF represented by Cpl. Foday Sankoh in the presence of West African leaders Eyadema, Obasanjo, Taylor, Compaore, the Foreign Ministers of Ghana and Côte d'Ivoire, and the representatives of the OAU, ECOWAS, UN, and the Commonwealth. The four international organizations and the government of Togo undertook to be 'moral guarantors' to ensure the implementation of the agreement 'with integrity and in good faith by both parties'. Kabbah called on the people to 'forgive and forget' while Sankoh 'deplored all atrocities' and asked for forgiveness from the people.

Under the Lome Agreement, the RUF entered into power-sharing with the government, the RUF being offered four cabinet positions, four deputy ministerial positions, while Sankoh himself became the Chairperson of the new Commission for the Management of Strategic Resources, National Reconstruction and Development (CMRRD), with the protocol status of

Vice-President. The Agreement also provided for disarmament of all combatants including pro-government militias under the supervision of a neutral UN peace-keeping force, the restructuring of the army, the transformation of the RUF into a political movement with access to posts in the army and administration. Article IX gave 'absolute and free pardon' to Sankoh as well as 'to all combatants and collaborators' who committed war crimes. The Lome Accord also made provision for the setting up a Truth Commission to allow victims 'tell their stories', a Human Rights Commission, and a Commission for the Consolidation of Peace to supervise and monitor the peace process.

The major difference between the Abidjan and Lome peace accord is contextual. When Abidjan was signed, the RUF was on the run; in 1999 it was on the offensive. All carrots and no stick, this agreement ran contrary to the general mood in Sierra Leone, where a mass protest against power-sharing with the rebels paralysed the capital (*Reuters*, 17 June 1999). In spite of the groundswell of opposition to power sharing, the President nevertheless decided to believe that it had 'the approbation of … the populace of Sierra Leone' (*Concord Times*, 20 July 1999). The Lome Accord shocked the conscience of the world, and gave rise to a veritable storm of protest. Human rights organizations condemned the agreement for providing a blanket amnesty as a violation of international law. Peter Takirambudde of Human Rights Watch gave a graphic summary:

> For civil society in Sierra Leone [and]…in Africa generally, the amnesty shook the concept of accountability to the core. It represented a major retreat by all the parties…For the rest of Africa, where there are rebels in the bush, the signal is that atrocities can be committed – especially if they are frightening atrocities. The lesson to other rebels is that half measures will not do (Quoted in Coll 2000: 27).

The mediators defended the agreement as the only practical way to achieve peace. But the appeasement policy which led to this 'peace without justice', was not only the wrong policy, it was both dangerous and disastrous. The major blunder was in the basic postulate underlying the whole approach to the negotiations which assumed that the RUF was genuinely interested in peace, and that in return for a share of power and other concessions, it would be willing to end the fighting and reinvent itself as a legitimate political movement ready to vie for power in a democratic context. It was hoped that by merely signing an agreement, the RUF would *ipso facto*, behave like a civilised movement (Seyon, 2000: 1–2; Reno, 2000: 1). Mr. Sankoh was misguidedly treated as a champion of the rural poor although the record of his movement's barbaric terror directed against them was very well known, making it difficult to fathom whether the mediators had indeed acted in good faith.

The power-sharing model too, was inappropriate, as free and fair elections had been held. So what the Accord did instead was to get the RUF to participate in a democratic political process by undemocratic means. The Agreement also failed to take into consideration the interests of other armed factions, principally the AFRC and the *Kamajoisia*. By allowing the rebels to remain in the diamond areas and making Sankoh responsible for the country's minerals, the agreement failed to remove the RUF's primary means to prosecute the war. Any incentive for upholding peace by the RUF was lost, and the agreement was a time bomb waiting to explode. As US Republican Senator Judd Gregg correctly observed this 'graveyard peace' called Lome 'gave the RUF at the negotiating table all the things it could not capture on the battlefield...It was surrender at its most abject' (*Washington Post*, 9 May 2000). A democratically elected government was forced to share power with a terrorist organization.

Back to square one: Even rewarding evil is not enough

But problems started almost immediately. A number of actions under the agreement were due for implementation two weeks after signing, including the formation of Sankoh's CMRRD, but Sankoh delayed coming home for another three months. Ironically, the self-proclaimed champion of the masses was afraid to be present in Freetown without sufficient security. In the meantime, RUF commanders attacked and assaulted the press for writing critical articles, and clashes began between the RUF and the AFRC because the RUF allegedly marginalized them at Lome and humiliated their leader. They asserted that the AFRC 'attack on Freetown made it possible for the release of Cpl. Foday Sankoh and the convening of the Lome Peace Conference' (AFRC: 1999a). Sankoh warned them against disturbing the peace process and began accusing them of being 'responsible for the atrocities and the amputations in January' 1999.

Sankoh and Koroma arrived in Freetown on October 3 after staying in Monrovia, and issued a very reassuring joint statement that peace was definite. However, it soon became apparent that Koroma was far more sincere in keeping the peace and disarming than Sankoh who was cautioning the following week that there should be no rush with disarmament. In October, the UN approved 6,000 peace-keeping troops for Sierra Leone (UNAMSIL), which together with ECOMOG, were to disarm and demobilise approximately 45,000 combatants. Sankoh complained that the Agreement did not ask UN for peacekeeping troops. But Sam Bockarie, Sankoh's most vicious terrorist commander, lashed out that the UN was jeopardising the peace process and later informed a press team that 'we will not disarm until total revolution is achieved in Sierra Leone' (Coll, 2000, 15; CCP Press Statement, 12 November 1999). While Bockarie was undiplomatically stating the true RUF agenda, Sankoh proceeded to register the RUF party (RUFP) as a diplomatic cover-up.

Meanwhile, Kabbah appointed Sankoh and Koroma to the National Committee for Disarmament, Demobilization and Reintegration (DDR), and few weeks later, appointed them respectively to head the CMMDR and the CCP. The AFRC began disarming immediately, but the RUF was slow and according to UNAMSIL, was turning in the least numbers. From about the middle of October, thousands of RUF fighters moved in from Liberia and Bockarie ordered massive movements of heavily armed troops from Kailahun in the east to Makeni in the north where they dislodged the AFRC. As December approached, a rift developed between Bockarie and Sankoh with a common concern that they might attempt to arrest or assassinate each other. After failing to seize the Daru military barracks, Bockarie fled to Liberia on December 16. Thus, disarmament, the real pillar for ensuring peace and the success of the whole agreement, was painfully slow, showing only 12 percent disarmed by the December 15 deadline for the total disarmament of the estimated 45,000 combatants. The UN Secretary-General decided to request an increase in the number of peace-keeping troops to about 10,000.

To divert attention, Sankoh called a press conference on violations of the Lome agreement at the end of December (RUFP, 1999; 2000). The government responded in a Reaction Paper (30 December 1999). An analysis of these documents reveals Sankoh's skill in the art of propaganda, distortion, and half-truths, through manipulation of facts including concealment, allegations, outright lies, exaggerations, and deception. Knowing fully well that he was scuttling the peace process, he presented himself as the only genuine party interested in maintaining peace. He reiterated for the umpteenth time that the whole peace process was a UN plot against Sierra Leone. This is not to say that Sankoh did not have any genuine grievances. There were some for which he already knew the answers, namely, government lack of funds, while others were loopholes created by the Kabbah government which he lost no time in exploiting. Interestingly, in all his litany of complaints, was the conspicuous absence of any reference, as provided in the agreement, to the immediate freedom of political prisoners, abductees, and child soldiers, whom the RUF was notoriously guilty of holding.

As the New Year opened, Sankoh decided to test the UN troops who, under no orders to fight, and hampered by bureaucracy and insufficient logistical and other support, were in no position to resist force from the RUF. The RUF successfully obstructed UNAMSIL from deploying at a disarmament centre, and then disarmed a few Guinean and Kenyan UN troops, all with impunity. On 14 January, a Guinean Battalion moving overland to join UNAMSIL was intercepted and their arms and two armoured vehicles carted away. Sankoh at first denied that the incident ever took place only to later revealed that the said seizures had been made without his permission. This set a pattern for rebel obstructionism, kidnapping, abducting, and disarming more UN troops in the next few months. All this while, Sankoh kept giving false assurances that he was committed to democracy and the Lome agreement, but he also managed to convey his complete abomination of the UN, describing it as a colonialist organization working to get control of the African continent (Lynch, 2000: 1-3)

It appears that the UN underestimated Sankoh, and did not treat him as seriously as they should have done. It was not until the middle of March 2000 that 107 Indian UNAMSIL peacekeeping troops were deployed in Kailahun, Sankoh's stronghold. The lack of any serious response from UNAMSIL emboldened Sankoh to launch more verbal and later physical attacks. Accompanying a high-level disarmament mission on 10 April to his strongholds of Segbwema and Daru where only 70 combatants showed up, some empty-handed, Sankoh described Parliamentarians who were on the mission as 'old crooks', 'thieves and criminals' and then admonished his supporters not to yield to any UN pressure. He then instructed them to disarm anyone who fired a gun, 'be it a UN soldier or not' (*Concord Times*, 11 April 2000).

The denouement: Masquerade unmasked

As May approached, Sankoh carefully chose the moment for the maturity of his plans. He had molested and disarmed UN troops with impunity and added to his own stockpile. He had verbally assaulted and insulted the UN and its Secretary-General, Members of Parliament and the government of Sierra Leone, also with impunity. As long as Sankoh kept making political digressions and falsely assuring everybody that he was committed to peace, no sanction seemed possible against him. Nigerian ECOMOG troops were pulling out and their replacement by UNAMSIL would take a while to arrive. The new government army had not been trained. It was time to make a move!

On 1 May, a disarmament mission to Magburaka in the North was stoutly opposed. Commotion broke out when Kenyan soldiers tried to recover a box of ammunition seized by the rebels, resulting in the deaths of seven UNAMSIL soldiers and an equal number of rebels. Almost simultaneously in neighbouring Makeni, rebels took nearly 50 UNAMSIL soldiers hostage (*Expo Times*, 5 May 2000). Sankoh denied his men were holding any hostages, but ordered search parties. Yet the number of hostages doubled the next day. The UN Secretary-General called on various regional leaders to put pressure on Sankoh to release the hostages. This policy of conciliation was to be carried out by Charles Taylor of Liberia and Moammar Gadhafi of Libya (*Washington Post*, 9 May 2000). Sankoh promised Taylor he would endeavour to secure the release of the UN hostages, but instead the RUF took more, bringing the total number to about 500 in just three days. Then, using 'infantry type weapons' and armoured cars seized from UN troops, the RUF immediately began to move south towards Freetown, capturing the town of Lunsar. This RUF action was no random event, but a carefully orchestrated plan which incredibly was reported to have caught diplomats by surprise (*Washington Post*, 5 May 2000). But the writing had all along been on the wall.

A full-blown crisis had now materialised, with the surrender of the UN troops to the RUF rebels. The first response to the crisis was to bring the UN troops up to the approved strength of 11,100 from the 8,700 on the ground. Britain decided to send five warships and about 1,600 troops to secure the international airport and facilitate the evacuation of her citizens while the US promised logistic support. But more immediately, Johnny Paul Koroma told Sierra Leone soldiers to prepare to defend Freetown against a possible RUF attack. Thousands responded, but it was the next day, Monday, 8 May, that the masquerade was unmasked. Parliamentarians and civil society groups organised a rally to call for peace and condemn the RUF seizure of UN troops. The crowd instead marched to Sankoh's house where his body-guards opened fire, resulting in several casualties. In the imbroglio, 21 people were killed including a journalist, and Sankoh whisked away in an amoured car belonging to Nigerian UNAMSIL soldiers. (*London Times*, 8 and 9 May 2000; *SLN-SLW*, 8 and 9 May 2000).

Meanwhile, supporters of Johnny Paul Koroma who had been contacted in Freetown by RUF officials to join them in a coup d'etat they were going to stage on 9 May, exposed the plan to Koroma, who immediately responded by arresting about 25 of the key players. Since UNAMSIL could not defend the country, Deputy Defence Minister Chief Sam Hinga Norman, also head of the *Kamajoisia*, announced that pro-government forces including Johnny Paul Koroma's loyal troops, now called West Side Boys, (WSB), were taking responsibility for security, and moved to ward off the RUF advance. At this point, the British sent troops, in part, to bolster the government. Sankoh's raided house turned up documents that revealed that indeed he had been trading diamonds for military equipment to prosecute the war and planned 'to stage a very violent and bloody coup' on 9 May. Other documents dealt with financial favours granted to RUF supporters, forceful capture of civilians, and abduction of children for use as soldiers (*SLN-SLW*, 13 May 2000). Koroma's men later captured Sankoh, who suddenly emerged in the area on the morning of 16 May 2000. The events of May 2000 salvaged the Lome peace accord: it lead to the deployment of more UN troops and the incarceration of Sankoh (*Washington Post*, 12 June 2000). It was the final nail in the coffin of a rebel leader who was doggedly determined to seize power through force.

Conclusion: Dancing with the chameleon all along

Achieving peace in Sierra Leone proved elusive because of the elementary, but difficult to perceive, reason that the RUF was never interested or committed in peace in the first place. Their terrorist monstrosities visited on the poor and innocent people continue to haunt them: what would be the guarantee against reprisal attacks from their respective communities and the country at large? No amount of legal guarantees in any number of peace agreements was sufficient to convince the ruffians. Sankoh was painfully aware of this. The conjuring tricks in Abidjan and Lome was to buy time to push forward the original RUF agenda: capture state power through violence. The RUF was therefore not sincere when it entered into negotiations with successive regimes throughout the period of the war. Otherwise it would have sincerely embraced the over-generosity of Lome in particular. All the negotiations meant nothing to Sankoh and his key field commanders except to buy more time for a suitable opportunity to seize power *vi et armis*. This would have been the only way to escape justice, *à la* Charles Taylor in Liberia. The RUF was also not willing to disarm because the predominantly illiterate rank and file were unsure of a future sans violence. The tragedy in the whole performance was that a bunch of bandits turned a small country into a serious problem for the world, humiliating the UN in the process, embarrassing the West, and making a fool of regional and national leaders. Everyone, it seemed, had his/her turn in dancing with the maverick chameleon.

Notes

1   See Human Rights Watch, 'Sierra Leone: Getting Away with Murder, Mutilation and Rape', 1999.

2   The violence in Liberia was initially driven by ethnic sentiments. After the failure of Quiwonkpa coup in 1985, Samuel Doe unleashed soldiers mostly of his Krahn ethnic group to systematically kill people in Nimba County, Quiwonkpa's home.

3   The RUF document, *Footpath to Democracy: Toward a New Sierra Leone* attempts to sell the RUF as a democratic organisation seeking a just and democratic society.

4   The 1995 foreign hostage crisis was resolved through the intervention of International Alert. The RUF surrendered the sixteen hostages to Alert envoy Addai-Sebo, and who personally escorted the captives to the Guinea border and handed them over to the Red Cross.

5   A South African based mercenary outfit hired by the NPRC in 1995 which proved effective in neutralizing rebel activity.

6   See Gberie for details.

7   For example a jury decision did not have to be unanimous any more. Only eight out of twelve votes were necessary for a decision.

8   Klein was convicted in Columbia in 1989 and in Israel in 1991 for selling arms and training the Columbian Medellin drug cartel death squads. See James Rupert, 1999.

9   In addition to the above, the RUF demanded four deputy ministerial positions to include defence and finance; six top diplomatic positions including Ambassadors to the US and Liberia, Deputy High Commissioner to the UK; High Commissioner to Nigeria; 11 parastatal headships including Governor of the Bank of Sierra Leone; Head of Ports Authority; Sierratel; State Lottery; Roads Authority; National Shipping; Sierra Leone Airlines; National Insurance Company; Commercial Bank; Customs Department; May of Freetown and Head of post-war reconstruction.

11

Nigeria, ECOMOG, and the Sierra Leone Crisis

'Funmi Olonisakin

We envisage to conclude the war soon despite the difficulties of terrain and logistic that we are faced with. Presently, we have been able to restore peace, law and order in more than 80 percent of the country. The remnants AFRC/RUF regime are still taking advantage of the unfavourable terrain and its imposed delay on our advance to inflict unimaginable cruelty on innocent civilian population. But time and international opinion are against them. We have taken the war to their last frontier and will soon bring them to justice[1] (Khobe, 1999).

Introduction

These were the words of Brigadier General Mitikishe Maxwell Khobe, the ECOMOG Task Force Commander in Sierra Leone in May 1998, about three months after the Nigerian-led force had flushed out the forces of the AFRC and the RUF from Freetown and opened the way for the reinstatement of Ahmad Tejan Kabbah's elected government.

General Khobe was not alone in this optimism. This statement was made in an atmosphere of enormous goodwill for the Kabbah regime and euphoria following the reinstatement of the President in Freetown. There was supreme confidence within ECOMOG, the Government of Sierra Leone (GOSL), and outside of these two establishments – among civil society groups in the capital, that junta and rebels would be wiped out in just a matter of time. This partly informed the policy of the Kabbah regime and raised the expectations of the people, many of whom had encountered untold human suffering at the hands of the junta and forces loyal to them.

The questions (regional and international) that preoccupied the minds of observers outside Sierra Leone were irrelevant to those inside the country, who had suffered under the AFRC, and who felt liberated from their junta oppressors. Did the ECOMOG intervention signify a new trend in regional security? Was international law broken in order to right a wrong? Why was it Nigeria, itself a pariah state and under a military strong man (Abacha) take the lead in the effort to unseat another military regime? Most importantly, did ECOMOG have the tools at its disposal to wipe out forces loyal to the junta and the RUF? How did this differ from the ECOMOG operation in Liberia? Questions like these appeared as academic luxury that Sierra Leoneans were least concerned with.

The crisis in Sierra Leone was the second since the end of the Cold War, that attracted the intervention of a sub-regional force, the Economic Community of West African States (ECOWAS) Cease-fire Monitoring Group (ECOMOG)(Adekeye, 2002). When this force was first despatched to Liberia in 1990, the magnitude of the Liberian crisis and the human suffering in the country made it difficult to challenge the need for this force, despite indications that some of its planners had motives other than the benevolent ones that were advanced to justify its deployment. The force was also thought to have been despatched at a time when it affected the balance of power between the conflicting parties, although the need for some form of humanitarian intervention was glaring. But for a force responding to that level of crisis, ECOMOG faced serious legal challenges not least because this was the first force of its kind in the sub-region.

In Sierra Leone, the sub-regional involvement took on different roles over a period of time. It occurred over several phases of the conflict and had wide-ranging implications. The ECOMOG intervention in Sierra Leone had both political and military dimensions, which ultimately impacted significantly on the peace process in the country. Prior to the arrival of the ECOMOG Task Force led by General Khobe, ECOMOG troops from Nigeria, Guinea, and a Squadron of the Ghana Air Force (42 personnel) were in Sierra Leone. They were in Sierra Leone supporting the ECOMOG operations in Liberia as well as assisting the Government of Sierra Leone in combat operations against the rebels and in the training of the national army.

Seven months after General Khobe's confident statement above, things fell apart in Sierra Leone yet again, and the Kabbah regime, the most glaring symbol of that state, was hanging precariously to power. The ECOMOG successes of the previous months had been reversed as AFRC/RUF forces made their way back to Freetown, wreaking havoc on the city, looting, maiming, and killing innocent civilians in the process. ECOMOG was caught completely off-guard and was only able to fight off these invading troops after significant reinforcements but not before the rebel forces had inflicted heavy casualties on them.[2] What accounted for this state of affairs? Had the questions that were apparently swept aside in previous months suddenly become more important? Could complete confidence be placed on outside actors when it comes to the maintenance of internal security? This chapter discusses the Nigerian-led

ECOMOG force in Sierra Leone, the legal, political and operational issues that influenced its activity in the country and the prospects for regional security in West Africa.

Did earlier predictions have a sound basis?

Apparent commitment by Abacha and Nigeria

The confidence reposed in ECOMOG and its ability by Sierra Leoneans could be understood from a number of perspectives. First, many Sierra Leoneans had been down in the depths of despair following months of battering and abuse by forces loyal to the junta and the RUF. That a force could come in, dislodge these fighters from Freetown, and take control of more than 80 percent of the country in a relatively short period of time, served to boost the confidence of many residents. The role of Nigeria – in particular, its leader at the time, General Sani Abacha – was central to this confidence felt by Sierra Leoneans – not least the Kabbah regime. And although the May 1997 coup drew attention to the Nigeria/ECOMOG involvement in Sierra Leone, Nigeria and ECOMOG's involvement in the country pre-dated the events of May. As earlier stated, ECOMOG troops (largely Nigerian and Guinean) were first despatched to Sierra Leone before the 1997 coup, when the border incursions by the NPFL and RUF threatened to create a security crisis in the country. The Nigerian Air Force was then based in Lungi, where it supported ECOMOG operations in Liberia and Sierra Leone.

Nigeria's role in the provision of security in Sierra Leone grew by accretion since war started in 1991. A more comprehensive security arrangement was later reached between Nigeria and Sierra Leone, with the signing of the Status of Forces Agreement (SOFA). As a result of this agreement, the Nigerian Army despatched Infantry and Artillery troops. But when the need to expand from single service to include the Navy and the Air Force, Nigeria and Sierra Leone returned to the 'drawing board'. This led to the formation of the Nigerian Forces Assistant Group (NIFAG), that was stationed in Freetown.

NIFAG was administratively under ECOMOG but its operations were however independent of the multinational monitoring group. Most Administrative and operational matters concerning NIFAG were handled directly from Lagos/Abuja. It is estimated that about 900 Nigerian troops were in Sierra Leone before the May 1997 coup as part of ECOMOG and this was not in addition to the Nigerian military training group (*The Economist*, 7 June 1997: 50). This was why when the coup took place, Brigadier General Jimmy Ojouojo, who was the NIFAG Commander, was authorised to take overall command of the Nigerian Forces on Sierra Leone soil. These troops had tried unsuccessfully to reverse the coup and despite rapid deployment of additional Nigerian troops from Liberia, bringing their total number to between 3,500 and 4,000, the junta could not be dislodged in the period after the coup until February 1998, when another Nigerian-led offensive was mounted (UN-IRIN-West Africa, Sierra Leone, 9 June 1997). Following Kabbah's reinstatement in 1998, Nigeria continued to be actively involved in the restructuring of Sierra Leone's security forces. This culminated in the secondment of General Khobe as Chief of Defence Staff. These developments were indeed a manifestation of Abacha's commitment and support for Sierra Leone, although personal interests rather than altruistic ones had motivated his actions.

ECOMOG's own confidence was based in part on the popularity of its Task Force Commander Mitikishe Maxwell Khobe. Khobe had excelled in the ECOMOG operations in Liberia as the first of the ECOMOG Ground Task Force, and Commanding Officer of the 221 Light Tank Battalion, Nigerian Army Armoured Corps. He was well known as a disciplined and professional soldier and well respected by colleagues, subordinates and ordinary Liberians who were familiar with ECOMOG's work in the field. He was trusted by his men and dreaded by the rebel forces. He had the experience of dealing with guerrilla forces in Liberia and was bound to take some lessons to Sierra Leone. Those who knew Khobe did not doubt that he was a good choice for the Sierra Leone operation. Khobe later explained that his confident statement about early defeat of the rebels were based on assurances that his request for additional battalions either from Liberia or Nigeria, to beef up the force, would be honoured. This was not to be. It was his successor who subsequently got all what Khobe had asked for by which time events had taken a different turn (Personal Interview with General Khobe, London, January 2000).

Tacit support by the international community

The apparent international legitimacy given to the Nigeria-led intervention right from the period after the May coup was also a contributory factor, which served to boost confidence and to raise expectations in Sierra Leone. In an international environment where coup making and the unseating of democratically elected governments had become a thing of the past, any means of reversing that trend in Sierra Leone was given tacit approval by the international community. In particular, the great sacrifices that the people of Sierra Leone had made to protect and defend their democratic system of government was admired by many in the West. Kabbah's reinstatement won kudos for ECOMOG action not only in Africa but from the donor community and the UN. Francis Okelo, the United Nations Secretary-General's Special Representative in Sierra Leone, confirmed that the world body supported Kabbah's reinstatement, referring to the ECOMOG action as a 'shining example of what ECOWAS can do' and that 'the sub-region should be proud of this achievement' (Panafrican News Agency, 6 May 1998).

The Nigerian-led operation was accorded legitimacy despite the suspicion that lay behind General Abacha's motives. It is difficult to see the real motives of Nigeria as one of benevolence and a genuine desire to alleviate the human suffering of the people of Sierra Leone. However, the events in Sierra Leone created an opportunity for the regime of General Abacha to accomplish valuable foreign policy objectives – to launder its image as an 'errant' state. Arguably, the element of a 'good' that was done in Sierra Leone was a matter of coincidence but understandably, this was of little import to many Sierra Leoneans, who had benefited from this intervention and, who saw the Nigerian leader as one who had rescued them from the hands of their tormentors, the RUF and AFRC.[3]

This was probably no different from the Liberian case, where it was difficult to challenge the humanitarian role of the ECOMOG force despite the fact that the intentions of its planners might have been completely different. ECOMOG and its humanitarian tag (albeit tarnished at times) might thus have been an accident of history. Nonetheless, the Sierra Leone situation raised a real question as to whether to decry an act whose intention or origin was not altruistic even if it accomplishes some good in the process of fulfilling the actor's selfish ends. Perhaps the feeling of the target country is what should matter more than other considerations, and in this case, Sierra Leoneans were less concerned about the motives of the Abacha regime.

Legal basis

Given the above reasons amongst several others, ECOMOG did not suffer the same legitimacy problems that it did when it intervened in Liberia seven years before. Not only did the recognised government of Sierra Leone had a defence pact with the leading nation, Nigeria, Sierra Leonean support appeared more solid – the conflicting parties were fewer (unlike Liberia). In Addition, despite its propaganda efforts, the junta, which was opposed to the intervention did not enjoy the co-operation of Sierra Leoneans in the capital and in many other places. The AFRC made co-ordinated efforts to secure the recognition of the international community, sending delegations to ECOWAS, South Africa, US, and several countries in Asia, Europe and the Middle East.

The one area where the ECOMOG operation would have had a sounder basis than its mission in Liberia concerns its legality. Yet this was not as straightforward as it should have been. The legal basis for a sub-regional operation had not been established in a situation where a unilateral operation by Nigeria, under the Status of Forces Agreement (SOFA), with Sierra Leone could have provided the needed legal umbrella for the operation.[4] However, legal questions more serious than those envisaged or those relating to the bilateral defence pact between both countries arose over the intervention in Sierra Leone, because Nigeria preferred to explain its actions as an ECOWAS/

ECOMOG intervention. Nigeria placed less emphasis on the SOFA/NIFAG agreement and chose to explain its intervention to stop the coup as action taken under a sub-regional umbrella. This created a number of problems. First, as at the time of the initial use of force in May–June 1997, there was no ECOWAS or OAU authorisation for this action. Second, there did not seem to be a consensus to use force amongst the sub-regional nations, many of whom were fatigued by the Liberian operation. This emphasis on action under a regional umbrella did indicate the preference of regional powers for multilateral action over unilateral ones.[5]

A regional stamp of approval later came from the OAU summit in Harare where the attending heads of state urged ECOWAS leaders to work towards the reinstatement of President Kabbah. Furthermore, ECOWAS leaders later agreed on a course of action, which expressed preference for a diplomatic and non-violent solution to the crisis, with the use of force becoming a necessity only when these options had been exhausted. ECOWAS Foreign Ministers set the scene for a sub-regional action about three months after the initial Nigerian-led intervention. A Contact Group, consisting of the Foreign Ministers of Côte d'Ivoire, Ghana, Guinea, Nigeria was established to co-ordinate and engage in negotiations with the junta. This group was later expanded to include Liberia. The Foreign Ministers' approval of the use of force as a means of restoring Kabbah's regime served to legitimise Nigeria's earlier action, whilst the decision to pursue diplomatic means thereafter limited Nigeria's actions momentarily (Final Communiqué, Extraordinary Meeting of ECOWAS Ministers of Foreign Affairs on the Situation in Sierra Leone, Conakry, 26 June 1997). What was previously claimed (by Nigeria) as ECOMOG action in Sierra Leone, can be described as such only in August 1997, when ECOWAS Foreign Ministers agreed and recommended the 'establishment of an ECOWAS Cease-fire Monitoring Group in Sierra Leone to be known as ECOMOG II' (Final Communiqué of the Meeting of Ministers of Foreign Affairs of ECOWAS, Abuja, 28 August 1997).

Keen not to lose the backing of potential allies for its sub-regional initiatives, Nigeria conceded to a less-belligerent response. It was a combination of negotiations and economic sanctions instituted by sub-regional leaders, with the backing of the international community, which led in part to the Conakry agreement with the junta in October 1997. Under the Conakry plan, the junta agreed to hand over power to Kabbah's elected government on 22 April 1998. By February 1998, when the Nigerian-led force drove the RUF and AFRC forces out of Freetown, following a number of incidents, there was no question about the legitimacy of its action. Thus, regional and extra-regional approval appeared to have been given for the Sierra Leone operation retroactively. The support of the UN for the ECOWAS action was apparent in its 8 October

1997 Resolution in which it backed the sub-regional action by an arms embargo and expressed

> strong support for the efforts of the ECOWAS Committee to resolve the crisis in Sierra Leone and [encouraged it] to continue to work for the peaceful restoration of the constitutional order, including through the resumption of negotiations.[6]

This marked a major departure from the Liberia experience, where the initial peace agreement was not accompanied by an arms embargo.

Factors that foretold a slim chance of success

Finding consensus and cohesion within ECOWAS

After the reinstatement of President Kabbah, ECOMOG and the Government of Sierra Leone proceeded with plans to flush out the rebels from the country side. This project was however fraught with difficulties. First, there were indicators that the longstanding problem of finding consensus within ECOWAS would continue. Events leading up to March 1998 were a glaring indicator of this. The element of cohesion in action that had developed in the Liberian operation after years of joint multinational operation did not bear fruit at the beginning of the Sierra Leone operation. Rather, as in 1990, political divisions within ECOWAS coloured the Sierra Leone operation, albeit for different reasons. Thus, following the return of Kabbah, the handwriting was on the wall: the military operations to mop up the remnants of the junta would not be an easy task. Evidence of this unfolded gradually. Nigeria, and to a certain extent, Guinea, appeared to be the only countries committed to the use of force to dislodge the junta. Ghana, which always contributed the highest number of troops after Nigeria, was initially opposed to the use of force in Sierra Leone and was weary of another long drawn-out enforcement operation as in Liberia. Indeed Nigeria had conceded to a less belligerent approach to the Sierra Leone situation when the immediate efforts to reverse the coup failed – largely as a result of reluctant allies. This situation had not altered much after Kabbah's restoration.

When ECOMOG returned to peace enforcement in February 1998, more troops were needed to reinforce the ones on the ground. And there were signs that other countries were not prepared to contribute troops that would be embroiled in battle with rebels and remain indefinitely in Sierra Leone. For example, Ghana, which had contributed the second largest contingent throughout the Liberia operation, called for clarification of ECOMOG's status and objectives in Sierra Leone before it would agree to commit troops to the mission (Ghana Focus, 4 May 1998). It was obvious that Ghana was keen to avoid a replica of the Liberia operation. According to Ghana's Foreign Affairs

Minister, Mr. Victor Gbeho, some of the issues, which required clarification, included:

> a clear definition of ECOMOG's status in Sierra Leone, the objectives it seeks to achieve, the rules of engagement, the strength of the forces required and the resources needed for this task.[7]

> ...The fact that ultimately it was the use of military action that led to the removal of the junta and reinstatement of President Kabbah should therefore be seen as more a matter of self-defence than a premeditated military action. It is perhaps because of this development and the continued activities of the remnants of the erstwhile junta that such a pronouncement is necessary so that none of us will be left in any doubt about how we intend to achieve our objectives in Sierra Leone (Ibid).

Potential operational difficulties

Some of the operational difficulties that would confront ECOMOG also became apparent during this period. Although additional 6,000 soldiers were pledged from Côte d'Ivoire, the Gambia, Ghana, Guinea, Mali, Niger and Nigeria to beef up the 10,000 mostly Nigerian troops on the ground after Kabbah's reinstatement, these pledges took much longer to materialise. The Liberian experience in which requests for additional troops were not always honoured or a situation were the deployment of troops was slow came to haunt the Sierra Leone operation. In most cases, Nigeria increased its troop contribution whilst other countries were unable to mobilise additional troops. In addition, the much-needed financial and logistic support from the international community did not materialise. Nigeria's Chief of Defence Staff at the time, General Abdulsalami Abubakar, had appealed to the international community for logistics support – particularly the provision of trucks and boots. There was also no guarantee that such request would be honoured in a timely fashion.

Domestic and external support for the junta

Although Khobe noted the support for the junta from amongst a cross-section of local actors in Sierra Leone, as well as sub-regional backers, it is doubtful that the full impact of such support was anticipated. Nor were their effective mechanisms through which their actions could be countered. Those believed to have constituted the forces that sustained the AFRC from the May 1997 coup until the reinstatement of President Kabbah included domestic interest groups, consisting of losers in the Presidential and parliamentary elections that brought Kabbah to power; business groups that either supported the previous regime or needed a support base in any government; and northern officers, politicians and elite amongst others (Khobe, 1999: 21). Strategies for containing these elements after Kabbah's restoration were perhaps not well thought-out. This proved to be a costly mistake.

Nigeria's military-politicians

The ECOMOG operation in Liberia was under the control of the Nigerian military regime and this had a noticeable impact on the ECOMOG force and the Nigerian military institution. The planning and execution of the Sierra Leone operation after March 1998 should have taken this factor into consideration. What was perhaps the most significant impact of the political control of the ECOMOG operation by the military regime in Nigeria was the cleavage that became apparent in the command structure of ECOMOG. There was noticeable conflict between the 'military politician' and the 'military professional' within the military establishment of the leading contributing nation, Nigeria. Since Liberia, there had been a clear division between the professional officer soperating in outside operations and their political counterpart at home.

ECOMOG officers on the ground in Liberia at least prior to the introduction of a Special Representative of the Executive Secretary of ECOWAS, were clearly dissatisfied with the lack of political presence or greater input from the political division at the secretariat. Although these officers technically perceived ECOWAS as the political authority, they were also keenly aware of the leadership role played by the military regime in Nigeria. What was in fact being witnessed, which was not clearly articulated at the time, was a fusion between the political and military authority (directing ECOMOG), which was now largely vested with the military regime in Nigeria, having bypassed the political body, ECOWAS. The Nigerian military government was seen to have given greater attention to political interests over military matters, as a result of which the military institution suffered at home and abroad under successive military regimes.

The problems confronting the Nigerian military were not just those of credibility, given the military's involvement in politics, but that of a weakening of its professionalism. It is indeed doubtful that Sierra Leone held Abacha's (ECOMOG's Benefactor) best attention after Kabbah's reinstatement. Abacha was himself gearing up for a referendum in Nigeria, which would return him unopposed as a civilian president. Thus, much resource had been diverted toward seeing this political project through. The Nigerian Armed Forces were not well equipped nor did they receive regular training. This was an issue of major frustration for the professional officers within the military establishment, some of whom happened to be in ECOMOG, as the issues of concern to the force were often relegated to the background.

This invariably affected the performance of the Nigerian armed forces in the regional operations. In Liberia, for example, Nigeria, the largest contingent suffered huge problems of logistics, morale and invariably, command and control. Commenting on the impact of logistics problems on the Nigerian contingent, General Olurin, one of the ECOMOG Field Commanders in Liberia, remarked on different occasions that

> The lack of centralised logistics has inherent command and control problems for the commander. Besides, it is bad for morale of troops who share the same accommodation or office or check points to have different standards of feeding and welfare amenities (Olurin, 1992–93: 13).

> It is however disheartening to note that of all the contingents in Operation Liberty the Nigerian contingent is the most badly turned out. Most of the soldiers had only one pair of boots and uniform. Our troops can easily be seen in tattered camouflage uniforms. Of late they have resorted to purchasing uniforms and boots from Ghanbatt and Leobatt contingents (Olurin, 1993: 30).

In terms of logistics and welfare, the Sierra Leone operation did not fare much better than Liberia. In addition to the inadequate number of men on the ground and the failure of other ECOWAS member-states to make contributions or deploy to Sierra Leone speedily, the Nigerian contingent on the ground suffered severe logistic problems. The troops suffered low morale due to poor provision of welfare. The same problems of irregular pay and long tours on duty encountered in Liberia were set to continue unless outside assistance was provided. Many of the same men that served in Liberia were diverted to Sierra Leone, whilst Nigeria continued to maintain a small contingent in Liberia. Thus, in all likelihood, it was over-stretched and fatigued Nigerian troops that were on the ground to face the RUF.

According to Brigadier-General Khobe, he had requested two additional battalions following the February 1998 defeat of the junta in Freetown but this request was not honoured. He argued that his optimism that the war would be brought to a swift conclusion was based on his expectation that additional troops would soon be deployed so that the momentum would be maintained (Personal Interview with Gen. Khobe, January 2000). It was with this expectation that he provided a timeline for concluding the war following pressures by the British to do so (Ibid). In the end, Khobe was replaced as ECOMOG Task Force Commander and appointed Sierra Leone's Chief of Defence Staff. The additional battalions were not deployed during Khobe's term whilst his successor was later provided with additional troops - by which time the strategic outlook had changed significantly in Sierra Leone, amongst other things.

It was under these circumstances that the junta and RUF forces, once again launched an attack on Freetown in January 1999, killing hundreds of ECOMOG soldiers (mainly Nigerian) and many Sierra Leoneans, maiming and looting in the process. Nigeria would later send reinforcements to Sierra Leone, to repel the rebel attack and maintain security in Sierra Leone. But the disaster was collosal: 5,000 civilians were killed and millions of property damaged.

January 1999 disaster: An explanation

Senior officers in the Nigerian contingent for example, have explained the failure of ECOMOG in January 1999, to contain and repulse the rebel advance into Freetown before the damage was done, in part as a result of over-reliance on an over-stretched Nigerian force. ECOMOG sources argued that inadequate logistics and human resources accounted for the failure of the force to deal with the junta forces. The most serious factor, which was seen to have contributed to this crisis within ECOMOG, was a 'command structure problem' (UN-IRIN, *West Africa*, 4 February 1999).[8] General accounts suggest that a combination of factors were responsible for the January 1999 invasion of Freetown. Amongst the explanations put forward are the failure of both the Kabbah regime and the ECOMOG High Command to heed warnings, or to respond in a timely manner to information about the rebel advance on the capital.

Kabbah's Strategy

What happened in January 1999 did not happen because the Kabba regime had not evolved a strategic policy. On the contrary, the events of January occurred precisely because the strategic policy was too ad hoc and heavily dependent on an over-streched and ill-equipped Nigerian troop. This strategy, according to Yusuf Bangura, had three key components: first, a reliance on ECOMOG both to create and maintain stability; secondly, the creation of a new national army, which would include a small number of the old army, who were considered loyal; and thirdly the support for the Civil Defence Forces (CDF) (Bangura, 2000). This strategy was designed to fulfil a number of objectives: elimination of the rebels, thereby removing the RUF and AFRC from the political equation; creation of a force that would guarantee the security of Sierra Leone and sustain it after the departure of ECOMOG; reaffirmation of the legitimacy of the Kabbah regime; and the upholding the rule of Law (Ibid).

At the core of this strategic policy was the security of Sierra Leone. The success of all other factors rested on the ability to defeat the rebellion and guarantee security in the interim, while the new army was being trained. This required unwavering external support and commitment, which would manifest itself in a strong force on the ground, capable of achieving military successes against the rebels and defending the resulting stability. The Government of Sierra Leone depended entirely on ECOMOG to achieve this and thereby, on Nigeria, as the main guarantor of the force. After the defeat of junta troops in Freetown in February 1998, Sierra Leoneans, including their political leaders, were won over by the seeming professionalism of ECOMOG and its capability not only to keep the rebels at bay but to eventually defeat them. The subsequent actions of the government underlined the confidence that was reposed in ECOMOG.

The other components in the strategic policy were not well laid out or properly executed. The Civil Defence Force (CDF) proposition, or the idea of a people's army was not given pride of place in part because it had the potential to transfer the strategic advantage from the President to his Deputy Minister of Defence who had overall control over the CDF. Retraining and keeping the disloyal renegade army was still considered as a way of maintaining the President's grip on power. Thus efforts to establish the CDF nationally as a subsidiary force to the national army did not go according to plan as this did not materialise because powerful sectional interests were against it. Furthermore, part of the old army being trained for the new national army did not remain loyal – their role in providing intelligence to the RUF/AFRC troops and in rejoining them, was crucial to the junta's initial success in the battle for Freetown in January 1999. Consequently, both ECOMOG and the Sierra Leone Police Force, amongst thousands of civilian casualties, sustained enormous casualties.

Leadership crisis within ECOMOG

ECOMOG failed to provide the security that was required to move the country forward to ensure the implementation of the Governments strategic policy and the continuation of other peace building activities. It also failed to contain the rebel advance and subsequent destruction of Freetown. A major problem for ECOMOG was not inadequate troops in Freetown but poor leadership in deciding what to do with what was available. Those who witnessed the events of January 1999 argue that the leadership question was central to ECOMOG's failure to prevent the attack on/defend Freetown. Information on the movement of the rebels towards Freetown was received well in advance of the attack. But the ECOMOG leader at the time, General Ahmadu was seen to have lost command.

Generals Khobe and Shelpidi provided Ahmadu with timely information on the security situation and movement of the rebels but the latter failed to make the right command decisions. Six battalions were on the ground as at January 1999 but they were not judiciously deployed. General Ahmadu kept the troops in Lungi, far away from Freetown, and at Jui and Allen Town on the outskirts of the city. The rebels were between Allen Town in the bush and Jui. Instead of deploying troops in the city, the Task Force Commander deployed them in Hastings and the Police Training Schools toward Waterloo. Some officers argued that if the troops had been deployed in the city, they would have been under the Brigade Commander, Col. Akpata, who was not aware that there were troops in Hastings and the Police Training School. Nor were the other troops in Hastings and the Police Training School aware of the location of the other battalions. Yet they were less than 2 kilometres from each other. The rebels wrought havoc in Freetown, because they succeeded in bypassing the bulk of the ECOMOG forces, advancing to Freetown, whilst encircling the others. Even when it was apparent that the city had been surrounded by the AFRC/RUF rebels, senior government officials and ECOMOG officers continue to inform the public that everything was under control. The Kabbah regime depended on these assurances and was perhaps right to do so, after all, ECOMOG had proven dependable in February 1998.

But General Ahmadu was in a difficult situation as any officer taking over the command of the Task Force from General Khobe would have been given the record set by the latter and the fact that his successor would be constantly measured by those standards. Every other problem at the time of the crisis revolved around this command problem. It was not that the senior commanders in ECOMOG were not aware of the rebel movement nor was it a human resource or capability problem. Contrary to claims that ECOMOG had inadequate men on the ground, the core of the problem was that they were not deployed wisely. The problem in part was that the military leadership at home permitted the recruitment of incompetent officers into command positions. Some did not live up to the expectation of their authority. At the time of the AFRC/RUF invasion of Freetown, Nigerian troops protecting the capital were reported to have had grossly inadequate logistic supplies, with many side arms without ammunition. This accounted in part for the heavy losses inflicted on ECOMOG by the AFRC/RUF forces.

Explaining ECOMOG's failure to prevent or repulse the advance on Freetown will be incomplete without reference to the domestic situation in Nigeria. General Abacha died in June 1998 and the political scene in Nigeria was thrown into pandemonium and uncertainty. General Abdulsalami Abubakar, who succeeded the dictator, was more inclined to pay more attention to Nigeria's domestic problems. The ECOMOG mission in Sierra Leone was seen as the personal project of his predecessor. Nigeria was undergoing a major transition and Abubakar was eager to restore some confidence in the Nigerian military, which had lost credibility at home and abroad. The new regime's approach was to seek to build Nigeria's image in the eyes of the international community, through improvement of the human rights situation at home and the preparation for elections, which were to culminate in the presidential elections in February 1999. In the aftermath of the January 1999 crisis, the force had to be significantly increased in order to adequately meet the security challenges in Sierra Leone. This would have meant getting more involved in Sierra Leone a decision the new leader was not ready to take.

Weak morale within ECOMOG

Added to Nigeria's political problems was the question of morale within ECOMOG. Nigerian troops were rotated infrequently (a problem common to all the contingents in Liberia, with the possible exception of Ghana). In many cases, Nigerian soldiers had been transferred from Liberia to Sierra Leone without any break. It was not unusual for the same troops to be in the area of operation for up to twenty-four months without being rotated. In the case of other ranks, they did not have the opportunity to visit their families during this period, a privilege that was only enjoyed by the officer corp. These problems were compounded by infrequent payment of operational allowance, which was sometimes delayed by several months.

In the Sierra Leone operation, morale was severely weakened not just among enlisted men but also within the officer corps. Enthusiasm was dampened by a number of factors. One is that the force suffered from poor reputation. Reports of gross indiscipline by ECOMOG soldiers had been rife since the Liberian operation. This was not in terms of human rights violations, but in terms of looting civilian property found in their area of operation. Arguably these incidents only involved a small percentage of the overall force. Yet it tarnished the image of the entire force. Indeed, this is an offshoot of the domestic problem at home as the military administration in previous years had shown a reluctance to punish those suspected of committing these acts, particularly when they were thought to be loyal to the regime at home. Officers and other ranks felt these experiences alike (although the latter seemed to have been more affected). It was difficult to ignore the conditions under which these troops operated in Liberia, many of which continued in Sierra Leone.[9] The plight of their men on the ground gradually took precedence in the minds of some of the officers and this sometimes created conflict with their counterparts in political circles at home. They seemed to be at loggerheads with the regime over delays in payment of operational allowance; long periods in an area of operation without rotation; and inadequate logistic supplies.

Lastly, the best of armies have found it extremely difficult to overcome small guerrilla armies. Those who confidently predicted an ECOMOG victory over the AFRC/RUF forces blatantly ignored this fact. It was relatively easy for a conventional Nigerian force to dislodge the rebel and junta forces in the capital, Freetown, where the latter had no choice but to fight a conventional battle. However, once in the remote country area, the RUF and indeed the junta forces were able to utilise the familiar terrain of the countryside - remoteness and thick forests – to their own advantage. Thus, even if ECOMOG troops were well armed and equipped, they were still likely to have found it severely difficult to dislodge the rebel forces.

Post-January 1999 operational difficulties

ECOMOG sustained heavy losses in their bid to take Freetown from the AFRC/RUF. But developments in the post-January 1999 period continued to reflect the operational difficulties encountered earlier. In post-January 1999 Sierra Leone, the problems of ECOMOG became even more apparent. In a new operational environment, although enforcement was not excluded from the task of ECOMOG, the main focus was the provision of security, particularly after efforts intensified to bring the Government of Sierra Leone, and the RUF/AFRC alliance to the negotiating table. The problems of command and low morale remained. Interestingly, unlike earlier ECOMOG operations where morale was often weaker among other ranks than officers, this was widespread among the officers and men. Within the officer corps, the factors that served to weaken morale transcended the welfare issues described above. First, after January 1999, many middle level officers and other ranks had lost respect for some of their senior commanders for the woeful manner in which they handled the January crisis. Second, the perception of Sierra Leoneans about the purpose of ECOMOG was a source of concern. According to a senior ECOMOG officer in May 1999:

> Sierra Leoneans think ECOMOG is contracted to solve a problem. They are not ready to provide any assistance. Some countries contribute to the war effort in their country but this is not the case here.[10]

Officers in the Nigerian contingent were especially critical of the attitude of their colleagues in other contingents, who assumed that they had less responsibility than Nigeria. Here are some of their comments:

> The attitudes of fellow West Africans are also part of the problem. They think they are assisting Nigeria. They cannot take orders from Nigeria [commanders] and they are not ready to deploy until their home government is consulted.

Nigerian officers serving in Sierra Leone were of the opinion that the assistance provided by the international community sometimes did more harm than good:

> The support from the international community comes in trickles. They promise much but little gets delivered. Yet they give a lot of publicity to these donations. Assistance received from the international community has served to create disaffection within ECOMOG. For example, assistance given recently by the UK

and Canada, instead of being given to ECOMOG as a unit, was divided between the contributing nations. Although Nigeria contributes more than 90 per cent of the troops, the assistance was divided almost equally between the contingents. Ghana, for example received the same, if not more than Nigeria even though Nigeria has 11,191 troops compared to Ghana's 680.[11]

Despite the uneven support received by each contingent, Nigeria was responsible for the movement of troops from Liberia to Sierra Leone in addition to the provision of petroleum products. Nigeria also provided assistance to Mali and Benin, with allowance and ration for their troops.

Another demoralising factor for Nigerian officers and men was that their country had no identifiable objective in Sierra Leone. Many officers and other ranks expressed a strong preference for returning home, and a complete withdrawal from Sierra Leone unless certain conditions were met. Some officers pointed out what they saw as a disparity between the standards applied to Nigeria in Sierra Leone and the US/NATO in Kosovo:

> After all, the US does not apply the same standards in Kosovo, where they (NATO) have continued to pound Serbia despite unilateral cease-fire and other offers. Yet ECOWAS is persuaded by the international community to accept the rebels' unilateral cease-fire(Interview with Nigerian Officer, 1999).

Though the overall command was left largely in the hands of Nigeria the other contingents were unwilling to submit to Nigeria's command. The Malians, for instance, refused to stay in their area of operation after the loss of a few men in May 1999 and instead requested a transfer to Lungi airport. Guinea, was for understandable reasons more concerned with protecting its border area with Sierra Leone than with fighting. They were also withdrawn from Sierra Leone during the elections. The Ghanaian contingent, showed preference for Lungi as an area of operation. Thus, command and control were even much more difficult to attain in Sierra Leone than in Liberia. Sierra Leoneans were quick to read these signs: they expressed their preference for Nigerian troops whom they believed were tough and could fight.

ECOMOG handed over control of the security situation to the United Nations in 2000. The last of its units departed from Sierra Leone at the end of April 2000. The efforts of ECOMOG in providing and maintaining a measure of stability in Sierra Leone was perhaps underplayed until the time of its departure. Inspite of its numerous shortcomings, the ECOMOG experience was instrumental in shaping the peace process and laying the foundation for the arrival of the UN. It is therefore understandable that a degree of nervousness was expressed by many when it was learnt that ECOMOG was to leave Sierra Leone. Many feared that they would be left unprotected from the RUF. It is not inconceivable that the RUF's attempt to seize power in May 2000, starting with the kidnapping of UN troops resulted in part from the departure of ECOMOG troops, which in all probability would have met any RUF attacks with deadly force.

A sign of things to come?

Beyond the Sierra Leone operation, these operational problems revealed the monumental challenges that still lie ahead for regional security in West Africa. ECOMOG is the first sub-regional peacekeeping effort in the post-Cold War period. However, its ad hoc nature coupled with the lack of a solid political structure ensured that only few positive lessons of the Liberian operation were applied in Sierra Leone. The structural changes which the new ECOWAS treaty and the Mechanism for Conflict Prevention promised have yet to be implemented. As a result, there is no structured response to complex regional conflicts as seen in Liberia, Sierra Leone and to a certain extent in Guinea Bissau. Ad hoc operations on the other hand ensure that individual states are able to influence such operations directly and that strong states are able to take over control of such operations as witnessed in Liberia and Sierra Leone. Where such a state is well meaning, these operations may have some chance of achieving some good. In the final analysis an unstructured response holds the risk that operations may be conducted to suit the leading nation's selfish ends. With ECOWAS moving towards a workable mechanism for conflict resolution in West Africa, the Sierra Leone ECOMOG operations could only serve as useful lessons for the planning of a standing force or similar organs, which will form part of the mechanism of conflict resolution and management within ECOWAS.

Notes

1   Brig-Gen. M.M. Khobe, 'Conflict Management and Resolution,' ECOWAS Regional Forum, Ouagadougou, 1998.

2   It is estimated that Nigeria lost about 1,000 soldiers as a result of the AFRC/ RUF invasion of Freetown in Jnauary 1999, under gruesome circumstances.

3   Indeed, Sierra Leone was the only country where General Abacha was publicly mourned. In his country, where he was regarded as a brutal dictator, thousands took to the streets jubilating when it was announced that he was dead.

4   The Status of Forces Agreement was not universally accepted as valid by commentators. For example, the agreement is thought to have excluded the use of force in support of the regime, and that the terms and the letters of the agreement might have been stretched beyond breaking point to accommodate the Nigerian actions. See, for example, Yusuf Bangura, 'Security in ECOWAS', *West Africa*, 30 June–6 July 1997, p. 1039; and Abass Bundu, 'The Case Against Intervention', ibid., p. 1041.

5 South Africa's intervention in Lesotho later that year would also be presented as one conducted under the umbrella of the South African Development Community (SADC). This was despite the fact that the troops consisted largely of South Africans and only a handful of troops from Botswana.

6 UN Resolution 1132 adopted by the Security Council at its 3822nd meeting, 8 October 1997.

7 Mr. Gbeho's statement at a meeting of Armed Forces Chiefs of Staff of West African countries in Accra, 4 May 1999. See Ibid.

8 General Khobe, for example, attributed the December 1998/ January 1999 rebel advance to this factor.

9 For a full account of the operational difficulties encountered by ECOMOG in Liberia, see 'Funmi Olonisakin, *Reinventing Peacekeeping in Africa,* The Hague, London and Boston: Kluwer Law International, 2000, pp. 145–188.

10 Interview with the Chief Military Information Officer (CMIO) at ECOMOG Headquarters, May 1999.

11 Size of ECOMOG as at May 1999: Nigeria –11,191; Ghana – 680; Guinea – 600; Mali – 427; Benin – one platoon; Niger – one platoon.

12

'Smallest Victims; Youngest Killers': Juvenile Combatants in Sierra Leone's Civil War

Ibrahim Abdullah

Ishmail Rashid

We feared them. They were cruel and hard hearted; even more than the adults. They don't know what is sympathy; what is good and bad. If you beg an older one you may convince him to spare you, but the younger ones, they don't know what is sympathy, what is mercy. Those who have been rebels for so long have never learned it.

Once, a rebel, a small boy in full combats, he couldn't have been more than twelve, called everyone out of the house across the street. The papa of the family, Pa Kamara, said, please my son, leave my family, but the boy said, listen, we can do anything we want in Freetown. We don't have mothers, we don't have fathers. We can do anything we wanna do. And that is how Pa Kamara died; the rebel boy shot him, in front of his wife, his children, his grandchildren. They are wicked, those boy soldiers. They spare no human life. [Adama, a 42-year-old secretary (Human Rights Watch, *Sierra Leone: Sowing the Seeds of Terror*, 1999)].

Late one evening, a ten-year old with a pistol came, alone, into our house. He told my husband his commander was hungry and wanted one of our chickens. While my husband was catching the hen, that boy sat down to wait. He was thin and exhausted. I brought him a biscuit and water. He said he was tired and weak and as he left with the chicken, he turned to me and said, 'thank you, mam'.

Later my neighbours criticized me for giving him that biscuit. I said I didn't care if he was a rebel or not. He's still somebody's child. May be he was abducted. God knows what they've done to him. I wanted to hide that boy and take him with us as we fled and just knew he would've come with us if he'd had the chance'. [Zainab, a 24-year-old market vendor (Human Rights Watch, *Sierra Leone: Sowing the Seeds of Terror*, 1999)].

The above quotations capture the two dominant approaches – conscious actors or villains – in the study of juvenile combatants in the civil wars raging across Africa, Latin America, and Asia (Machel, 1996). Both quotations, however, presents the problem in the form of a binary either/or situation: children are either seen as conscious agents, 'fighting with their eyes wide open' or as victims of wars they had no hand in originating (Peters and Richards, 1998). This either/or problematic, raises the old argument of structure versus agency. Are juvenile combatants willing partners in war or are they reluctant actors being manipulated by unscrupulous army officers and warlords who press-ganged them into action with drugs after destroying their families and communities? When is agency not agency; or is structure a one-way street that leads only in one direction? These questions are difficult to answer but they begin to cast some doubt on the explanatory power of an either/or problematic. To get away from this binary, this chapter examines the problem from the point of view of labour recruitment and mobilization. It argues that the initial recruitment drive by the rebels and the national army in Sierra Leone did not involve juvenile combatants, that juvenile combatants only became a factor after it became evident that able bodied adults were either difficult to come by or were just not available. As the war progressed from the border region to engulf the whole country, the increasing presence of juvenile combatants became a marked feature of the RUF. As in Rwanda during the 1994 genocide, the atrocities committed by juvenile combatants were seen as work by their RUF commanders. Commanders repeatedly congratulated their juvenile combatants for work well done, seeing the whole machinery of violence as part of the labour process of war (Mamdani, 2000). Key to understanding the phenomenon of juvenile combatant is the centrality of labour.

The exploitation of child labour is common to all societies throughout history. One of the most insidious forms of child labour is the use of children as combatants and auxiliaries in war. Children have participated in military conflicts in Asia, Europe, Latin America and Africa. In Angola, Somalia, Uganda, Sudan, Rwanda, Ethiopia, Democratic Republic of Congo, Sierra Leone and Liberia, children as young as seven years have been armed and allowed to participate in senseless civil wars (Machel, 1996; Dodge and Raundalen, 1991; Furley, 1995; Wessels, 1997; Human Rights Watch, 1994; Honwana, 1999). Between 1991 and 1999, the Republic of Sierra Leone Military Forces, the RUF and the Civil Defence Forces (CDF) used children who were 15 years and younger in combat and support roles in their war effort. Whereas the RUF abducted, kidnapped, and press-ganged their juvenile combatants, the Sierra Leone army and the CDF seemed to have been swamped by under-age volunteers eager to avenged the death of their loved ones. All three military machines however fed drugs to their under-aged combatants, encouraged them to commit atrocities, and deployed them in dangerous frontline positions (Interview with demobilised juvenile combatants, 1996; 2000).

Juvenile combatants: Towards an explanation

From 1991 to 2000, Sierra Leone experienced a brutal and nasty war that engulfed all regions of the country and all sections of the population. From the moment when the RUF fired its first bullet in Bomaru village in March 1991 with the ostensible objective of ousting the decadent APC regime of Major-General J.S. Momoh, to the combined RUF/AFRC invasion of Freetown in January 1999, the country experienced an unprecedented orgy of violence, destruction and untold human suffering. Close to 50,000 people were killed or maimed in the process. Another 300,000 persons were internally displaced or fled into exile in Guinea, Liberia, the Gambia and Ghana. Nearly all the country's economic and social infrastructure disappeared under the rubble of the war. The war brought unprecedented social and economic disaster to the country.

The paradox of this brutal war was that children were its most vulnerable victims as well as some of its most vicious prosecutors. Between 1992 and 1996, more than 4,500 children were drawn into the war as spies, porters, sex-slaves, carriers and combatants for the RUF, the national army and later the CDF (Olanisakin, 2001). Children bore arms and took part in all aspects of the various military campaigns. They killed, collected and relayed intelligence, conducted reconnaisance mission, and disseminated propaganda (Human Rights Watch, 1994). Many children, particularly those who fought on the side of the RUF, took part in many atrocities, including the amputation and the disembowelment of pregnant women. Apart from fighting, children helped in the transportation of military supplies and looted items (Interview, 1996; 2000). Older male combatants raped female children or made them their 'concubines' or 'wives'. In the ten years of conflict, many young girls had their first sexual encounter with combatants, and grew into unwilling mothers and wives.

How do we make sense of these terrible crimes perpetrated by people barely old enough to go to school or pronounce their names correctly? What kind of society produces such murderous impulses and behaviour in children? What kind of military organizations arm such tender hands and then compel them to execute such hellish acts? Any research into the problem of juvenile combatants should start by looking at the partial disintegration of state and society in Sierra Leone in the 1980s and 1990s. This process arguably contributed to the weakening of social bonds and the restraining influences of family, communal and institutional structures. The state, for its part, could neither provide support to shore up these social structures nor establish any durable mechanisms to deal with the ensuing consequences. One of those consequences was the expansion in the pool of children who strayed away from home hanging out with lumpen youths and participating in their anti-social culture (Abdullah, 2002). This category of children, some in foster homes, others staying with blood or distant relatives, would become the partial reserve army for the warring factions, especially the RUF, and the national army.

If the partial disintegration of state and society constitute an appropriate point of departure for our understanding of the phenomenon of juvenile combatants, the character of the different contending factions in the war begins to explain why juvenile combatants are to be found in the current senseless wars raging across the continent (Furley, 1994). The RUF, the national army and the CDF share one thing in common: they were highly indisciplined. They lacked clear ideological focus, esprit-de-corps or guidelines on the conduct of war. For the RUF, this was not surprising since it drew its membership mainly from the lumpen urban and rural population. This population, long marginalized and alienated from mainstream society, felt no compulsion to conform to internationally agreed standards of war which protect innocent civilians, especially women and children. The RUF's idea of combat was the putting into practice of the cynical adage that all was fair in love and war. And as its leadership repeatedly pointed out, the ultimate goal was to 'level' Sierra Leone society and out of its ruins, create a new utopia. As the rate of attrition among its combatants increased with the prolongation of war, the RUF gradually lowered the age-range of its recruits by press ganging pre-teen boys, and some girls, to serve as combatants. There were no child soldiers amongst its ranks when the RUF entered Bomaru in 1991. Yet by 1997 when they occupied Freetown in alliance with the AFRC, half of their combatants were under-aged.

The national army, which was supposed to be the professional standing army of the country, behaved no better than the RUF. In the course of the war, it converted its boy-soldiers into active combatants. Like the RUF, it also recruited under-aged boys to create an auxiliary army of irregulars. These irregulars were put together early in the war by the late Lt. Ben Hirsch to serve specific purposes: intelligence gathering and support network in their home community. But as the war progressed these irregulars also came from the ranks of children who had been orphaned by the war, and made the revanchist decision to join the army to avenge the death of a loved one. In character and behaviour, these irregulars were no different from the combatants of the RUF. The morale and professionalism of the army declined almost in inverse proportion to the number of irregulars that were brought in its fold. The irregulars prosecuted the war with the same brutality and disregard for the civilian population as the RUF combatants. They became *sobels*: soldiers by day and rebels by night. In the blighted economic climate of war-time Sierra Leone, many destitute children and families came to regard the military and the war as a source of 'employment'.

While some children may have found 'employment' in the ranks of the RUF, not all child-soldiers 'voluntarily' joined the fray. As the testimony below demonstrate, majority were kidnapped and abducted from their homes, schools and communities. The RUF seized the children of families and the communities that it ravaged and converted them into military labour. Specific raids, such as the one in Pujehun in 1994 and Kambia town in 1996, were organized to capture young school children. The kidnapped or better still captured children experienced their initial baptism of fire when the older combatants forced drugs down their throats, threatened them with execution mafia-style or made them witness or participate in atrocities against their communities. Such initiation rituals were common with all the fighting forces more but so with the RUF; they went the extra mile to brand their recruits with RUF tatoos.

Why did the RUF and RSLMF use children in support and combat roles? Who made the decisions to recruit and employ children? What were the reasons they gave to support the recruitment of children? The first reason was the shortage of able-bodied male to fight for the RUF and the RSLMF. The high death toll, the wretched conditions of service, the meagre salary which forced some soldiers to augment their pay through looting or mining, the summary executions, and above all, the senselessness of the war, discouraged responsible adults from enlisting on either side. Unable to tap the labour of the adult population, the two main fighting factions turned to children and the under-aged. As the war progressed, more children and under-age combatants were recruited to serve in various capacities, so that by 1998, close to about 25 per cent of the fighting forces were children and the under-aged.

For the top military officials of the national army and the 'revolutionaries' of the RUF, children represented a cheap and exploitable form of labour. By 1993, the war had become a profitable business for the senior military officials in the NPRC. Millions of dollars were requisitioned and allocated for the army which never found its way to intended recipients. Some of them were 'ghost soldiers', many of them irregulars who had never been formally registered as recruits into the army. 'My intention was to stay with the military until I could get a number. It is only when I get a military number that I will start receiving my salary. Until then, I only get what my commander gives me' (Interview with demobilised juvenile combatant, October 1996). Apprenticed to an army officer, these child soldiers never got paid or receive any benefit. And the senior military officials rarely accounted for the allocations set aside for the 'irregulars', which included the child-soldiers, who were officially not in the army pay roll. Since the military were in control of state power during the NPRC period, and various officers controlled their own little fiefdoms, no one could compel them to account for the allocations or even audit them. Regular soldiers in the military usually received salaries and compensation in loot. The military was less concerned with compensating juvenile 'irregulars'. These irregulars had less clout than regulars and because of their age and position had less inclination to resist authority. Most of their compensation came from the largesse, looted and otherwise, of their patron officers. The ability of the leadership of both the RSLMF and RUF to appropriate resources at the expense of child-soldiers made them more attractive than adults, especially if they could perform similar military functions like them.

By drawing children into their military organizations, the RUF and the national army deprived them of the protection, sustenance and authority of their families, communities and social institutions. This displacement or capture of parental responsibility was not a new phenomenon. Parents have routinely given up their children, particularly the troublesome ones, to the military to discipline them (Interview with rank and file soldiers, 2000). The institution thus became their surrogate parents. Once within military institutions, the children came under the heavy and despotic hand of older soldiers and combatants. The RUF underlined its own surrogacy over its child-soldiers with its national anthem : 'Go and tell my parents they can see me no more I am fighting forever' (*Footpath to Democracy*, n.d). The military institutions took over the role of 'disciplining,' or more exactly, manipulating these young minds to serve a variety of purposes.

In return for the 'discipline' and 'protection' that these institutions provided during the war, the officers and commanders, demanded the unflinching obedience of the child-soldiers. It is this blind obedience, usually bolstered by psychotropic drugs, that the military organizations manipulated to get children to commit an array of violent, destructive and atrocious acts. Older combatants, more independent and needing longer periods to break in, may question superiors, disobey orders or desert. Children rarely exercised such options because of fear and dependence on the protection of the military organizations. The harrowing confessions by ex-child soldiers point to conflicting 'zeal' and 'pain' with which they carried out their military duties (Interview with demobilised juvenile combatants, 2000).

Regardless of the zeal with which they executed their duties, child-soldiers were expendable to the two military organizations. The 'protection' and surrogatehood/ parenthood provided by the RUF and RSLMF were limited. Older combatants had greater access to scarce food resources during lean periods. Child-soldiers had the least access to resources and starved when food was unavailable or in short supplies. Child-soldiers were usually haggard, poorly attired and lean. One of the quotations at the beginning of this chapter captures the plight of the child soldier. His commander had sent him to get chicken so that he can eat but the woman whose house he went to obtain the chicken noticed that he was lean, hungry and tired and therefore offered him biscuit and some water. The lives of child soldiers had the least worth. They performed dangerous tasks and were sometimes sent recklessly into dangerous military situations by their superiors to draw enemy fire. Without strong family or the communal ties or institutional protection, both the RUF and RSLMF had no obligation to account for their juvenile combatants, whether alive or dead. Many ex-juvenile combatants got missing. Families and communities are still trying to account for children who disappeared during the war between 1991 and 1998. Life and death is even more tragic and pitiful for destitute children whose family had given them up, even before the war.

Telling their own story: Juvenile combatants speak

Below are four testimonies by juvenile combatants. Two of them were abducted by the RUF the other two willingly enrolled in the national army. One of these saw action with ULIMO-K – one of the armed factions in Liberian war – and later with the national army. The testimonies of those who fought with the national army were obtained from the office of the Children Associated with War project (CAW), those of the RUF were interviews conducted by us. The testimonies obtain from the Children Associated with War project are reproduced here as they appeared in the original.

> In 1992, I was a form two student at the Koidu Secondary School in Koidu Town. Then on 23 October of the same year, rebels attacked Koidu Town. It was on this day that I got separated from my parents and family. The family had escaped to the town of Kwakor together with retreating soldiers of the Sierra Leone army. In the ensuing confusion, I got separated from the rest of my family. Because of this I was forced to stay with the soldiers. I knew no one else and the soldiers were kind to me. Later on, I learnt that my family had gone on to a village called Kamba Yondeh, which is near the Guinea border.
>
> On the 25 October, news reaching the soldiers at Kwakor indicated that reinforcement from Freetown had recaptured the town of Koidu. So, that same day, the soldiers moved from Kwakor to join forces with the new comers in Koidu. I went together with the soldiers.
>
> While I was with the soldiers at Kwakor, I came in contact with a former school mate called Tamba Komba. He was a soldier. I admired him so much that when we reached Koidu Town I asked him to recommend me for recruitment into his battalion. This he did, and on 28 October, just five days after the attack, I was recruited into the sixth battalion of the Sierra Leone Army based in Koidu Town, together with fourteen (14) other boys of about the same age group as vigilantees.

We were trained for a period of about two months. Our training was basically centred around the use and maintenance of the gun (cock and fire).We were also instructed on some ambushing techniques. After this short training, we were sent to fight in various places in the Kono District. Some of the places I fought included Njabwema, Manjama and Baidu.

It was in Manjama that I shot and killed my first rebel. We had caught and tied up a rebel suspect after we recaptured the village. I was ordered by our officer Lieutenant 'T'(then a Sergeant), to stay and guard the suspect till he was interviewed. My companions had gone into the house to loot. Then suddenly, the suspect got loose somehow and stood up. I was so scared that I ran and stood some distance from him. Then I started shouting and calling for help. No one came to help. I was so small and the man was such a big fellow. When the man saw that I was scared he started backing away from me. It was then that I realised I held a gun in my hands. There and then I became bold and told him to stand still or I would fire. At this, he turned sharply and began to run. I followed him slowly. He turned and saw me following, so stopped and stepped into some bushes by the side of a hut. I called him to come out or I would fire. There was no response from the bush. After some time I thought he had escaped and gone further into the bush, so I decided to fire some shoots after him so that I would tell my boss that I tried to stop him but he ran faster. I set my gun to rapid position and let go at the bush. I was really surprised when I heard a cry of pain coming from the bush. I removed my fingers from the trigger and listened. On hearing the shots my companions left their looting and raced to where I was standing. I couldn't answer any of their questions until our officer himself came rushing up to the scene of the firing. I explained exactly what had happened. The officer then ordered some of the men to enter the bush and investigate. They came out barely two minutes later dragging the body of the rebel suspect between them. I will never forget that sight. The bullets had entered his one side and came out with all his intestines on the other side. I felt very bad for the rest of the day and night. I could not eat anything for almost two days. My friends praised me, but I did not feel I had done anything brave.

I fought until August 1995. By this time I had gained contact with my family. Luckily I had been part of a patrol sent to the area around Komba Yendeh. While in the area I had made inquiries about my family. As my father was a very popular hunter, there was no problem in locating them. I found them in the Loi Chiefdom of Kono District. It was a joyful occasion. All my people were happy to see me. My father told me that they had long since given me up for dead. I stayed with them for three days and before I left to join my fellow soldiers, my parents and other relatives begged me to leave the army and stay with them. I told them I would consider and left.

After some time I was visited by my father in Njagbwema, where my group was then based. He talked to one of our officers – one Corporal Ballah who was in charge of medical affairs. My father told him that he had come to take me home because I was still a child and so he wanted me to continue my schooling and got some education first. Corporal Ballah agreed and I was called from the billet and disarmed. I was given civilian clothes to wear. This was in August. I cannot remember the date. My father took me to Senehun to join the family.

I felt sad at leaving my friends with whom I had stayed and fought with for more than two years. Moreover, I was not happy to return home because my father was a very strict and no-nonsense man. While at the war front I had been used to an unruly way of life. If I stayed with my father, I know sooner or later, there will be problems. I stayed with my parents for only two days and I left to join my uncle (mother's brother) in Koidu Town.

I stayed with my uncle until I heard about CAW and decided to join the programme. The CAW officers were based at Koidu Secondary School (K.S.S) compound, which was visited by us children. That was how I learnt of the programme and what they can do for us children who had taken part in war.

The second account is by Foday Sesay (not his real name) who was in Kenema District when the area was attacked by rebels. He was born in February 1978 and started fighting when he turned twelve in 1992.

Around the early part of 1992, while I was living with my parents in Panguma village, we got wind of rebel attacks in a nearby village called Talama because of this, my parents left our village for Kenema town. I stayed behind with a friend called Mustapha who was later killed in one of the many ambushes we do regularly fall in.

As the rebels were now on the rampage in many places, a ULIMO General called Gbupleh recruited me together with Mustapha and many others and we were taken to a training base at the Moa Barracks where we were subjected to vigorous military training for a month. By the end of this exercise, I was taken together with 51 others back to Tongo field where rebel activities were now very frequent. In Tongo under the command of General Gbupleh, I fought in almost all the villages in the chiefdom including Lowuma, Bomi, N'geyima and Wima amongst others.

When asked as to how many times he was involved in direct combat, and ambushes and how he survived them, Foday said thus,

I was a platoon commander and in fact one's survival in an ambush does not depend on what you know but God. Since he said such attacks do come by surprise.

After about six months, in Tongo, I was taken along with others for further briefing to Daru from where I was deployed to fight in Zimmi, Koidu, Kwiva, Pendebu, Mabgie and Nomofama villages.

When asked as to how many of his friends were killed during his time of fighting, with the ULIMO group Foday said they were many and that was the more reason why he continued to fight because 'each time we had cause to fight, we do have a few some times many'.

> All of these ... do frustrate people leaving them with no alternative but to avenge the loss of a colleague.

> While we were at Koidu in 1993, our boss, one Captain Keitta, told us that UNICEF was now concerned with the way children were been used in the fighting and he suggested that we (about twenty of us) were taken back to Daur Barracks from where we were conveyed on board a UNICEF mini bus to Freetown to a place known as Conakry Home in the Westend of Freetown.

> I spent about seven months in this camp and I was finally taken to my mother in Kenema around December, 1993. I stayed with my mother for sometime until early 1994 when I decided to again take up arms under the command of one Captain Messeh, this time with the Sierra Leone Army. While I was with Messeh, I fought in places like Mano-Junction, Bo, Kenema Highway and others until Captain Messeh was transferred to the Moyamba Operational area and I together with a few others were taken along. We lived and fought along side the Sierra Leone Army Forces in the Mokanji Rutile and the surrounding villages. As the fighting in this area was now getting tough and tougher every day, I decided to travel unauthorised (AWOL) on my own to Bo town where I again rejoined other troops at the Brigade Headquarters then under the command of one Colonel Samura. There again I was in almost all the fighting and ambushes in areas like the Bo Mile 91 highway until we at one time lost track and spent three days in the bush feeding on wild fruits but we finally surfaced around Tikonko where some Nigerian troops covering that area were alerted by civilians and we were captured by the Nigerian contingent and taken to base in Bo.

> After a while, Colonel Samura was re-deployed back to Freetown and I was his personal bodyguard, I had to come to Freetown with him. In Freetown, I lived with Colonel Samura for about a month going to work, and around town with him until he was sent to Ghana on a staff course, leaving me in his house with his family. While there, I used to go around town with the driver one Sergeant Conteh with my military uniforms on. It was during one of these shopping arounds that we ran into Tom Yuma a Captain then who said that I was too small to be in the army, and that I should be taken to Major Max Kanga. At Major Max Kanga's office in Cockrill, I was strip off all military gears and was later taken to the CAW office where I was made to answer few questions after which I was given a hand written note and Le 500.00 in cash to travel and report to Mr. M'briwa the home administrator in Benin.

> I arrived in Benin around three in the afternoon on 1 February 1995 and was alocated to the care giver in domitory two after few minutes of question and answer session.

When asked why he rejoined the army, Foday said it was because he was not visited by CAW field workers as promised so he lost hope.

As to how many rebels he killed during the time he fought Foday said it is indefinite but he said he can remember a few times when he was ordered to kill captured rebel. On how this was been done, he said these normally depends on the circumstances in which rebels were captured. When asked to comment, he said,

> if we catch any during a bloody battle, these are taken to our base, where they are made to dig their own graves, and depending on orders given we will plug eyes, cut off the nose, ears, fingers and then bury them half dead. While for those who were caught during fact finding mission, depending on the officer commanding and our position on the ground the rebels will dig their graves, and then either shot to death or buried alive or kept in custody and encouraged to obtain information.

On his responses and intension to get back to the Army, Foday said he is now happy to have been with CAW again.

As to what he would do on CAW field component's failure to visit him again after resettlement he said that he will do his best to stay with his mother and then go to school. As to what his going back to school was aiming at, Foday said he plans to become a motor mechanic, in the future and as such a carrier will require some reading and writing knowledges, he said he will try to attain a fourth form level in school before embarking on the carrier.

The account by juvenile combatants who fought with the RUF stands in sharp contrast to those who fought with the national army. Below are two accounts of juvenile combatants abducted by the RUF.

'What is your name?'

'My name is Momodu, I was born in Masiaka, Port Lokko District in 1982'.

'Did you live with your parents before the war?'

'I lived with my parents, both mother and father, not too far from the Masiaka police station before I was kidnapped'.

'Who kidnapped you?'

'The RUF. It was on a Saturday, early in the morning, and I was going to meet my father in the farm. The rebels were in the bush, about twenty of them, some looked tired and were resting, but the others were busy doing something with their guns. I was scared when I saw them and wanted to run but they threatened to open fire so I cried and waited until one of them came and grabbed me'.

'What did they want you to do for them?'

'They started asking me questions about soldiers on the Freetown-Masiaka highway. I told them that I did not see any soldiers that morning but that the police were on the road with guns at a check point. They also asked me where I was going that morning and I replied that I was going to meet my father in the farm. We went round and round in the bush and by the afternoon we got to their base'.

'How did you know it was their base?'

'There were many people there – young boys and girls, old men, but they were mostly young men. It was in this place that they taught me how to use a gun'.

'For how long where you there?'

'I was there from the time I was captured to about the middle of 1995 when we were told to leave because of the Nigerian Alpha jet'.

'What was the Alpha jet doing?'

'They were shooting from the sky. They started one morning and we were told to leave the place because it continued for about two days'.

'Where did you go when you left the place?'

'We went to the bush because the place is on a hill and we walked for about two days in the bush. It was very tiring, there was no food, and water was a problem'.

'How did you survive?'

'I think I was lucky because some boys collapsed on the way and we just left them there. It would have been easier if we just had to walk by ourselves but we had to carry weapons and ammunitions. It was when I noticed that everybody was tired on the second day that I started planning my escape'.

'What do you mean by planning your escape?'

'I was in that camp for about ten months and I saw what they did to two boys who were caught escaping'.

'What happened?'

'They chop off their feet with cutlass (matchetes) and we buried them alive'.

'Who buried them?'

'I mean we the small boys'.

'So the RUF did such things?'

'Yes, it was the wounding (violence) and killing that made me want to escape. I did not understand why they were doing it'.

'Did they not explain to you why they were fighting?'

'No they only told us that Sankoh wants to make Salone (Sierra Leone) a better place for children so that they could go to school and after school get a good job.

I did not understand what they meant and they only told us that one night when the Commander came with about forty young men'.

'So this is why you escaped?'

'Yes, but the wounding (violence) and killing was the big thing for me'.

'But you only saw them do this once. That is true but when you stay in a place for a long time and you do not see people you ask questions'.

'What do you mean?'

'Well, I had a man who liked me, Commander Wan Bone, and I asked him about people in the camp. He would tell me that so and so has gone on a mission or that so and so has been killed'.

'Did you ask him why they got killed?'

'I did but his answer was always the same: *dis nar revolushon* (this is a revolution) people get killed by the revolution if they fail to carry out a task assigned to them'.

The other interview was with a teenager abducted in December 1998 by the renegade national army. This interview was conducted in February 2000.

'What is your name? My name is Momoh Sesay'.

'How old are you? I am fourteen'.

'Where you a soldier? They did not give me uniform because I am too small but they thought me how to use a gun'.

'Did you kill anybody? Yes, I killed many people and everyday I pray to God for forgiveness'.

'When did you join the army? My brother and I were kidnapped together with eight other boys in Songo'.

'When was this?'

'In December 1998. We woke up one morning and saw soldiers in our compound. They told our father that they want all the men in the compound to accompany them to Freetown. My father pleaded with them that we were small boys but they insisted and threatened to burn all the three houses in the compound. My mother and all my sisters were crying and begging but they refused'.

'So what happened after they took you? We trekked to Benguema where we stayed for about three weeks. It was in Benguema that they thought us how to use an AK47. This took about three days'.

'Did you fight at Benguema? No, we were in the bush most of the time until after Christmas when we were ordered to move to Kossoh, were we stayed for another two days, and then advanced to Allen Town. At Allen Town we washed our bodies for the first time and we were given some powder to put in our nose'.

'What kind of powder? It was a kind of white powder. Everybody was given a pinch after which we were ordered to advance to Calbah town (on the outskirt of Freetown). We stayed there for a while before we were ordered to move to the hills over looking Kissy'.

'Did you enter Freetown?

'No I did not I only fought in Kissy'.

'What did you do?'

'We killed people and burnt houses'.

'For how long where you doing this? We started after New Year and continued until ECOMOG pushed us out of Kissy'.

'So you were a rebel?'

'No I was not a rebel. I did what I was told to do but I am sorry for what I did'.

'Where you not afraid of anything?'

'In the beginning I was, but after taking the powder and when they killed my brother, everything changed. I mean I became crazy (mad)'.

'Who killed your brother?

I don't know. He went on a mission and did not return'.

'Why did you not escape after you discovered that your brother was dead?'

'There was nowhere to run to. I was in a war situation and if I had gone to any civilian they would have identified me as a rebel'.

'But you just said you are not a rebel'.

'What I mean is that one can easily identify me as a rebel'.

'How so?'

'I was dirty, scruffy and smelling. I went on for days working without eating or sleeping. It was the most difficult time in my life'.

'Where you working?'

'Killing people and burning houses is work. We were not paid but our commanders always congratulated us for a job well done'.

'Where you involved in amputation?

Yes, I did it many times'.

'Did you know why you were doing these horrible things?'

'I did them because I was ordered'.

'Will you do anything you are asked to do?'

'No, that was a different situation. I think the powder was also a factor'.

Understanding juvenile combatants: By way of conclusion

The testimonies presented above reveal the pattern of recruitment of juvenile combatants by both the Sierra Leone Army and the RUF. Whereas the national army attracted combatants bent on avenging the death of a loved one, the RUF had to resort to unconventional methods of recruiting their under-age combatants. Both armed factions, however, treated their juvenile combatants as expendable commodities to be captured or recruited as the situation demands. But combatants also had a choice, however, limited to fight with one faction or another, or to leave the theatre of war and re-enlist if and when they choose. This element of choice is key to unlocking the victim vs villain prism through which the issue has been studied. RUF recruits did attempt to escape, while those with the national army could switch sides or withdraw from combat voluntarily if they so desire. This was because the national army, unlike the RUF, had to justify or explain why they were using juvenile combatants.

The deliberate targeting of children in Mozambique and the indiscriminate supply of drugs to keep children as combatants in Liberia underscores the nature of both RENAMO and the NPFL. Lacking a clear ideological thrust or a concrete programme of societal transformation, these two movements came to rely heavily on violence as a form of terror directed principally against civilians. It is therefore not coincidental that the RUF, similar in make up to RENAMO and the NPLF, also deliberately targeted children and fed them drugs. The terror in Mozambique and Liberia were reproduced ten fold in the Sierra Leone context. The character of these movements contrast sharply with that of the NRM in Uganda. The *Kidogos* in Uganda, as child soldiers are refered to in Kiswahili, were marked by their discipline and orderliness. The atrocities committed by juvenile combatants in Mozambique, Liberia, and Sierra Leone were totally absent in Uganda. And this was not because Ugandan children are well behaved. Rather, it was because the NRM had a clear direction about why it took up arms and why it wanted political power. The NRM did not press-ganged or abducted its *Kidogos* nor did it fed them with drugs or forced them to commit atrocities in their communities. An armed political group without a concrete programme of societal transformation that could attract members willing to fight and defend that programme, would sooner than later turn to children to replenish its fighting forces so as to continue fighting. In such contexts fighting becomes a campaign of terror against the very civilians that such movements claim to be fighting for.

By historicising the phenomenon of juvenile combatants we begin to understand why only a fraction of children in conflict situations are recruited or abducted and why these 'recruits' are predominantly from the rural areas. With the possible exception of the RPF in Rwanda, where juveniles were recruited before the outbreak of hostilities, all the other armed movements only turned to children as the war progressed to replenish their labour needs. Labour shortage and the nature and character of armed movements are therefore central to understanding the phenomenon of juvenile combatants. To broach the subject from the perspective of total state collapse and the absence of institutional structures to contain a looming anarchy leaves us with too many unanswered questions. These questions range from the ingenious ways in which some children are able to negotiate their way out of war situations to the use of voluntary enrollment as a survival strategy. The element of choice is crucial to understanding the phenomenon of juvenile combatants.

Bibliography

Documents

Address by His Excellency Ahmad Tejan Kabbah, President of the Republic of Sierra Leone, to the 52nd session of the United Nations General Assembly, Wednesday, 1 October.

Armed Forces Revolutionary Council. 1997a. Position Paper on Negotiation, July.Freetown.

Armed Forces Revolutionary Council. 1997b. List of Members of the Supreme Council. Freetown.

Armed Forces Revolutionary Council. 1997C. AFRC Chairman, Johnny Paul Koroma's Letter to Alimamy Pallo Bangura, 31 July, Freetown.

Armed Forces Revolutionary Council. 1999a. *Grievances and Demands of Soldiers of the Sierra Leone Army with regards to the Lome Peace Agreement.* Press Release, 3 September.

Armed Forces Revolutionary Council. 1999b. *Position Statement of the Sierra Leone Army (SLA) and the Armed Forces Revolutionary Council.* Press Release,18 September.

African-American Institute. 1996. *Sierra Leone: Final Report.* Democracy and Governance Programs, December 16.

Community Leaders, 1997. Letter to General Sani Abacha, 10 August.

ECOWAS. 1997a. Meeting of ECOWAS Committee of Four on Sierra Leone. Abidjan, Côte d'ivoire, 17-18 July.

ECOWAS. 1997b. Twentieth Session of the Authority of Heads of State and Government; Decision A/D/8/97 On Sanctions Against the Junta in Sierra Leone, 28-29 August.

ECOWAS. 1997c. ECOWAS six month Peace Plan for Sierra Leone, 23 October, 1997–22 April 1998, Conakry.

ECOWAS. 1997. Final Communiqué, Extraordinary Meeting of ECOWAS Ministers of Foreign Affairs on the situation in Sierra Leone, Conakry, 26 June.

ECOWAS. 1997. Final Communiqué of the Meeting of Ministers of Foreign Affairs of ECOWAS, Abuja, 28 August.

Government of Sierra Leone. 2000. *The Anti-Corruption Act 2000.* February.

Government of Sierra Leone. 1997. Position Paper on the Reactivation of Local Government and Decentralization in Sierra Leone. February.

Government of Sierra Leone. 1967. *The Beoku-Betts Commission of Inquiry into the Sierra Leone Produce Marketing Board.* Freetown: Government Printer.

Government of Sierra Leone.1967. *Report of the Dove-Edwin Commission of Inquiry into the Conduct of the 1967 General Elections in Sierra Leone and the Government Statement Thereon.* Government Printer: Freetown.

Government of Sierra Leone. 1996. *Address by His Excellency Ahmad Tejan Kabba, on the occasion of his swearing-in as President of the Republic of Sierra Leone on Friday, 29th March 1996.* Government Printers: Freetown.

Government of Sierra Leone. 1991. *Constitution of Sierra Leone*, Supplement to the *Sierra Leone Gazette Extraordinary*, 25th September 1991. Government Printers: Freetown.

Government of Sierra Leone. 1997. Government of Sierra Leone's Reaction to the AFRC Junta's Position Paper to the ECOWAS Foreign Ministers in Abidjan, August.

Government of Sierra Leone. 1999. *Government's Reaction to the Position paper of the RUFP Relating to Alleged Violations of the Terms of the Lome peace Agreement.* Press Release, 30 December.

Revolutionary United Front/SL. n.d.. *Footpaths to Democracy: Toward a New Sierra Leone.*

Revolutionary United Front.(n.d.) *The Basic Document of the Revolutionary United Front of Sierra Leone(RUF/SL): The Second Liberation of Africa.*

Revolutionary United Front Political Wing. 1999. *Call for Independent Investigations.*

Revolutionary United Front Party. 1999. *Position Paper.* Press Release, 27 December.

Revolutionary United Front Party. 2000. *Violations of the Lome Peace Accord.* Press Release, 24 February.

Sierra Leone Gazette. 1997. Government Printers. Freetown. April 3.

United National People's Party. 1996a. *Manifesto of the United National People's Party.* Freetown.

United National People's Party. 1996b. *Comments on the Presidential Run-Off Election.* Freetown.

United Nations Security Council. 1997. The Security Council Resolution on Sierra Leone 1132 of 8 October.

UN Resolution 1132 adopted by the Security Council at its 382nd meeting, 8 October 1997. Ghana Focus, 4 May 1998.

Secondary Sources

Abdullah, I. 2002. 'Youth Culture and Rebellion: Understanding Sierra Leone's Wasted Decade'. *Critical Arts*, 12, 2.

Abdullah, I and Muana, P. 1998.'The Revolutionary United Front: A Revolt of the Lumpen Proletariat'. Christopher Clapham (ed.) *African Guerillas*, James Currey: London.

Abdullah, I. 1997. 'he Colonial State and Wage Labor in Post-War Sierra Leone: Attempts at Remaking the Working Class, 1945-1960'. *International Labor and Working Class History*, 52, 1.

Abdullah, I. 1996.'Violence, Youth Culture, and War: A Critical Reading of Paul Richards', Sierra Leone Electronic Discussion Forum, Leonenet, 19 May.

Abdullah, I. 1995. '"Liberty or Death": Working Class Agitation and the Labour Question in Colonial Freetown' *International Review of Social History*, 40.

Abraham, A. 1993. 'Regional Politics and the Social Services Provision Since Indepdence'. In Fyle (ed.) *The State and the Provision of Social Services in Sierra Leone Since Independence, 1961-91.* CODESRIA: Dakar.

Abraham, A. 1978. *Mende Government and Politics under Colonial Rule: A Historical Study of Political Change in Sierra Leone 1890-1937.* Oxford University Press/ Sierra Leone University Press: London/Freetown.

ActionAid, 1995. *The Reality of Aid: An Independent Review of International Aid.* England.

Adi, H. 2000. 'Pan-Africanism and West African Nationalism in Britain' *African Studies Review*, 43, 1.

Adi, H.2000. *West Africans in Britain, 1900-1960: Nationalism, Pan-Africanism and Communism.* Lawrence and Wishart: London.

All People's Congress (APC), 1982. *The Rising Sun: History of the All People's Congress Party of Sierra Leone.* A.P.C Publications: Freetown

Amnesty International. 1996. *Sierra Leone: Towards a Future Founded on Human Rights.* London.

Apter, D. 1996 (ed.). *The Legitimization of Violence.* UNRISD and Macmillan Press: London.

Bangura, Y. 1997.'Reflections on the Abidjan Peace Accord', *Africa Development*, 22, 2&3.

Bangura, Y. 2000. 'Strategic Policy Failure and Governance in Sierra Leone'. *Journal of Modern African Studies*, 38, 4, Dec.

Boas, M. 2002. 'Civil Society in Sierra Leone: Corruption, Destruction (and Reinvention)' *Democracy and Development*, 3, 1.

Cabral, A. 1969._Revolution in Guinea.* London.

Cartwright, J. 1970. *Politics in Sierra Leone,1947–1967.* Toronto.

Cary, J. (1947). *Mr Johnson.* London.

Chabal, P. and Daloz, J-P. 1999. *Africa Works: Disorder as Political Instrument.* James Currey: Oxford.

Chole, Eshetu and Jibrin Ibrahim (1995) *Democratisation Processes in Africa: Problems and*
Perspectives. CODESRIA: Dakar.

Clapham, C. (ed.). 1998. *African Guerrillas.* James Currey: London.

Cohn, I and Goodwin-gill, G. 1994. *Child Soldiers: The Role of Children in Armed Conflict.* Clarendon Press: Oxford.

Cole, D and Raundalen, M. 1991. *Reaching Children in War,* Nordiska African Institute: Uppsala..

Cohen, R.and Michael, D. 1973.'The Revolutionary Potential of the African Lumpen Proletariat: A Skeptical View'. *IDS Bulletin,*5,no.2/3.

Collier, Paul (1999), 'Doing Well Out of War'. Paper prepared for Conference on Economic Agendas in Civil War, London, April 26-27, 1999.

Collier, P. and Hoeffler, A.(2001) 'Greed and Grievance in Civil War'. Ms.

Collins, John. 1992. *West African Pop Roots.* Temple University Press: Philadelphia.

Conteh-Morgan, E.and Dixon-Fyle, M(1999) *Sierra Leone at the end of the Twentieth Century.* Peter Lang: New York.

Davies, Victor A.B., 2000. 'Sierra Leone: Ironic Tragedy'. *Journal of African Economies,* 9, 3.

Daramy, S. B. 1993. *Constitutional Development in Post Colonial Sierra Leone, 1961-1984.* Edwin Mellen: New York.

Denzer, L., and Spitzer, L. 1973. ' I.T.A Wallace-Johnson and the West African Youth League'. *The International Journal of African Historical Studies.*

Douglas, M. 1986. 'The Social Precondition of Radical Scepticism in J. Law(ed.) *Action and Belief: a new sociology of knowledge.* Routledge and Kegan Paul: London.

Duffield, M. 1995. 'Complex Emergencies and the Crisis of Developmentalism'. *IDS Bulletin,* 25, 4.

Dumbuya, A. 1999.'Parliament and the Enforcement of Democratic Accountability in Sierra Leone. Mimeo:Freetown.

Dumbuya, P. 1999. 'Post-Election Peace-Making in Sierra Leone: Opportunities and Pitfalls in the Restoration of Peace and Democracy in a War-Torn State'. Mimeo.

Editorial Board. April 1985. 'Editorial, The Review, Intellectual and the Left in Africa'. *Review of African Political Economy,* 32.

Ellis, S. 1995. 'Liberia 1989-1994: A Study of Ethnic and Spiritual Violence'. *African Affairs,* 94, 375.

El-Kenz, A.1996. ' Youth and Violence'. Stephen Ellis (ed.) *African Now.* London.

El-Khawas, M. 1986.*Momar Qaddafi: His Ideology and Practice.* Maple Leaf Press: Battlebro.

Emerson, Donald K. 1968. *Students and Politics in Developing Nations.* Praeger: New York.

Esler, A (ed.) 1974. *The Youth Revolution: The Conflict of Generations in Modern History*. D.C. Heath and Co.: Lexington, MA.

Fanon, F. 1961. *The Wretched of the Earth*. London.

Fatton, R. 1992. Predatory Rule: The State and Civil Society in Africa. Lynne Reinner: Boulder, Co.

Fofana, L. 1997. 'Sierra Leone-Children: Young, Armed and Dangerous,' Inter Press Service, 1 July.

Fofana, U. 1999. 'The Conflict in Sierra Leone and its Effects on the Media'. Lord, D and Onipede, A (eds). *Africa and the Media*. Conciliation Resources: London.

Furley, O. 1994. 'Child Soldiers in Africa' in Oliver Furley (ed.) *Conflict in Africa*. Taurus Academic Press: London.

Fyle, C. M. 1994. ' The Military and Civil Society in Sierra Leone: The 1992 Coup D'etat'. *African Development*, 18, 2.

Fyle, C. M.1979. *The Sulima Yalunka Kingdom: Precolonial Politics, Economics and Society*. Nyakon Press: Freetown.

Gberie, L. 1999. ' The Sierra Leone War: Background and Key Actors'. Briefing Paper for Canadian Foreign Affairs Department and CIDA.

Gberie, L, 2000, 'Bandit Country'. *African Now*. August/September.

Hanna, W.J., Hanna, J.L. & Sauer, V. 1975. 'The Active Minority'. William J. Hanna *(ed.) University Students and African Politics*. African Publishing Co.: New York.

Hanna, W. J. (ed.). 1975. *University Students and African Politics*. African Publishing Co.: New York.

Hargreaves, J. 1985. 'British Policy and African Universities: Sierra Leone Revisited'. *African Affairs*, 84, 336.

Harrell-Bond, B., Howard, A., and Skinner, D.1978.*Community Leadership and the Transformation of Freetown (1801-1976)*. Mouton Publishers: New York.

Hayward, F. M. 1989. 'Sierra Leone: State Consolidation, Fragmentation and Decay'. Donald B. Cruise et al, *Contemporary West Africa*. Cambridge University Press: Cambridge.

Hayward, F. M., 1972. 'Development of a Radical Political Organisation in the Bush: A Case Study of Sierra Leone'. *Canadian Journal of African Studies*, 6,1.

Hayward, F. M and Kandeh, J. D., 1987. "Perspectives on Twenty-Five Years of Elections in Sierra Leone'. F.M. Hayward (ed.) *Elections in Independent Africa*.Westview Press: Boulder, Co.

Heilbrunn, J. and Stevens, M. 2000. Anti-Corruption Agencies and World Bank Clients'. Controlling Corruption: Towards an Integrated Strategy. World Bank Insitute.

Herman, E. and Chomsky, N.1988. *Manufacturing Consent: The Political Economy of Mass Media*. Pantheon: New York.

Honwana, A. 1999. 'Negotiating Post-War Identities: Child Soldiers in Mozambique and Angola,' *CODESRIA Bulletin*, 1& 2.

Human Rights Watch. 1994. *Easy Prey: Child Soldiers in Liberia*. New York.

Human Rights Watch. 1999. *Sierra Leone Sowing the Seeds of Terror*. New York.

Human Rights Watch 1999. *Getting Away with Murder*. New York.

International Alert. 1995. *Sierra Leone Mission Report*. April.

International Alert. 1996. *Sierra Leone Mission Report*. May-September

Johnston, M, and Kpundeh, S. 2001 'Building the Clean Machine: Anti-Corruption Coalitions and Sustainable Reforms'. Draft World Bank Working Paper (forthcoming).

Jones, K. 1999. 'United Nations Intervention in Conflict Resolution: the Case of Sierra Leone'. M A Term Paper. Long Island University, Brooklyn Campus. N.Y.

Kandeh, J. Forthcoming. 'Sierra Leone's Post-Conflict Elections'

Kandeh, J. 1996. 'Predatory Regime Continuity and the Demise of the Sierra

Leonean State,' Canadian Association of African Studies, May 1–5, 1996, Montreal, Canada.

Kandeh, J. 1999.' Ransoming the State: Elite Origins of Subaltern Terror in Sierra Leone'. *Review of African Political Economy*, 26, 81.

Kaplan, R. 1995. *Ends of the Earth: A Journey at the End of the 21st Century*. Random House: New York.

Kaplan, R. 1992.'The Coming Anarchy'. *Atlantic Monthly*, February.

Karefa-Smart, J. 1997. Suggestions for a National Conference for Peace, Reconciliation and Enduring Democracy in Sierra Leone. Freetown, July.

Kaufmann, D.1998, 'Revisiting Anti-Corruption Strategies: Tilt Towards Incentive-Driven Approaches' in *Corruption and Integrity Improvement Initiatives in Developing Countries*. Sahr Kpundeh and Irene Hors (eds.) UNDP/OECD.

Kaufmann, D, Pradhan, S and Ryterman, R. 1998. New Frontiers in Diagnosing and Combating Corruption. *Premnotes*, 7, Oct.(World Bank).

Keen, D. 1995. '"Sell Game": The Economics of Conflict in Sierra Leone'. Conference paper, 'West Africa at War: Anarchy or Peace in Liberia and Sierra Leone'. University College, London.

Khobe, M. 1999. 'Anatomy of the Sierra Leone Conflict' Paper delivered at the CDD Workshop, Lome.

Khobe, M. 1998. 'Conflict Management and Resolution' ECOWAS Regional Forum. Ouagadougou.

Kilson, M. 1966. *Modernisation and Change in a West African State*. Harvard University Press: Cambridge, MA.

Koroma, A.. 1996. *Sierra Leone: The Agony of a Nation*, Afromedia Publication, Freetown.

Kpundeh, S. 1999. 'Controlling Corruption in Sierra Leone: An Assessment of Past Efforts and Suggestions for the Future'. K.R. Hope and B. Chikulo (eds.) *Corruption and Development in Africa: Lessons from Case Studies.* Macmillan: London.

Kpundeh, S. 1998. 'Political Will in Fighting Corruption'. Sahr Kpundeh and Irene Hors (eds.) *Corruption and Integrity Improvement Initiatives in Developing Countries.* UNDP/OECD.

Kpundeh, S. 1995, *Politics and Corruption in Africa: A Case Study of Sierra Leone.* University Press of America: Lanham, MA.

Kpundeh, S. 1993. 'Prospects in Contemporary Sierra Leone' *Corruption and Reform,* 7, 3.

Lappia, J. N.L, Gaima, E.A.R., Konteh, F.H., Jalloh, A. , 2000 *Survey Report on National Perceptions and Attitudes Towards Corruption in Sierra Leone.* UNPD.

Lavalie, A. 1985. 'The SLPP in Opposition'. *Sierra Leone Studies at Birmingham.* Vol. 5.

Lipset, Seymour M. 1967. *Students Politics.* New York. Basic Books Inc.

Makannah, T. 1995. *Population Size, Growth, Composition and Distribution: Handbook of Population of Sierra Leone.* Toma Enterprises: Addis Ababa.

Mamdani, M. 1987. 'Uganda Today'. *Ufahamu.* 15, .3.

Mamdani, M. 2000. *When Victims Become Killers.* Princeton University Press: Princeton.

Mazrui, A.1996. 'Global Africa: From Abolutionists to Reparationists'. Tajudeen Abdul Raheem (ed.) *Pan Africanism: Politics, Economy and Social Change in the Twenty-First Century.* New York University Press: New York.

Marx, K and Engels, F. 1848. *The Communist Manifesto,* Lawrence and Wishart: London.

Mbayo, R. 1999. 'The African Press: Prospects for Freedom in the New Millennium'. Richard Mbayo (ed.) *Press and Politics in Contemporary African States.* Edwin Mellen: New York.

Mkandawire, T. 1991. 'Crisis and Adjustment in Sub-Saharan Africa'. D. Ghai (ed.) *The IMF in the South: The Social Impact of Crisis and Adjustment,* UNRISD (Geneva), ISER (Kingston) and Zed Press: London.

Muana, P. 1997. 'The Kamajoi Militia: Violence, Internal Displacement and the Politics of Counter-Insurgency'. *Africa Development,22,* 3 /4.

Mukonoweshuro, E. 1993. *Colonialism, Class Formation and Underdevelopment in Sierra Leone.* University of America Press: Lanham, MD.

Musa, A. and Fayemi, K. 2000. *Mercenaries: An African Security Dilemma.* CDD: London.

Museveni, Yoweri. 1997. Sowing the Mustard Seed: The Struggle for Freedom and Democracy. Macmillan: London.

Nkomo, M., Nkomo O.1 984. *Students Culture and Activism in Black Africa South African Universities: The Roots of Resistance.* Greenwood Press: Westport, Connecticut.

Nunley, J. W. 1987. *Moving with the Face of the Devil: Art and Urban Politics in Urban West Africa .* University of Illinois Press: Urbana.

Olanisakin, F. 2001. 'The Impact of Armed Conflict on Children in West Africa.' IPA/ ECOWAS Seminar, Abuja, Nigeria 27-29 Sept.

Olowu, D, 1993, 'Roots and Remedies of Governmental Corruption in Africa', *Corruption and Reform*, 7, 3.

Olurin, A.I 1993. "Peacekeeping in Africa: The Liberian Experience' in *The Peacemaker*, 2, 1, Sept.

Olurin, A.I. 1993. Lecture on Military Operations in Liberia, National War College, Lagos, 2-3 October 1993.

Opala, J. 1994. "'Ecstatic Renovation!'": Street Art Celebrating Sierra Leone's 1992 Revolution', *African Affairs*, 93

Pan African Union. 1982. *Pan-African Union Information Brochure.* Freetown

Parfitt, Trevor W. and Riley, S. P. 1989. *The African Debt Crisis.* Routledge: London.

Peters, K and Richards, P. 1998. 'Why We Fight': voices of youth combatants in Sierra Leone'. *Africa*, 68, 2.

Qathafi, M. 1978. *The Green Book.* Martin Brien and O'Keefe Ltd: London.

Reno, W. 1995. *Corruption and State Politics in Sierra Leone.* Cambridge University Press: Cambridge.

Reno, W. 1998. *Warlord Politics and African States.* Lynne Reinner: Boulder, Co.

Revolutionary United Front. (n.d) *Footpaths to Democracy.*

Revolutionary United Front. 1990. *Basic Document.*

Richards, P. 1995. 'Rebellion in Liberia and Sierra Leone: Youth in Crisis'. Oliver Furley (ed.) *Conflict in Africa.* London: I.B. Tuaris Publishers.

Richards, P. 1996. *Fighting for the Rainforest: War, Youth and Resources in Sierra Leone.* James Currey: London.

Riley, S. 1997. 'The Militariat Strikes Again'. *Review of African Political Economy*, July.

Riley, S and Sesay, M.. 1995. 'Sierra Leone: The Coming Anarchy'. *Review of African Political Economy.*

Roberts, G. O. 1982. *The Anguish of Third World Independence.* University of America Press: Lanham, MD.

Schedler,1. 1999. 'Conceptualizing Accountability'. Andreas Schedler, Larry Diamond and Marc F. Plattner (eds.) *The Self-Restraining State: Power and Accountability in New Democracies.* Lynne Reinner Publishers: Boulder, Co.

Sankoh, F. 1996. 'War would have started in 1988'. Interview with Foday Sankoh. *Concord Times*, 6 December.

Seyon, P. 2000. 'Peace Never had a Chance in Sierra Leone Under the Lome Agreement'. *The Perspective*, June 1.

Sesay, A. 1992. 'Civil Society and the Democratisation process in Africa: A case Study on the Sierra Leone Experience'. Omoruyi, Schlosser, Sambo and Okwosa (eds.) *Democratization in Africa,* Vol 2, Lagos.

Smillie, I.1996. Sierra Leone: NGOs in Complex Emergencies, Unpublished Paper.

Spivak, G. 1995 'Can Subalterns speak'. Bill Ashcroft, Gareth Griffiths, Helen Tiffin (eds.) *The Post Colonial Studies Reader.* Routledge: London and New York.

St. John, R. B. 1988. *Qaddafi's World Design: Libyan Foreign Policy, 1969-1987.* Sagi books: Worcester.

Straker, G and Moosa, F. 1997. 'Child Soldiers in South Africa: Past, Present and Future Prespectives' in Efraime Boia et al, *Children, War and Persecution—* Rebuilding Hope, proceedings of the Congress in Maputo, Mozambique, 1-4 December.

Tarr, B. S.1993. 'The ECOMOG initiative in Liberia: A Liberian Perspective'. *Issue,* 21,1-2.

Tungamirai, J. 1995.'Recruitment to ZANLA: Building up a War Machine'. Ngwabi Bebe and Terence Ranger (eds.) *Zimbabwe's Liberation War.* James Currey: London.

UNDP Human Development Index. 2000. *Human Development Report 2000.* Oxford University Press: New York.

UNDP. 1990–1996. *Human Development Report.* Oxford University Press: New York.

Wessel, M. 1997. 'Child Soldiers,' Bulletin of the Atlantic Scientists in Chicago, Nov/Dec.

Young, T. 1990.'The MNR/ RENAMO: External and Internal Dynamics'. *African Affairs,*89,357.

Zack-Williams, A.B. 1993. 'Sierra Leone: Crisis and Despair'. *Review of African Political Economy,* 56.

Zack-Williams, A.B. Riley. S. P. 1993. 'The military and civil society in Sierra Leone: The coup and its consequences'. *Review of African Political Economy, 56.*

Zartman, I. W. (ed.). 1995. *Collapsed States: The Disintegration and Restoration of Legitimate Authority.* Lynne Reinner: Boulder, Co.

Newspapers and Magazines

Awareness Magazine (Freetown, Sierra Leone)

Focus on Sierra Leone (London, U.K.)

For Di People (Freetown, Sierra Leone)

New Citizen (Freetown, Sierra Leone)

The New Republic (USA)

Sierra Leone Progress (New York)

Standard Times (Freetown, Sierra Leone).

Tablet (Freetown, Sierra Leone)

Tablet International (New York/Washington, USA)

Tawakaltu (New York/Washington, USA)

The New Republic (USA)

The Times (London, UK)

Unity Now (Freetown, Sierra Leone)

Vanity Fair (USA)

Vision (Freetown, Sierra Leone)

Washington Post Magazine (USA)

Washington Post (USA)

West Africa (London)

Lightning Source UK Ltd.
Milton Keynes UK
UKOW052112150512

192641UK00002B/262/A